T0367126

MUSLIM WOMEN of the FERGANA VALLEY

MUSLIM WOMEN
OF THE FERGANA VALLEY
A 19th-Century Ethnography
from Central Asia

Vladimir Nalivkin and Maria Nalivkina

Edited by Marianne Kamp
Translated by Mariana Markova
and Marianne Kamp

Indiana University Press

Bloomington and Indianapolis

This book is a publication of

Indiana University Press
Office of Scholarly Publishing
Herman B Wells Library 350
1320 East 10th Street
Bloomington, Indiana 47405 USA

iupress.indiana.edu

English translation © 2016 by Marianne Kamp and Mariana
Markova

⊗ The paper used in this publication meets the minimum
requirements of the American National Standard for Information
Sciences—Permanence of Paper for Printed Library Materials,
ANSI Z39.48-1992.

Manufactured in the United States of America

Cataloging information is available from the Library of Congress.

ISBN 978-0-253-02127-4 (cloth)
ISBN 978-0-253-02138-0 (paperback)
ISBN 978-0-253-02149-6 (ebook)

1 2 3 4 5 21 20 19 18 17 16

Contents

Central Asia, including the extent of Russian conquest, late nineteenth century.
Source: Margo Berendsen, 2015.

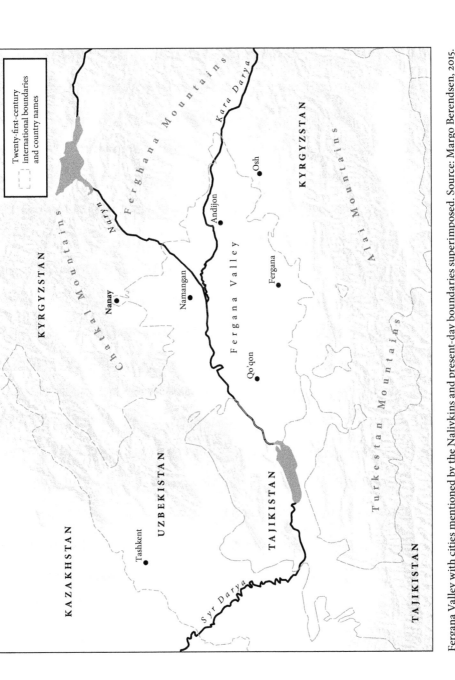

Fergana Valley with cities mentioned by the Nalivkins and present-day boundaries superimposed. Source: Margo Berendsen, 2015.

Editor's Introduction

Marianne Kamp

THIS WORK, originally titled *A Sketch of the Everyday Life of Women of the Sedentary Native Population of the Fergana Valley* and first published in Russian in 1886, offers readers a nineteenth-century ethnography focused on women in an Islamic society, as observed by Maria and Vladimir Nalivkin. The Nalivkins were Russians who lived in a "Sart" (Uzbek) village in a territory new to the Russian Empire, the Fergana Valley. With the exception of Edward G. Lane's *An Account of the Manners and Customs of Modern Egyptians*, very few nineteenth-century ethnographies of Muslim societies were based on the ethnographer's long-term participant observation, and accounts by women were even rarer. Maria Nalivkina learned the Sart language and lived in the village of Nanay from 1878 to 1884, during which she befriended her neighbors and tried to learn all she could about their lives and the ways that Islam shaped their lives. The authors' focus on explaining Islam will be familiar to those who have studied nineteenth-century Orientalist scholarship: the authors wrote with all the hubris of Western cultural superiority but also with an attention to detail and effort at description that arose from genuine curiosity. The exploration of women's lives is unique, but the Nalivkins' focus on everyday life in rural communities exemplifies a dominant trend in nineteenth-century Russian ethnography.

This introduction provides brief biographies of Vladimir and Maria, focusing on their intellectual formation, the milieu within which they worked, and their scholarly production. Comparisons are drawn between their ethnographic work and those of several of their contemporaries in Russian Central Asia. An overview of the book's themes is followed by a discussion of choices that we made in translation.

The Nalivkins

In 1878, a young Russian couple, Vladimir Petrovich Nalivkin and Maria Vladimirovna Nalivkina, purchased a courtyard home and some land in the *kishlak* (village) of Nanay in the Fergana Valley. Nanay, situated in the hills between the Tian Shan Mountains to the north and Namangan to the south, was home to people whom the Nalivkins identified as Sarts. I discuss the meaning of this term later. The Nalivkins lived in Nanay for six years, where they learned to speak and read the local languages, dressed like Sarts, farmed using local techniques, raised a family, and wrote several books.

Until 1876, the Fergana Valley had been part of the domain ruled by the khan of Kokand.[1] The Khanate itself was founded in the 1780s and by the 1850s grew to encompass the Fergana Valley, parts of the Kazakh steppes, and the city of Tashkent. In the same period, the Russian Empire expanded south and east, and the Russian military command in Central Asia became dissatisfied with the perimeter it had established at the fortresses of Vernyi (Almaty), Ak-Mechet (Kyzylorda), and Shymkent, in what is now southern Kazakhstan. General Mikhail Cherniaev's forces conquered Tashkent in 1865, taking control of Kokand's largest city and most important center of trade; the khan's territory shrank to focus on the Fergana Valley. In 1875–1876, after Russian forces defeated and made treaties with the khan of Khiva and the emir of Bukhara, Turkestan's governor-general Konstantin von Kaufman found reason to attack Kokand, after an internal coup drove out the cooperative Khan Khudoyar. Kaufman "feared that the new Khoqandi regime might ally itself with Bukhara" or other of Russia's opponents, and he ordered Russian forces to take control of Kokand and the Fergana Valley. The Russian administration dissolved the Khanate in a brutal conquest and absorbed its remaining lands into Russia's Turkestan Territory, under Governor-General von Kaufman's Tashkent-based administration.[2]

Vladimir Petrovich Nalivkin

Vladimir Nalivkin, an officer under Russian general Skobelev's command, had served in several Russian campaigns, including the campaign against Khiva (1873) and another against Turkmens. He arrived in the Fergana Valley with this Russian force but then left military service and took up farming in Nanay. Later he wrote that he resigned his commission because of the conduct of Skobelev's forces at Gurtepa, where Russian soldiers "hacked" fleeing Sarts, men, women, and children "with sabers."[3] Historian Natalia Lukashova interprets Nalivkin's choice thus: "His unmediated impression of the Turkestan campaign broke the faith of the young, enthusiastic officer that Russia was carrying out a positive civilizing mission in Central Asia." He viewed Russian conquest as colonialism, Russian military attitudes as hostile to natives, and their actions as cruel toward a peaceful population.[4] If Nalivkin's depiction of his motivation for this career change was honest, those feelings were slow to overcome him and were of a passing nature. In a form that he filled out in 1906 explaining his military service, Nalivkin wrote that he resigned his commission in 1878 because of "illness." After Russian forces subjugated Kokand, Nalivkin was transferred to the military administration in Namangan, where he served as assistant to the director and worked for a time with the land-organization commission. In 1878, having built

Nalivkin family photo, ca. 1898. Left to right: Vladimir (b. 1878), Maria Vladimiovna Nalivkina, Grigorii (b. 1895), Vladimir Petrovich Nalivkin, Natalia (b. 1891), Boris (b. 1876). Source: Personal file of Vladimir Petrovich Nalivkin, Uzbekistan State Archive, F. 2409, op. 1, photos.

his knowledge of Fergana Valley geography and land use, Vladimir Nalivkin re-signed his military post and signed up for the reserve, and only then did he and his wife purchase land in Nanay.[5] The Nalivkins moved to Kokand in 1884, when Vladimir was recalled on reserve, after which he took up new service positions in the Russian colonial administration of Turkestan.[6]

Vladimir Nalivkin was neither a trained ethnographer nor a trained Orien-talist. Other scholars who constructed imperial knowledge of Central Asia for the empire were university graduates, and some were specialists in Oriental stud-ies, trained at Kazan or St. Petersburg, but Nalivkin had a military education.[7] He was the son of a military officer and was born in either Kazan or Kaluga, Russia, in 1852.[8] He followed in his father's footsteps and entered St. Petersburg's military preparatory school, Pavlovskii Kadetskii Korpus (Pavlov Cadet Corps, a school for young boys) in 1863. He graduated from the Pavlovskoe Voennoe Uchilishche (Pavlov Military Training School, a two-year institute for those who had fin-ished gymnasia or high school) in 1872. The training for a military officer at this

Vladimir Petrovich
Nalivkin (undated).
Source: Personal file
of Vladimir Petrovich
Nalivkin, Uzbekistan State
Archive, F. 2409, op. 1,
photos.

institution focused on topography, mapping, and military law but also included sciences and languages. Lukashova writes that "early he proved to have extraordinary linguistic ability: while still in gymnasia, he became acquainted with the Georgian language, and in the Training School he perfected his French."[9] Nalivkin's ancestors belonged to the service noble (*dvoriianin*) estate, meaning that they were hereditary gentry who had originally earned their privileges through military service, but he later remarked that he rejected an appointment to the prestigious Izmailovskii Guards because he lacked the financial means. He took a posting to Orenburg, joining a Cossack brigade there in 1872, and thus became involved in the Russian military campaign against Khiva. He moved to Central Asia and lived there until the end of his life.

While Nalivkin did not undergo the philological training that would have been available to him at the Staff Academy in St. Petersburg, he was nonetheless the product of Russia's military professionalization. According to historian Alexander Marshall, Russia's General Staff "during the nineteenth century, undertook a unique and distinctive historical role in mapping, studying, strategically analyzing and statistically categorizing" the newly conquered peoples in Russian Asia. The Russian military invested in training officers to gather intelligence, creating "military-statistical" portraits of the Russian Empire and neighboring states, producing detailed maps based on travel and surveys, and gathering textual and observational knowledge to describe cultures of the conquered.[10] However, Nalivkin was not trained at either of the military institutions that offered instruction in Tatar, Persian, and Arabic, the General Staff Academy in St. Petersburg and the Nepluevskii Military College in Orenburg. Nalivkin was clearly interested in all things Central Asian, and he took opportunities to join in geographic mapping expeditions in the late 1870s and early 1880s. He contributed to military reports and published articles about his observations in the Tashkent newspaper *Turkestanskie Vedimosti*. He read widely and was an active participant in Russian Orientalist debates.

Nalivkin may have studied Turkic languages using such works as A. K. Kazem-bek's *Turko-Tatar Grammar*, and he probably took advantage of any opportunity to learn Turkic languages while posted in Orenburg and Tashkent. He referred to Budagov's *Comparative Dictionary of Turko-Tatar Dialects*, but he perfected his knowledge of Uzbek by living in Nanay, where he worked to master the language in all its regional dialects.[11] He also learned Persian and its local, spoken variant, Tajik, to the degree that he was able to translate Persian texts, such as histories and medical tracts, into Russian. He made reference to Arabic when explaining Islamic terms, but Lunin's claim that Nalivkin knew Arabic seems overstated. In any case, he and Maria relied on a Russian translation of the Qur'an (Koran) and translations or verbal explanations of other religious documents in Arabic.

After six years in Nanay, Vladimir Nalivkin again began serving the Russian administration as an adviser, a producer of a study of desertification processes and an inspector of schools in the Fergana Valley, and in other positions that made use of his knowledge of the languages, cultures, geography, and history of Central Asia. Although Nalivkin did not have formal higher education, he established himself as one of the leading Orientalists in Russia's Turkestan administration. He published articles and books on a wide range of topics, including geography, history, grammar, Islam, and contemporary issues, but scholars criticized his paucity of citation and his somewhat uncritical use of historic texts. However, V. V. Bartol'd judged Nalivkin "'probably the best expert on the language and culture' of Uzbeks."[12] His *Short History of Kokand* was published in

1886, in the same year as *A Sketch*, and the introductory chapters of both volumes are based on several of Vladimir Nalivkin's newspaper articles.

Maria Vladimirovna (Sartori) Nalivkina

In 1875, Nalivkin married Maria Vladimorovna Sartori. She was born in 1858 in Saratov, in a privileged household, and was educated through the secondary school level, though whether she studied at Saratov Women's Institute or at the prestigious, though not necessarily rigorous, Smolny Institute is uncertain.[13] Smolny, in St. Petersburg, was founded in the eighteenth century to educate girls from noble families, preparing them to manage elite households. However, in the 1860s, the Russian Ministry of Education established secondary institutes for girls of all social classes in Russia's main provincial cities, including Saratov, and in 1870 renamed them as gymnasia, reforming the curriculum to resemble that of the male gymnasia and preparing girls for modern, public life. Maria's grandson, Ivan, described her education this way:

> From her childhood years, Maria Vladimirovna was raised to become the mistress of a comfortable home and hearth, as an enlightened woman to whom were available all the benefits to forever protect her from any hardship, and for whom physical labor would have been simply unthinkable. Maria Vladimirovna graduated, with highest honors, from an institute for well-born maidens, and if you don't consider her excellent knowledge of French and German languages, which she gained there, then the rest of her institute education did nothing to prepare her for the life that stood before her.[14]

It is doubtful that Maria had an "excellent" education, as Pugovkina asserts, but she was one of a tiny minority of Russian women who were graduates of a high school in 1875, and she certainly had the intellectual talent to capitalize on that education.[15] Many of Smolny Institute's students became wives of military officers; perhaps Maria and Vladimir had crossed paths while they were both studying in St. Petersburg, but records do not reveal how they met or why they married. Vladimir traveled to Saratov in 1875, marrying Maria as soon as she finished her education. At age seventeen, she embarked across the Kazakh steppes on horseback to join her new husband in Tashkent.

By 1878, Maria had given birth to two sons, and when her husband resigned his military commission, they used Maria's dowry to purchase a house and land in Nanay. In a memoir written many years later, Vladimir Nalivkin noted his admiration for Maria's fortitude:

> In another year, she was in the remote village Nanay, in an Uzbek hut; she wore a *paranji* [veiling robe], and she was supposed not only to bake bread but also milk the cows and camels, do laundry and mending, make fuel out of manure for heating, and move up to the mountains in summertime with her

fellow villagers [for pasture], all this with the arrival of two children and with a shortage of monetary means. And bear in mind at that time in the whole large district of Namangan lived only three Russian families, not counting soldiers and administrators in the city.[16]

The Nalivkins had two small sons when they moved to Nanay, and Maria did her own housework, cooking, baking, and tending livestock. Somehow she still found time to work with Vladimir on researching and writing two books.

Maria Nalivkina was named as Vladimir's coauthor on their 1884 Russian-Sart and Sart-Russian dictionary, which included Maria's essays on grammar.[17] Maria was also Vladimir's coauthor on *A Sketch of the Everyday Life of Women of the Native Sedentary Population of the Fergana Valley*. The Nalivkins refer to themselves as "we" throughout the text, never attributing a particular observation to one or the other. It is clear from the repetition of entire paragraphs in his *Short History of Kokand* that Vladimir wrote much of *A Sketch*'s first chapter, a geographic introduction to the Fergana Valley.[18] It may be inferred that materials emerging from intimate conversations with Uzbek women must have come from Maria; as an unrelated male Vladimir simply would not have been admitted to the inner courtyards of houses and would not have spent time talking with Uzbek women about child rearing, sewing, marriage, and love affairs. Nalivkin acknowledged that this ethnography depended on Nalivkina's access and perceptions, writing later that he could study these aspects of daily life only "in partnership with (my) wife, without whose collaboration it would have been impossible to penetrate into the midst of the almost entirely closed off daily life of the native family."[19]

The dictionary and this ethnography were Maria Nalivkina's only published works. She gave birth to a daughter in 1891 and another son in 1895.[20] Vladimir continued to be a prolific writer, and recollections about Vladimir noted that she continued to work with him on his scholarly publications even though her name did not appear as coauthor. She died in 1917. Aside from those mentions, the rest of her life is unrecorded.

Vladimir Nalivkin's Career and Death

Although most of Nalivkin's career took place after this work was published, a brief synopsis seems appropriate. Nalivkin served as an inspector of schools and then periodically as a consultant to the Russian administration. Anthropologist Sergei Abashin notes that although much of Nalivkin's published work in the 1880s was sympathetic to Sarts and somewhat critical of Russian administration, following the 1898 Dukchi Ishan uprising in which Muslims in Andijon attacked Russian troops in their barracks, Nalivkin's report leaned toward the more widely held Russian position that Muslims were fanatics and must be controlled. Following the 1905 Russian Revolution, which established the Duma as Russia's body of elected representatives, Nalivkin was elected to represent Russian Turkestan (in a contingent that grossly overrepresented Russian colonists and underrepresented indigenous Central Asians). The elections took place too late for Turkestan's delegates to participate actively in the first Duma, but Nalivkin's entrance into politics revealed his affinity for socialists and his antimonarchical inclinations. Although Turkestan's right to Duma representation was then eliminated, Nalivkin continued to be recognized as a Turkestan deputy and known as a critic of Russia's colonial policies.[21]

In February 1917 the revolution overthrew the tsar, and the role of governor-general of Turkestan also disappeared. In April, Russia's Provisional Government named Nalivkin to one of three positions for Commissars for Civil Administration of Turkestan, along with Orest Schkapsky and Muhammadjan Tinishpaev. In July he was named president of the Turkestan Committee, the "first person" in Turkestan's government, as Abashin puts it.[22] In this position, he supported the idea that indigenous Turkistanis should become politically dominant in Turkestan, rather than that Russian colonists should continue their dominance; however, as historian Daniel Brower noted, the Provisional Government could not undo the violence between colonial settlers and nomads unleashed in the 1916 uprising.[23] In September 1917, the contest for political control of Tashkent became more complicated when Bolsheviks attempted to seize power from the Provisional Government, forcing Nalivkin to mobilize its defense. Nalivkin could please neither the Bolsheviks nor the Provisional Government; the latter relieved Nalivkin of his position before the October 23/November 9 Bolshevik Revolution disbanded the government.[24] According to one of his obituaries, from October 1917 to January 1918, Nalivkin had to flee from his home and hide, "and because of this, he could not even attend the burial of his wife," who died of cancer in November. On January 20, 1918, Vladimir Nalivkin went to Maria's grave in Tashkent and committed suicide there, using his own revolver.[25]

Russian Imperial Expansion and the Nalivkins

Although Nalivkin later wrote that he had resigned his position because of Russia's harsh and immoral methods of warfare, *A Sketch* never evinces any hint of that dissatisfaction. The Nalivkins' criticisms of Russians in Central Asia are mild, presenting Russian administrators and soldiers as bumbling and naïve, overpaying Sarts for goods and services, rather than wise and judicious, or venal. However, they convey a judgment that Russian conquest had harmed "natives" morally by liberating men and women from religious restrictions and thus allowing an explosion of certain sins and crimes. They repeatedly allude to the perspectives of Sarts in Nanay, Namangan, and Kokand, who told them that vices such as prostitution and drinking alcohol existed under the khans' rule but were neither so pervasive nor flagrant as they became when the Russian administration relieved the *rais* (the community-level enforcer of morality and law) of his authority.

Twice, the Nalivkins mention a belief that Sarts would become equal members of the Russian imperial family of nations, using the term *grazhdanstvennost'*. A Russian *grazhdanin* (citizen) had been granted new rights to legal status and representation in the 1860s reforms, which created zemstvos (organizations for local self-government) in the provinces of central Russia. Many historians have pointed out that the Russian "citizen" was in many ways still a subject; autocracy undermined reformers' aspirations to rule of law and guarantees of rights. In the imperial peripheries, Russia traditionally pursued integration of ethnic others in a limited way, by incorporating "native" elites into Russia's military and landowning noble ranks. In the Caucasus, Russian administration established policies designed to integrate newly conquered peoples into the rights and duties of Russian citizenship by enforcing taxation and labor service requirements, establishing zemstvos, and opening Russian schools.[26] The Nalivkins expected that Turkestan would become more integrated with Russia in these same ways, bringing benefit and progress to both, and they declared that "citizenship" had released Sart women from the arbitrariness of Islamic law and given them support from the Russian administration. In 1886, the Nalivkins believed that Turkestan, which was under special military rule, would eventually follow the patterns established in other reaches of the Russian Empire. However, as Alexander Morrison explains so clearly, the Russian Empire never transitioned Turkestan to its normal, if hybrid model of governance. Turkestan remained under the special regime of the military governor-general; Turkestan's elites were not integrated into Russian nobility; the zemstvo organization was not applied in Turkestan; and native Turkistanis were treated as legally different from, and inferior to, Russian citizen-subjects. Turkistanis were subjects in a colonial empire, not Russian citizens-in-the-making.[27]

While the Nalivkins imagined a harmonious future in which Central Asians would benefit from Russia's civilizing influence, they rejected the policy of Russian colonization. Repeatedly, they emphasize the Fergana Valley's population density, intensive agriculture, limited irrigation capacity, and lack of land open for Russian colonial settlement. This seems almost ironic, given that the Nalivkins themselves purchased and farmed land in the Fergana Valley. Unlike wealthy Russian colonists whom the Kaufman administration encouraged to form cotton plantations near Tashkent, the Nalivkins lived and farmed in the same manner as their Sart neighbors, not seeking to introduce Russian agricultural or cultural practices. Their ownership was temporary; they relinquished their farm to local Nanay owners when they left.

A Sketch, like other published works in Imperial Russia, obtained approval from the government censor before publication, and one wonders how this shaped the publication. The authors make their way through topics from geography and economy to the stages of Sart women's lives, but the work ends abruptly, terminating in what seems to be the middle of a narrative about attending parties with prostitutes (a section that probably reflected Vladimir's direct experiences rather than Maria's). This may reveal a censor's cut. Overall, it seems fair to assume that Russia's regime of censorship encouraged the Nalivkins to produce a text that they knew would be publishable.

Even though the end of the volume is dissatisfying, a well-known Russian Orientalist, Nikolai Veselovskii, nominated *A Sketch* for one of the Russian Imperial Geographical Society's highest honors. The Imperial Geographical Society granted the Grand Gold Medal for Ethnography and Statistics jointly to Maria Nalivkina and Vladimir Nalivkin in 1886, making Maria the first woman, and one of only two, that the society so recognized. The work continued to be read and studied by Russian Orientalists.[28] The book also earned the Nalivkins praise from one of the leading Orientalists of their time, Arminius Vambery. In a letter to Vladimir, Vambery wrote, "I found your sketch of the lives of women in Kokand the more striking, in that there is no comparable essay on women, even about those Muslim women who are closest to us."[29]

The Nalivkins as Russian Ethnographers

A Sketch is typical of Russian ethnography of its time but unusual in its subject matter. Governor-General von Kaufman had initiated a project for collecting ethnographic and scientific knowledge of Russia's new Central Asian lands, recruiting linguists and other scholars to carry out and publish new research, and continuing and expanding on the military's ethnographic and statistical studies. However, this particular contribution to Russia's ethnography of Central Asia was voluntary, not commissioned. Vladimir participated in military ethnographic and geographic expeditions, and he and Maria were both well read and aware of new Russian works about Central Asia. They assumed that their reader, an educated Russian with interests in the expanding empire, had read about many facets of Sart culture and Turkestan's geography, described by A. P. Fedchenko, N. A. Maev, A. von Middendorff, L. F. Kostenko, and others, but had no understanding of Sart women's lives.[30]

In particular, they may have been inspired to write in response to Fedchenko's *Travels in Turkestan* (1875). Fedchenko, who noted that he was a founding member of the Imperial Society of Amateurs of Naturalism, Anthropology and Ethnography, published an account that described roads, fortresses, and the state of Khodayar Khan's government in the final years before Russian conquest of Kokand. He also depicted his interactions with male "natives," goods in the bazaars, plants and animals, houses and shrines. Given the date of publication and the details included, such as the floor plan of one of the khan's palaces, one might surmise that the Russian military force that assaulted and defeated Kokand used Fedchenko's work as a valuable source of information. Fedchenko had very little to say about women, who merit mention only in passages such as this one:

> We found the chief watchman [*qorovul-begi*] terribly irritated. The problem was that the young soldiers [*jigit*] who had gone ahead had prepared nothing; they were in a deep sleep. Either on the road or when they arrived, they had smoked *nash* (hashish) very heavily and had given themselves over to sweet dreams. As is well known, after smoking nash, which most of the natives do habitually, a person plunges into sleep and experiences the most attractive dreams. Nash is prepared from the flowers and surrounding leaves of the cannabis plant. These parts of the plant are pounded in water; the resulting, powderlike mass shrinks into crumbs; these are added to tobacco in a water pipe for smoking. A few draws are enough to make one intoxicated. In Muslim countries, these dry narcotics (in addition to nash, the natives also use opium) entirely replace hard liquor, which is severely forbidden by the Koran; but it has nothing to say about nash or opium, so it follows they are permitted: and so the demands of law and the need for diversion are both met, though the latter in a way that is more harmful to the body. And this is the case not only with nash. Among these same Muslims we see that women, following dictates of the Koran, cover themselves, turning themselves into scarecrows, even more ugly than those we use to scare the birds from our gardens: the goal is evidently to cut women off from the surrounding world—and for men, to turn away their every glance. And in fact? Men, who have no access to women's faces and figures, ogle young boys, fall in love with them, flirt with them, go trolling for them, and so on, leading to the most unnatural acts. While women, following the law, disfigure themselves, but of course, you cannot overcome nature, so there are uncivilized results: the special product of Uratiube's industry, or couplings, even though there is a certain death sentence (burying the body neck deep in a hole and then stoning the head with rocks) if it becomes public.[31]

Fedchenko managed to combine a variety of exotic images to fortify his own Russian superiority: Sarts were drug addicts, the women made themselves deliberately ugly because of Islamic law, and men turned to boys to fill their sexual needs. The scope and imagery of this passage leave no doubt that Russia's Orientalists could rival England's Lord Cromer in the realm of contempt for "the natives."[32] Fedchenko's work was indeed "an intellectual tool for ensuring the West's domination over the East," to borrow David Schimmelpenninck van der Oye's words.[33]

An ethnographic publication that may have influenced the Nalivkins' study of Sart women was A. P. Khoroshkhin's 1876 *Collection of Articles regarding Turkestan Territory*, in which the author, another officer in a Cossack regiment, offered descriptions of Sart women in Tashkent and Tajik and Uzbek women in

Bukhara and Samarkand. Khoroshkhin collected his evidence by living in these communities for months or years, but he offers no explanation for the source of his interpretations of Sart women. He wrote of their clothing and their external appearance, "It is remarkable that among Sart women, many are pockmarked, but this does not disturb the fact that Sart women still fully conform to European understandings of beauty." He described some of their domestic tasks and presented what he imagined or was told of the influence of Islamic laws on women's lives. A girl might be married young, as one of multiple wives of an older man, but she would find a way to "breathe free air" no matter what conditions Sharia placed on her. "Her husband? He was either elderly or loved another woman or was in the shop or was, after all, a member of the circle of devotees of masculine beauty, and she was always alone."[34] His version of the character of the Sart woman, a theme that the Nalivkins also enjoyed, was this:

> Marks of character that are common to women of all peoples are not foreign to Sart women: they are coquettish, quarrelsome, and will even get into a fist-fight over trifles and gossip about each other. They hold their husbands in their hand and at the same time suffer under their yoke and finally run off to lovers. In a word, inherent in Sart women are all of the passions, great and small: she is vengeful, jealous, and more dangerous than other women in her jealousy.[35]

Khoroshkhin had nothing more positive to say about women's lives among Tajiks and Uzbeks in Samarkand and the Zarafshan Valley, where he declared they simply were used as men's servants and possessions, that women were not taught their rights according to the Qur'an, and that Tajik men were prone to murder each other and rape women. He also wrote that Uzbeks of the Zarafshan Valley did not permit prostitution or drunkenness and did not commit murder or rape but would kidnap girls to show their bravado.[36]

While in many ways the Nalivkins' interests overlapped with Fedchenko's and Khoroshkhin's, their portraits of Sart women and men were less judgmental, less interested in stirring shock and fear in their reader, and far more humane. Like many other foreign travelers to Turkestan, Fedchenko selected images that he could judge as exotic and debauched. The Nalivkins expressed their point of view in *A Sketch*'s final words: "For a farewell, we want to tell our reader a Sart saying: *Hamma odam bir odam*. All people are the same." Their closing reflects the tone of much of this work: the Nalivkins assumed that human needs and motivations are universal; therefore, unfamiliar Sart practices could be explained and understood and were more similar to Russian practices than the reader would first imagine.

The Nalivkins revealed their awareness of the norms of Russian ethnographic writing, which emphasized defining and describing nationalities. Historian Nathaniel Knight discusses the development of scholarly ethnography in

Russia under N. I. Nadezhdin: "While Nadezhdin's interests lay primarily with Russian folk, his methods were equally applicable to the various peoples of the empire. Thus, as ethnography took deeper root from the 1850s onward, its classic genre became the free-standing ethnographic portrait of an individual national group."[37] Russian ethnographers were eager to delineate and describe Turkestan's various ethno-linguistic groups, and the Nalivkins took an active role in debating what defined group identity, characteristics, and belonging.

The ethnonym Sart had a wide range of meanings in Central Asia in the nineteenth century. As Sergei Abashin explains, the Nalivkins participated in an ongoing disagreement with other Russian Orientalists over whether "Sart" was a meaningful or derogatory term and, if meaningful, then what the parameters of Sart identity might be.[38]

The Nalivkins' efforts to delineate Sarts contradicted Middendorff's influential arguments, found in his 1882 book, *Sketches of the Fergana Valley*. Middendorff, a zoologist and member of the Russian Academy of Sciences, devoted a section of his work to ethnography, by which he specifically meant a scientific categorization of the types of peoples found in the Fergana Valley. The peoples connoted by Tajik, Sart, Uzbek, and so on could be definitively distinguished using data on language, livelihoods, and physiognomy. Middendorff devoted many pages to describing Tajiks and very few to defining Uzbeks, while he determined that Sarts were "a mixture." "Most Sarts are so crossed with the Tajik type that they hardly differ at all from real Tajiks. It is commonly thought that this mixture may be differentiated according to a single attribute that remains of the Mongol physiognomy—namely, that the jawbone (jugular arc) protrudes more than among Tajiks."[39] Middendorff, steeped in biological sciences, sought his answers through reference to a variety of historical and scholarly works and his own research expeditions to the Fergana Valley, where measures of crania accompanied inventories of flora.

The Nalivkins, however, did their ethnographic work through long-term participant observation, not yet named as an anthropological method but one that, Lukashova notes, they undertook intuitively.[40] The Nalivkins noted that they used the term "Sart" because it had meaning for their audience but that in Nanay, the nontribal, sedentary speakers of a Turkic language called themselves Uzbeks. The Nalivkins used self-name, language, and lifestyle to differentiate Nanay's sedentary, agriculturalist Uzbeks from Kyrgyz, who were tribally organized, Turkic speaking, and seminomadic. Farming, trade, and settled life were associated with Sart (Uzbek), and herding and nomadic life, with Kyrgyz. Many specific customs and practices were linked to these fundamental differences. The Nalivkins viewed the formation of sedentary Uzbek communities as a process: Turkic-speaking nomads had settled and mixed with the Tajik-speaking indigenous peoples of Central Asia, and the domination of Persian terms in Uzbek for food and agriculture served as evidence of this transition. While Uzbeks in Nanay did not seem troubled by identity questions, scholars and nationalists in Central Asia continued to debate whether Sarts could really be considered an ethnic group and why so many sedentary Central Asians became identified as Uzbeks.[41]

However, Sart identity was not the Nalivkins' core focus; instead, they were offering their Russian ethnography-consuming readers an in-depth study of Muslim women. Nalivkina, like other educated Russian women of the 1870s, was probably familiar with salient themes in Russian thought on women and the "woman question." In the 1860s, Russian feminist thought and activism emerged in the context of Alexander II's Great Reforms. Maria Vernadskaia argued for women's equal education with men on the basis that women and men are "equal beings."[42] As urbanization and industrialization in Russia created more opportunities for women to enter wage labor, members of the intelligentsia and reformers emphasized women's right to work outside the home and earn money, whether out of necessity or for fulfillment. In the process of judicial reforms, begun in 1860s, Russia's legal experts began to reject the patriarchal concepts of Russia's *Domostroi* (the sixteenth-century code of household conduct) and instead "formulated a new ideal of the family . . . as a union of individuals in which mutual affection . . . gave rise to a combination of individual rights and mutual obligations." Legal reformers promoted "reduction, and even elimination, of the control of a husband over the economic activities of his wife" and the expansion of the state's role in protecting "wives from abuse."[43] This growing concept that marriage should be based on affection and on economic cooperation rather than on patriarchal protection and dominance shaped Maria and Vladimir's own marriage as well as their questions about Sart women and families.

The Nalivkins took up their farming life in Nanay in a period when intelligentsia members of Russia's *Narodnik* movement were "going to the peasants" to stir up peasant political consciousness and bring their own versions of progress to the Russian countryside. The Nalivkins, however, did not present themselves as radicals or social reformers or as interfering with those Sart customs that they criticized. The only exception to their stance as noninterfering observers arises in their account of spreading the idea that husbands and wives should work as partners. They write, "Several times we have either been asked to lend money or invited to become a participant in a commercial company or a trade or agricultural enterprise. If the husband agreed, we would ask him whether his wife also agreed; if he refused, he was asked not to hurry but to discuss it with his wife, since she may find the offer interesting or beneficial." In describing women's lives, the Nalivkins were especially interested in what kinds of work women performed, how they contributed to the family economy, what property ownership meant for women, and how property relations and sources of income shaped husband-wife relations. These themes were prevalent in Russia's "woman question" and were at the core of the novel that epitomized feminist thought in the reform period, Nikolai Chernyshevsky's *What Is to Be Done?*

Russian intelligentsia discourses on women and work explored and critiqued the economic conditions underlying prostitution, a theme that the Nalivkins engage repeatedly.[44] In 1843, the Russian government began regulating prostitution: prostitutes could register and ply their trade legally if they were associated with a recognized brothel. After 1876, the Russian military forces in the Fergana Valley opened brothels that, according to the Nalivkins, attracted Sart girls and women who were seeking escape or adventure. Historian Laurie Bernstein writes, concerning Russian thought on selling sex, that "gender ideology functioned as the underpinning of regulation and prostitution, couching the existence of commercial sex in terms of male need and female depravity."[45] By the 1870s, researchers, political activists, and feminists published competing interpretations of prostitution: Did women enter prostitution out of economic need? Because of coercion or men's oppression? Because of social and economic problems? Because of their own immoral desires? Although every interpretation regarded prostitution as a problem to be solved, the Nalivkins present prostitution as a normal part of life rather than as a problem, and their questions focus on why Sart women prostitutes entered prostitution, what they gained from it, and why and how they could leave prostitution.

The Nalivkins were aware of Russian discourses about the oppression of women, and they allude to their expectation that their reader imagined Muslim women to be even more oppressed than European women. The authors were skeptical, at times offering their opinion that Sart women were less oppressed than European women and at times refusing such sweeping generalizations in favor of analyses of Sart women as agents able to strategize and accomplish their own purposes, even under unpleasant and oppressive circumstances. They were interested in the ways that Islamic norms articulated in the Qur'an and in Sharia limited women and also gave women opportunities, illustrating their interpretations with evidence from everyday life in Nanay.

A Sketch begins with a geographically situated view of ethnography that was widespread among members of the Imperial Geographic Society: the writer first had to examine geographic conditions because they were assumed to shape human societies. For example, the Nalivkins wrote that Sarts relied on agriculture because the climate made it profitable but that this pleasant climate also resulted in "the population's comparative lack of needs," and thus there was little development of industry and "a lack of strong and progressive development of people's minds." This geographic introduction was then integrated with a Russian scholarly trend toward examining the lives of Russian working women and peasant women. While nineteenth-century imperial ethnography in Russia and in other empires tended to use study of ethnic "others" to advocate for greater imperial intervention, this volume's focus on women raises the reader's anticipation that the authors would call for particular Russian administrative interventions to relieve Sart women of oppression or to civilize women, meaning draw women toward Russian culture.

The Nalivkins wrote of their hopes that commercial relations with Russia would improve Turkestan's forms of production but pointed out that so far this connection "has contributed too little that could influence native life in the direction of progress." They criticized Khudoyar Khan's regime as wasteful and proposed that Russian style, state-sponsored charitable and socially beneficial organizations like orphanages might improve the lives of Sarts.[46] They told of their own interactions with their Sart servant girl, pointing out that by providing her with plenty to eat, they cured this poverty-stricken child's propensity toward petty theft. Since their own marital economic relations were apparently very interdependent and transparent, Maria and Vladimir expressed some disdain over Sart wives who "steal" from their husbands to provide food for their children. Yet they repeatedly expressed doubt that Russian intervention in Sart life would produce any positive results; instead, they adhered to the view that Russia was wreaking moral harm on Sart life.

Overview of the Text

The volume begins with a physical description of the Fergana Valley, the plants that grow there, the irrigated oases, and the people who live in the mountains and valley. To keep this description from becoming tedious, the authors chose to present themselves as hosts, speaking directly to the reader as "you" and inviting the reader to come along on a ride from the mountaintop down to Nanay. This journey takes the reader through kishlaks, their streets, mosques, and shops, and then begins to describe in more detail the livelihoods of those who farm and those who carry out trade, noting in both cases the ways that Islamic religious ideas shape attitudes and ordinary processes.

This leads into a discussion of religion, starting with a very lengthy translation of passages from the Qur'an, followed by a description of some beliefs and practices. They introduce the Qur'an by commenting that it "was written by Muhammad" and, disparagingly, that "there is often no logical connection between chapters or even among verses in a single chapter." The Nalivkins selected and presented several hundred verses concerning women or family life. Neither Vladimir nor Maria knew Arabic; instead, they reproduced a Russian translation by G. S. Sablukov, first published in 1877.[47] Other than stating that these verses concern women, the Nalivkins give no additional explanation for their choices. Were these verses that their local informants frequently cited? Were these verses particularly important to local practice? How did local imams or judges interpret and use these verses? The Nalivkins imply that these verses were important to understanding the lives of Sart women, on the assumption that a normative text like the Qur'an must be shaping daily life. Throughout the volume, they make frequent reference to "religion" and occasionally to a specific verse or hadith as the explanation for particular choices in dress and social interaction. The selections from the Qur'an are followed by an explanation of Islamic educational institutions and practices in the Fergana Valley and a discussion of the ways Islamic thought shapes attitudes about various ways of making a living. After the quotations from the Qur'an, very little in this chapter concerns women.

As a theme, Islam surfaces throughout the text largely as an explanation for attitudes and common practices. The Nalivkins refer to Islam as a system that shapes everyday practices and guides people's understanding of right behavior, but they do not discuss Islam as individual faith. They describe a woman praying at home and note that women went on pilgrimages. They initiate a discussion of women's religious knowledge but soon turn to the more general theme of women's lack of formal education. If Sarts in Nanay appreciated their own faith in internal and spiritual ways, the Nalivkins apparently did not ask questions leading to discussion of that aspect of religion. In their understanding, Sart women who made pilgrimages to shrines did so to seek resolution to specific problems, such as childlessness. Perhaps this was exactly what their interlocutors told the Nalivkins about faith, or perhaps this reflected the Nalivkins' own attitude toward religion. The Nalivkins' daughter, Natalia, reported that when Vladimir was younger, he attended church "either out of conviction or coercion," but later in life he said, "Religion arose when the first con man met the first fool."[48] Accounts of Vladimir's suicide note report that he requested a civil funeral, "as I long ago ceased belonging to any religion."[49] If the Nalivkins were themselves believers when they were doing their research in Nanay, their text leaves no trace of this: none of their comments about Islam implied any contrast or comparison with Russian Orthodox or other Christian beliefs.

After the chapter on Islam, the Nalivkins turn to daily life, means of earning a living, houses, and food. After explaining how houses are built, the authors mention women when they note the construction of spaces meant to separate women from men who were not members of the family. This chapter appears almost a series of notes, without argument or direction, although the authors follow a theme of class differentiation, illustrating the variance in wealthy and poor families' consumption patterns. Passages disparaging Sarts' lack of cleanliness, such as one warning the European visitor to avoid sleeping on bug-ridden bedding, contrast with others admiring outhouses for their hygienic conditions and lack of odors. The Nalivkins were shocked that "the natives manage not to catch colds and die in the hundreds because of staying near the *sandal* [heater] all day," a practice that flew in the face of their own beliefs about the source of colds.

At last, the essay addresses its core topic: women. A chapter that describes its subject in terms of dress and appearance is in fact about far more than this, presenting family life, birth, marriage, relations within the household, holiday practices, and many other topics while repeatedly returning to sartorial details. The paranji, a head-to-toe veiling robe, always featured prominently in Russian descriptions of Sart women, but the Nalivkins tried to move beyond this image so that description of clothing would lead to examinations of social class, stages of life, work and leisure, and women's activities inside and outside the home. Direct observation and Sart women's own explanations of their interests shaped Maria's writing, but the Nalivkins also articulated numerous rather inexplicable assumptions of their own, such as that "the concept of fashion must have appeared fairly recently." For the reader seeking images that correspond to this chapter's detailed descriptions of clothing and jewelry, Johannes Kalter's *The Arts and Crafts of Turkestan* (1984) provides an accessible collection of photos and explanations in English.

Like others who attempted to present a general picture of Central Asian peoples to a Russian audience, the Nalivkins describe "typical" Sart body and facial types, but in these seemingly objective passages, they refer to two views of beauty: their own and the view Nanay residents communicated to them. The Nalivkins deemed long torsos and short foreheads as "shortcomings," as though their judgment conformed to some universal standard, while they also point out that Sart women viewed facial birthmarks, light skin, and long dark hair as the epitome of beauty. This variation between the imagined, abstract, universal view and the situated, reflexive view runs through the entire work. At times, the Nalivkins consciously contrast their own Russian preferences with Sart preferences, though they concede nothing at all about the ways their own class backgrounds shaped their view of self or of Russianness. At other times, the Nalivkins present the fact that Sarts sat on mats and ate from low tables or cloths spread on the floor as an absence, a lack of civilization.

Successive chapters examine Sart women's labor, their sources of income, and the roles of older and younger women in an extended family household. After explaining the intricacies of silk production, the authors return to the stylistic device of hosting the reader, this time on a walk through the bazaar, to observe women's actions in buying and selling, with attention to poverty, wealth, and women's efforts to overcome difficulties. Here some of the descriptions verge on maudlin, for example, when the Nalivkins portray the struggles of a widow thus: "Only Allah knows how she manages not to die from hunger." They then consciously highlight their own use of such images to elicit the reader's pity and discomfort: "Do I need to tell you, reader, what is going on here? Should I tell you that this morning the corals were taken from her daughter; how the girl cried at losing her only treasure, which her late father gave her a year ago for a holiday? Should I explain why this is being done? Of course not. It is too dreary."

A more thorough description of goods sold in the bazaar leads into other consumption patterns, a lengthy list of the most commonly consumed foods and the most prized foods. The reader who is familiar with Fergana Valley cuisine may notice continuities such as the social value of *plov* (pilaf) and the way it is made and the variety of noodle-dough-based dishes. Obvious contrasts would be the absence in the nineteenth century of potatoes and of today's ubiquitous tomatoes and cucumbers. The Nalivkins make no mention of the fresh herbs that are so widely used in modern Uzbek cuisine. They do pay close attention to patterns, recording the kinds of details about expenditures and diet that Russian administrators collected for taxation purposes and that social activists used to demonstrate that peasants were ill fed and overtaxed.[50]

The chapter on the character of the woman is both a full-fledged construction of stereotypes and a close observation of women's family interactions, their festivities and customs. Maria Nalivkina's conversations with her friends and neighbors become evidence for observations about women's love affairs and sexual habits. The authors freely judge Sart women throughout this chapter, declaring their tears to be contrived and their mannerisms studied, while the word "natural" identifies the main criterion for judgment. The Nalivkins wavered between two quite different explanations for behavior. They knew that all societies raise their members, both male and female, to manifest their own culture's proper behaviors, and they illustrated this process of child rearing in Nanay. At the same time, the Nalivkins viewed the ways that they themselves felt and expressed emotion as natural: they recognized their own form of grieving, "the kind of grief that erases all other thoughts," as the only real grief and deemed all of Sart women's ways of mourning as unnatural.

Although their comparisons frequently present bourgeois Russian ways as a norm against which Sart practices are measured, they sometimes reverse the weight, valuing Sart women's actions as logical and superior to Russian cultural patterns. They were impressed by Sart women's wit in conversation and their ease in social situations. In depicting Sart emotional relationships, the Nalivkins voice criticism, intimating the superiority of their own middle-class Russian norms over Sart ways. They declare,

> If the moral aspect of the local kin relations between children and parents is weak, other kin relations are literally nonexistent, although there is a lot of talk about feelings and relations. . . . We can safely claim that local adult men and women have no feelings toward relatives at all in most cases, except for feelings toward small children, which exist only because of their helplessness.

Sarts did not express their feelings in the same way that the Nalivkins did, and the Nalivkins felt confident characterizing this as a lack of the tenderness they would have thought characteristic of Russians, at least those of their social class. But later, they write of other Sart child-rearing practices:

> In the child's presence, they discuss everything and everyone, calling everything by its name. . . . Thus, six- or seven-year-old Sart children know all about things that are often kept as a mystery from many of our fifteen- to seventeen-year-old young ladies. . . . The only thing that we can attest in this regard is that most Sart children talk with extreme sensibility and credibility.

This observation implies a critique of Russian, or at least bourgeois Russian, silences about bodies and sexuality and the idea that Russians might learn something from Sarts. The Nalivkins also subject men's character to examination, covering topics as diverse as styles of fighting, the morality of theft and waste, and fears, folk healing, and magic.

After these widely scattered themes, the Nalivkins address women's lives in what they considered a logical order, by illustrating women's journeys from birth through childhood, to marriage, divorce, widowhood, and death. This structure for ethnographic writing may have influenced the much better-known (but later) Russian work *Zhizn' Ivana* (The life of Ivan; 1906) by Ol'ga Semenova Tian'-Shanskaia, which follows a rural Russian male's life from birth to death.[51] Maria's close interactions with women allowed her to describe birthing practices and Sart ways of ensuring a newborn's health. They found Sart preferences for sons the same as Russian preferences; the arrival of a daughter was celebrated, not to the same degree as a son's birth, but they depicted no hint of attitudes that would have reduced survival rates for daughters.[52] They noted that all children were exposed to poor nutrition, smallpox, and "unhygienic" conditions such as going barefoot and wearing no pants: "Why they do not die by the thousands boggles the mind." The Nalivkins' section on marriage includes discussion of topics that non-Muslims found interesting about Muslims, such as polygyny and marriage of young adolescent girls, and they argue that *qalin* (bridewealth) given at marriage was not to be equated with selling a daughter; rather, it was one element in a series of exchanges that provided for the newlyweds. The Nalivkins write that both men and women obtained divorce easily and that being divorced posed no obstacle to remarriage. They offer no evidence to support these claims, so the reader is left wondering whether this impression could indeed be proven or whether the Nalivkins perceived Muslim divorce as common and easily obtained simply because it contrasted with the situation among Russian Orthodox Christians in the Russian Empire, for whom divorce was nearly impossible.[53] Linda Benson's studies show that many foreign observers of the same time period shared similar impressions about the ease of marriage and divorce among Muslims in Eastern

Turkestan (Xinjiang province, China).[54] Here, more than elsewhere in the text, the Nalivkins provide extensive footnotes to the Qur'an and to Hanafi jurisprudence (Sharia) to either explain Sart practices or to demonstrate a variance between Sart practice and Islamic law on marriage and divorce.

Finally, the Nalivkins turn to an analysis of prostitution, examining what they could find out about pre-Russian-conquest practices and developments since the conquest, Russian ways of encouraging prostitution, Sart women's motivations for becoming prostitutes and means for leaving prostitution, and Sart social attitudes regarding prostitution. One of their explanations makes men the initiators of prostitution: "The owners of brothels are almost exclusively men, and the women in the brothels are their legal wives, which is the reason why there are not more than four prostitutes in each brothel. A Sart takes three or four wives and trades in them." Other sections of this chapter ascribe more agency to women: "A wife who could not legally divorce her husband or a maiden who was still dependent on her parents ran away and came to the owner of the brothel to take her as a prostitute. . . . In the beginning, she enjoys her unprecedented freedom and merry pastime so much that she becomes afraid that her husband might track her down." However, women who spent time in prostitution could leave and successfully marry again, the Nalivkins reported, a story that may have been a selective view but was similar to what Benson's sources showed for divorced women and prostitutes in Kashgar. The Nalivkins seem to be winding up with an extensive example of interacting with prostitutes, an account that probably reflected Vladimir's experiences or stories that were told to Vladimir and Maria, but the account stutters. First they mention an 1883 performance by gymnasts in Namangan, but after noting that tickets were in high demand, that narrative line disappears. Then they begin describing a party with prostitutes, and again, the story stops after only a few sentences. The whole volume comes to an abrupt ending, as though the censor simply cut some pages and then sent the manuscript on for publication.

An Ethnography of Lasting Value

The Nalivkins illustrated the lives of Sart women in multifaceted ways. Readers of their own time regarded their efforts as successful, and it is my hope that readers of this translation will find it valuable for its descriptions of Nanay Uzbek women in the 1880s and as an example of late nineteenth-century ethnography. The historian Schimmelpenninck van der Oye posits that "many Russians have been conscious of their own Asian heritage" and that this factor shapes Russian Oriental studies. The Nalivkins, to the extent that they discussed themselves or Russian identity, never suggested anything other than absolute difference: they were Russians, and they were observing Sarts, and the two belonged in utterly different categories. Although they did not posit shared Asian heritage, they did believe in shared humanity. Their approach to this study was largely "sympathetic and respectful," guided by their belief that "hamma odam bir odam" (all people are the same).

Soviet-period ethnographers and historians found the Nalivkins' book on women to be of lasting value, citing it repeatedly as a source of information about Uzbek and Fergana Valley culture in the imperial period. Post-Soviet ethnographers who read the Russian version of this text continue to make use of it.[55] The Nalivkins' attention to details of customs, dress, food, housing, and family relationships and their apparent appreciation of many aspects of Sart life made this project more valuable as a source of ethnographic and cultural information than most of the contemporaneous nineteenth-century Russian publications about Sarts.

Contemporary historian Natalia Lukashova assesses the Nalivkins' standpoint as one that sought to

> avoid many negative and positive stereotypes in understanding the traditional social order in the Muslim East that had already become fixed in Russian and European consciousness and that sometimes continue into the present. Most demonstrative of this is the final chapter [on prostitution], but in every preceding chapter as well the reader finds quite a lot that contradicts his stubborn preconceptions about prerevolutionary Central Asia. At the same time, while the authors' respect for the local civilization is evident, it is also obvious that they share a positivist and Eurocentric view of it [local civilization] as a stage that is lower than that of the European.[56]

I concur with Lukashova's summary. I have found many of their descriptions helpful as I sought to understand early twentieth-century Uzbek women's attitudes and practices about veiling. Their comments about Sart preferences for arranging marriages for daughters to men who lived nearby are echoed in anthropologist Peter Finke's present-day findings on Uzbek preferences for marriages. Instructions on the etiquette of bread and how to sit properly are still followed today. Descriptions of festive occasions and holidays show continuity in many practices but some important shifts as well: Nanay Uzbeks called their spring holiday Sayil, not Navruz, and celebrated it later than the vernal equinox, with picnicking and watching *bachcha* (young boy dancers) performing in the grassy fields outside town.[57] Portrayals of houses and uses of domestic space shed light on many features still common in present-day Fergana Valley homes, although Soviet efforts to change gender practices led to the demise of the division into women's and men's courtyards.[58] Foods that the Nalivkins described still appear in ordinary meals in Fergana Valley rural homes, as well as on menus in cafés specializing in "national cuisine." The descriptive details offer ethnographers and historians materials on everyday life in a Fergana Valley village as the Kokand Khanate ended and the Russian Empire brought a wave of change.

Like anyone who attempts to cross a cultural and linguistic divide and observe another culture, the Nalivkins brought themselves, their own assumptions, prejudices, and knowledge to their sojourn in Nanay. Russians of a rather privileged class but not wealthy, educated and well read but not academically trained, they became respected ethnographers by writing and publishing this book. Readers of this translation should be aware that the Nalivkins' lens frames every image and that their association with the Russian administration of Turkestan shaped their interactions with Sarts in Nanay in ways they did not reveal and perhaps did not even consciously consider. However, this does not mean that we should read this ethnography solely to understand how Orientalism shaped Russian visions of Central Asian cultures. The Nalivkins were not impartial observers; nor were they inventing what they described: they wrote about what they saw, what they experienced, and what Uzbek women and men in Nanay and elsewhere in the Fergana Valley told them. Their work provides us with an enduring portrait of a moment after the Kokand Khanate was defeated, when its forms of Islamic rule were officially gone but before Russian imperial law, administration, and culture came to dominate rural Central Asian communities.

On the Translation

Although *A Sketch* was deemed an extraordinary work of ethnography in its time, this is the first translation of the work into English. Copies of the original Russian publication are held by various libraries, and a PDF of the text can be found online. I first read *A Sketch* at the Library of Congress around 1990, and in 1993 Dr. Dilarom Alimova allowed me to make a photocopy of her copy of the book. An opportunity to translate this work arose thanks to Dr. Daniel Waugh, who was able to make funding available from the Silk Road Foundation to pay for primary translation.

Mariana Markova, who holds a PhD in anthropology, undertook the task of translating the whole text from Russian to English. I edited that translation, reading Markova's translation against the original, correcting, rephrasing, and rendering the Uzbek words as they appear in the early twenty-first-century Uzbek Latin alphabet. The Nalivkins used and defined many Uzbek terms. Where they provided an in-text translation, I do so as well. Where they left terms untranslated, I provide a translation in brackets or a longer translation and explanation in a note on first use. If a term is used repeatedly, I do not provide an explanation every time, but these terms can be found in the glossary.

The Nalivkins put some of their explanations and citations in footnotes; I identify notes that appear in the original text with the designation "Authors' note." All other notes are mine and Mariana Markova's. Annotations about specific topics, from nineteenth-century vernacular architecture to food and customs, draw heavily on Soviet-period ethnographic works listed in the bibliography. Throughout the text, parentheses ( ) are used in places where the Nalivkins used parentheses in the original; brackets [ ] indicate my additions.

I use widely accepted spellings of Central Asian names or words that are already familiar to an English-language reader, such as Tashkent (Toshkent) and Fergana (Farg'ona). In cases where place-names are less familiar, I follow the Nalivkins' spelling, as in the case of Turkestan with an "e," Russian style, rather than Turkistan, although I decided to use the modern Uzbek spelling Qo'qon, rather than the Nalivkins' Kokan.

When the Nalivkins included an Uzbek word in the text, I present that word in its modern Latin Uzbek spelling. In making this choice, I deliberately part ways from the practices of my fellow philologists and Orientalists. Some historians and philologists conform to a consistent system of transliteration for the Arabic alphabet; such a practice renders Qo'qon as Khoqand. Others adopt an unused medial alphabet that attempts to render all Turkic words with one set of letters so that modern Uzbek *so'yla* becomes *soylä*. These choices enable the scholars to present words in ways that their fellow scholars approve but that would not be understood by ordinary Uzbek speakers. I contend that we do not change German, French, Turkish, or Vietnamese spellings from their version of the Latin alphabet to some other form for the sake of history or philology, and we should not do that to Uzbek spellings either.

Others, generally those scholars who know Russian but not Uzbek, transliterate through Russian. This would lead to including all of the Russian pronunciation norms that crept into the Nalivkins' presentation of Uzbek words, for example, making Uzbek *chorikor* into Russianized *chairiker*. Furthermore, the Nalivkins considered Uzbeks to have corrupted the pronunciation of various words by turning the vowel sound "ah" into the vowel sound found in the English word "awe," a shift that is seen in the word "namoz," so they would "correct" this back to the letter "a." In the glossary, I provide the Uzbek Latin version of a word first, followed by a transliteration of the Nalivkins' Russianized version of the word.

Some of my choices are inconsistent: I use kishlak rather than the Uzbek *qishloq* because kishlak is widely used in Turkic languages and in English-language scholarly work. However, I use the Uzbek versions of certain words that would be better known to a reading audience with a different transliteration: imom rather than imam, and namoz rather than namaz. In some cases, the distinction is important: Uzbek *ulomo* (Islamic scholars) is different from Uzbek *ulama* (hair extensions).

Many of the Uzbek terms that the Nalivkins used are found and defined in one of two dictionaries, the *Uzbek Language Explanatory Dictionary* and the *Uzbek-Russian Dictionary*.[59] However, in numerous instances, for obscure Uzbek terms, as well as for terms where the Nalivkins' transliteration is too imprecise or too unlike modern renderings, I relied on the expertise of Donoxon Abdugafurova, who grew up in rural Namangan region and whose university specialization in Uzbek language and literature built her knowledge of archaic and modern terms. In some cases, Abdugafurova marshaled her parents' and grandparents' knowledge of folk customs, objects, and practices to explain terms and phrases to me. Rahimjon Abdugafurov shared his expertise on Uzbek approaches to Islam to explain some religious terms, names of historic figures, and texts. I owe both Donoxon and Rahimjon many thanks. I also owe Ol'ga Pugovkina gratitude for her research, providing me with archival files and articles about the Nalivkins.

I went to Nanay for an afternoon in 1991, taken there by a friend from Namangan, Ikrom Nugmanxo'jaev. In early summer, Nanay was small and cool and pleasant after hot, bustling Namangan. The river still flows through Nanay, and there were teahouses along its banks, but Soviet modernization had brought new kinds of roads, housing, clothing, transportation, goods, work, and lifestyles to Nanay, and those have surely changed even more in the twenty years since Uzbekistan became independent.

A Sketch of the Everyday Life of Women of the Sedentary Native Population of the Fergana Valley

Vladimir and Maria Nalivkin

V. Nalivkin, M. Nalivkina.

A Sketch of the Everyday Life of Women of the Sedentary Native Population of the Fergana Valley.

Kazan. The printing house of the Imperial University, 1886.

Permitted by the censor, Kazan 4 July 1886
Preface

The relatively small acquaintance of Russians with the everyday life of the native population in general, and more specifically with the daily life of women here, gave us the idea of sharing with the reading public the results of those observations that we have been able to carry out in several years among the Sarts of Fergana Oblast when we were living under external conditions that were thoroughly Sart.

Those conditions, together with some knowledge of the language, made it measurably easier for us to draw near to native society.

Whether this has allowed us to draw, reliably and smoothly, a picture of this life, while remaining sufficiently objective, let the gracious reader judge.

We will be entirely satisfied if, in spite of notices of inadequacies, blunders, and omissions, the reader still says that our humble work presents him with something interesting.

The Authors

1   A Short Sketch of the Fergana Valley

Fᴇʀɢᴀɴᴀ ɪs ᴀ ᴠᴀʟʟᴇʏ that runs from northeast to southwest, surrounded by mountain ranges that open up only to its southwestern corner, near Khujand.

The length of the valley from Khujand to Uzgentom (in [geographic] projection) is approximately 300 versts.[1] The greatest distance between the base of the foothills is about 130 versts, and the smallest (near Maxram), about 30 versts. Longitudinally, the valley is cut by the river Syr-Darya, formed from the junction of the Naryn and Kara-Darya Rivers, a few versts to the south of Namagan. Many small rivers and streams run down the mountain slopes and partly in the foothills, but mainly when they flow into the valley, their flow diverges into an enormous network of *ariq*s, artificial irrigation channels.

The major cities, the most populated trade and industrial settlements, are Qo'qon [Kokand], Marg'ilon, Andijon, Namangan, Osh, and Chust. Apart from these cities, which correspond to six current *uezd*s [administrative divisions or regions] of Fergana *oblast'* [province], there are *kishlak*s (villages), some of which—for example, Isfara and Rishtan of Qo'qon region, Shaxrixon and Assaka of Marg'ilon region, and Uzgent of Andijon region—compare in size and population to such cities as Osh and Chust.

Depending on the local climate, all cultivated crops (grains, vegetables, fruit, and nonfruit trees) can be grown only provided that the soil is artificially irrigated, and that is why cultivated lands, planted trees, and sedentarization can be found only where local conditions were conducive to construction of ariqs.

If you could look at Fergana in the summer *a vol d'oiseau* [with a bird's-eye view], its lowlands would appear in hues of gray and yellow from the sand and saline steppes, almost devoid of vegetation, with occasional patches of greenery. These spots are cultivated oases nurtured by the local irrigation systems, large and small, the beauty and grandeur of middle Asia.

The characteristic features of the modern oases are so similar that they really differ only in size. In general, each large oasis that contains a city (or a large market kishlak) appears thus:

The external border of the elliptically shaped oasis has rather large plots of unfenced, cultivated fields where wheat, grain, lucerne [alfalfa], cotton, and beets are grown. The closer we get to the center of the oasis, the smaller the plots become, their cultivation visibly improves, and the more frequently one finds fields protected by rammed earth walls 1½ to 2 arshin in height,[2] inside of which grow mulberry (for sericulture), poplar, and other trees, with the above-mentioned crops plus vegetables (melons, watermelons, carrots, and onions), tobacco, and occasional vineyards. Further, there are almost no unfenced fields; the plots are bordered by few or many trees, in one line or in a double row. These are mainly mulberry trees, poplars, willows, and Russian olives.[3] Many places are shaded by elms and walnuts. Grain crops are almost completely replaced by vegetables, lucerne, and vineyards; on the roads one meets more and more *araba*,[4] some empty and some loaded; more people walking or riding horses; on all sides at every step there are gardens with vineyards, pomegranate trees, apples, pears, plums, cherries, walnuts, mulberries, poplars, and elms. Finally, the city itself begins.

The streets are always narrow; often two arabas can pass each other only with difficulty by scraping axle tips on neighboring fences and the walls of the houses, or in cases when they cannot pass, one of the arabas has to be backed by its horse till it reaches the nearest cross street, which it enters to let the other cart pass by. That is how narrow the streets are. The streets are lined by gray, rammed-earth walls[5] of one-story houses, with flat, earthen roofs and no windows facing the street; the fences, also of clay, are similar; the gates and wicket doors are small. The town turtledoves look like Egyptian doves; slim, suspicious-looking, scabby dogs in the streets, on the roofs, and on the walls, from which they bark at people that pass or drive by. Half-naked, dirty, and nevertheless very good-looking boys and girls play in the dust of the street, and if they are not run down in dozens, it is only because Sarts regard riding at a swift pace as unacceptable. Sart women, with faces covered by a black [horse]hair net, in gray *paranjis*, robes with long sleeves, draped from the head, while the hem and the ends of the sleeves drag behind or at least reach the ground, move along alone or in twos, carrying children in their arms and bundles of silk cocoons on their heads, in a light, slightly hasty gait, by their gray figures reminding one more of mummies than living human beings.

[Male] Sarts in cotton-print, quilted, or occasionally silk robes or white or striped shirts in the same style as the robes and made from local cotton fabrics, in turbans and skullcaps, barefooted or in leather boots with outer galoshes, walking, riding horses, or on arabas; Jewish dyers wearing similar dress but with long side locks and hands always blue from dye; two or three Indians;[6] a Kyrgyz in a fur hat riding a small, bony nag with a roped-together line of camels; a small ariq cutting the street, with a stone slab over it instead of a small bridge. On the left, you can see the mosque with a flat, earthen roof open from the eastern side, its inside covered with white plaster, niches in the walls, various pillars, and a brightly painted ceiling; the yard has a pond with huge, shady elms planted around it; the entrance gate's base is a good arshin below ground level, with a grating at the bottom to prevent animals entering, which could desecrate this holy space for every Muslim; the faithful have to climb over that grating to enter.

The bazaar. From afar, one can smell the unpleasant, sharp odor of sesame oil, which is used right on the spot in the bazaar to prepare various foods; the buzz of hundreds or thousands of human voices, carrying out trade; the rattle of blacksmith's hammers and the neigh of horses. From time to time, there is a shrill bellow of a camel. Streets in the bazaar are much wider than the town's other streets. Shops, small or tiny, line both sides of the street; most have small, bulrush sunshades standing on thin willow switches. This is where blacksmiths, harness makers, saddlers, tailors, silversmiths, and coppersmiths work and trade; in the midst of these, *qassob* (butchers) and *baqqol* (petty grocers) sell meat, melons, carrots, peppers, onions, oil, rice, and tobacco.

Here is a small shop with books; next to it dumplings and pies are made and sold;[7] further on, fur coats are curried; here a *kudungar* uses a mallet made of elm to beat a brightly colored, intricately patterned *atlas* [silk fabric];[8] a *Maddah*, covered with sweat, his eyes popping out in ecstasy, walks up and down waving his hands and striking his chest with a fist, shrilly reciting the biography of some Muslim saint. Further on, there is a line of open-air stores with felts, lassoes made of [horse]hair, woolen sacks, and other similar items; the halvah seller screams "shakar-dak" (like sugar) at the top of his voice; from another direction, as if in answer, comes "muz-dak, sharbat!" (sherbet cold as ice!). On the corner in the *choy-xona* (teahouse) several well-dressed Sarts sit in a half circle, facing the bazaar, with a *bachcha*, a cheesy, dolled-up boy in their midst, drinking tea and smoking *chilim*, the local water pipe made of cane. Further on, there are long lines of covered shops with expensive goods, cottons, red calico, padding, scarves, most of them in the brightest of colors. In front of one of the shops a whole company of holy fools, *devona*, wearing *kuloh*, high conical hats from a red fabric, with long staffs, with gourds at their waist instead of our beggar's bags, sing and beg for alms; the storekeeper avoids looking at them and starts a conversation with one of the Sarts passing by. On the other side of the street, an *isiriqchi*, another holy fool, runs around in the crowd, fumigating the passersby with smelly smoke of an herb, *isiriq*, to protect them from the approach of *shaitan* (the devil) and begging for alms in return. On the left, there is a line of stores with pieces of cloth hanging on the walls, atlas, *kanaus, iparkak, adras*,[9] and other silk fabrics; further on, *attors* are sitting selling buttons, different kinds of fasteners, medicines, looking glasses, cosmetics, and other things; there are several shops with skullcaps of various patterns and colors. A group of loiterers is entertained by an Afghani with a dancing monkey that also performs a soldier walking with a rifle, a hunter crawling to catch game, and other tricks. A large open gate reveals the inside of a caravanserai, a spacious yard with a line of tiny *hujra*, or cells, along the walls, with huge scales, piles of leather, iron fetters, pots, and yokes, with potbellied Sart merchants, with nimble, comely clerks, with Kyrgyz cart men, and, finally, with a Russian clerk in a service cap carrying a thick notebook.

Not far from the bazaar is the *o'rda*, the citadel or former residence of the *bek* or *hokim* who managed this *viloyat* [province], where one can still find an old-fashioned copper artillery cannon on the bulwark and a sentry wearing a white shirt with epaulettes and a service cap. In the distance, beyond the thick willows and tall poplars, the windows and white walls of Russian houses appear. An officer in a white military jacket and service cap heads toward the citadel; a soldier's wife is carrying a bundle of washed and starched laundry;[10] a Russian fine lady and her daughter, wearing hats, are hiding under umbrellas; a Sart cart driver passes in a very wobbly hackney cab; several soldiers follow; a Russian store with two windows and a sign "Trade in groceries"; another one across the street says, "Take-out Drinks"; a post office with two lampposts painted in the ordinary brownish-green color; a telegraph; empty streets lined with trees planted very close to each other; a long white military barrack at one end; quiet, and above all of this a transparent blue sky, the sun so bright that it is impossible to look at any of the gray, clay fences for a long time because their shimmer reflects its burning, nearly vertical rays; and to finalize the picture, 41 degrees Celsius in the shade [106°F].

Kishlak village bazaars are, naturally, much smaller than in the cities; the trade is mainly bread and other agricultural produce; the selection of other goods is very limited, and most of them, including items of indigenous mastery, cannot be found at all. With exception of Qo'qon and Marg'ilon, bazaar days occur once a week. The other six days of the week, other than meat and vegetable shops and the choy-xona, only a few shops are open and only in the cities.

In the cities, between sunset and sunrise, only night watchmen can remain in the bazaar. (The Muslim religion recommends not carrying out trade at night, first, so that there is no competition with those sellers who cannot work at night, for some reason, and, second, because things should be sold when they can be measured and viewed without impediment.)

The number of kishlaks with a bazaar is relatively large. For instance, there were five bazaars in Namagan district, which has an area of 5,600 square versts and a population of about one hundred thousand.

As we mentioned earlier, cultivation and sedentary life depend here, first, on building ariqs, which, in turn, depends on the presence or absence of water suitable for irrigation as well as on land contours. The same reasons underlie the vast differences in the sizes of the oases and the distances between them.

Kishlaks vary between one hundred and two hundred households. In places where Kipchaks, Karakalpaks, Kurama, and the recently settled Kyrgyz make up the majority, kishlaks (unwalled villages) are relatively rare, and instead, there are *qo'rg'oncha*, settlements surrounded by tall walls, with battlements that have arrow slits. In the murky past, these served as small fortresses, which is how they got their name. (Qo'rg'on means a fortress; qo'rg'oncha, a small fortress.)

Now we would like to say a few words about the climate of the country that we are describing. Spring, and the start of agricultural fieldwork, begins in late February or early March. In terms of vegetation, spring is observed when some grasses (iris) appear and almond and apricot trees blossom. In May, heat brings the strongest flow of water in rivers and mountain streams because of mountain snowmelt. At about the same time, mulberries, apricots, and barley ripen. Wheat ripens in June. Grapes and maize, in July. Nights in June and July are sweltering, and myriad mosquitoes and sand flies make the heat even more unbearable. In August, the heat gradually recedes, nights become cooler, and mosquitoes slowly disappear. The warm, dry autumn starts in early October. By late October, *jugara* (sorghum), cotton, and rice ripen.

Winter, when temperatures drop below 0 degrees Celsius [32°F], usually starts in late November or early December and lasts till the middle of February. In the years when winters are cold, the temperature often drops below 23 degrees C; while, generally, the average temperature for December and January is between 5 and 15 degrees C.[11]

This description applies to the valley floor (Namangan, 1,340 feet above sea level; Marg'ilon, 1,480; Andijon, 1,512; see the map of Fergana Province published in 1879).[12]

As we approach the mountains, the landscape gradually rises above sea level, and the length of the summer and the average annual temperatures decrease. Sorghum, rice, melons, grapes, pomegranates, and cotton cannot ripen at 4,000 feet in altitude, and crops of flax and millet, which are not planted on the valley floor because of their low profit margin, enter the crop rotation.

Starting from the above-mentioned height, we can find birch trees along the northern mountain ridge and, further, at 7,000 to 8,000 feet, spruce and mountain ash. At 10,000 feet the snow stays until the end of April; it falls starting from the middle of September, though it usually melts; it covers the ground in mid- or late October.

Most precipitation falls in the mountains. No matter how warm the valley is in winter, the mountains remain snow covered above 5,000 to 6,000 feet.

Precipitation is lowest in July and August in the mountains, and in the valley after warm, snowless winters [precipitation is low] in May, June, July, August, and September, sometimes even until October.

Before we move to the topic of Fergana's population, we would invite the reader to mount a horse and take a short ride with us.

It is mid-June, and you are in Dzhaik, in the mountains, about 75 versts [50 miles] to the north of Namangan. The mountains part to form Dzhaik, a wide, green valley cut from east to west by two medium-size streams that fall into the Padshaat River [Padysha-ata River]. Quick and crystal clear, it flows noisily along its stone-covered bed by the very foot of the mountain on the western side of the valley. The banks are covered with birch trees, wild rose, *asamusa*,[13] and barberry; erosion exposes some birch tree roots, and the trees lean over to touch the water with their branches. From east to west, steep or slightly sloping green hills covered with shrubs have formed *soi*, ravines, leading toward the valley. An almost vertical stone range locks Dzhaik from the north; it is cracked in the middle, and the Padshaat River escapes through this almost 10-*sazhen'*-wide[14] crack, the so-called Kapchigai [Kapchagai Gorge]. Its waters roar, foam splashing the cliffs on its banks and over the boulders sticking up from below, sweeping down and piling broken spruce and birch trunks, and leaping the final rapid, loudly rush out of the narrow Kapchigai into the wide Dzhaik Valley.

At the far end of Kapchigai you can see giant granite masses of mountains with dark spots along their cliffs and white snowcaps. There are the upper courses of the rivers Kashka-su and Ming-Ilik, and the dark spots are spruce and other groves. The peaks are covered with alpine flora, such as a creeping evergreen (*archa*) that is similar to our juniper, fields filled with wild onion and small bright green alpine grasses, with intermittent cliffs, snow slowly melting below them, with snowcocks (*ular*) and mountain goats their sole inhabitants.

Below them, giant carpets of splendid greenery with bright, intricate patterns of mountain flowers spread along the sloping hills; dark groves of wide-branching juniper, graceful spruce, and occasional mountain ash cover the slopes.

Below these, a mix of birches, maple and apple trees, barberry, raspberry and currant, asamusa, wild rose, and other shrubs grows at the bottom of a deep, narrow crevice covering and obscuring the noisy, cold stream as it jumps the moss-covered boulders.

But let us return to Dzhaik. Kyrgyz *auls* made up of five to six yurts[15] are scattered all over the valley. It is midday and almost hot. *Tuurduk*, felts forming the yurt walls, are lifted and stuck under *kyrchoo*, a band encircling the yurt like a belt. In the evenings, the place is lively; Kyrgyz scatter in circles on the grass to hear storytellers' legends; children and teenagers are catching calves and tying them to fences and lassoing goat kids to a yoke held up by two posts in the ground. Women hurriedly milk the goats and cows into wooden buckets. One hears voices all around, the neighing of horses driven close to the auls, mooing of the cattle and bleating of the goats and rams; in other words, the place is alive. But not now. It is quiet. Men sleep in the yurts, children sleep or play by the river, and only the women keep spinning tufts of goat or camel wool on their eternal spindles.

A herd of horses stands atop the nearest mountain, heads down, waving off the flies with their tails; below them restless goats appear among the bushes, and down near the river well-fed bulls and cows lie at ease, breathing heavily, eyes half-closed.

Facing the heat, you mount the horse and ride to Namangan.

The road is poor and rocky, which is why after riding 20 versts along the riverbank through the valley, you have only reached Nanay kishlak, where you will stay with our mutual acquaintance Mullah-Tash-Bai for the night. He has a spacious, high *mehmon-xona* (guestroom in the front courtyard) and a pleasant, newly planted garden, watered by a large ariq flowing from the clear, cold Padshaat.

At the moment, however, Nanay has little to recommend it. All the trees except the so-called autumn red apple tree are finished blossoming, and cherries and apricots are not yet ripe. The cherries are turning yellow, and the apricots will ripen in two or three weeks.

The road to Nanay, as we mentioned, passes through the valley, sometimes along the river and sometimes diverging to the side, going around the thicket of osier, seaberry, and other shrubs, around small bogs and cultivated fields that stretch intermittently up to Nanay.

At first the mountains are high, their northern ridges covered with shrubs, becoming lower and more barren on both sides as we approach Nanay, and finally, near the kishlak, they flatten into the wide plain Karavan-dala, which runs southward from Nanay 8 versts [5.3 miles], terminating at the mountains Bospu and Ungar.

Starting from Karamashat (a natural boundary about 12 versts from Nanay), you encountered tilled soil; you noticed barley forming grains and budding wheat; flax breaking into bloom, arshin-high maize without a hint of ears, and sprouting millet. On the road, you met two or three Kyrgyz men in pointed, white felt hats and yellow camel-wool robes, riding small, worn-out horses.

In one place, four men were cultivating maize with their *ketmon* (large hoe); when you approached them, they raised their heads, turned, and stared at you for a long time, after which they all started talking loudly among themselves. Closer to Nanay, here and there, you saw people walking barefoot with pants rolled above their knees, their long shirts tucked in, carrying ketmons; they directed the water coming from the ariq toward the crops of flax and corn.

Chivin, small mountain flies, hassled your horse; it shook its head despairingly throughout the whole journey, constantly tugging the reins, tiring you so much that you sleep like a log in the garden, lulled by the quiet whisper of the leaves and the rapid ariq. Sleep calmly. There are no mosquitoes, gnats, or scorpions here, though you will encounter them further on your journey. The early hours of the morning get chilly, but the caring host has already prepared a local padded quilt for you.

The next morning after breakfast you climb back on the horse and continue. It is hot, so you do not trot but drag.

The road meanders from Nanay to the foot of Ungar along the Karavan Valley among the fields of wheat, millet, flax, and fallow land. If it were not for

Ungar with its granite cliffs and green top, you could easily forget where you are and imagine yourself riding in the Russian countryside. The borders of the road, covered with grass, look the same; they run from the road and disperse in the crops; the same rutted, almost empty road; the same chatter of grasshoppers; the same cornflowers rise from among the grain; the same quails and skylarks.

Skirting Mamai village at the foot of Ungar Mountain, you cross the rocky verst-wide riverbed of Padshaat, split here into several channels; and passing Zarkent on your right, you continue along the ever dustier road into the flat, bare, sun-singed Iskovut steppe. The further you go, the hotter it gets. It is nearly noon; there is hardly a breath of wind; your head starts aching, and your eyes droop.

Ahead you see two Kyrgyz men, one walking and the other on horseback, driving a herd of fat-tailed rams; stretching their necks and nuzzling at the ground, they raised a cloud of loess dust that hovers in the air. This merchant's herd came from Aulie-ata, from Tokmak, across the mountains. Two or three fat rams that sprained a leg when crossing the rocky mountain pass are limping on three legs now.

Groaning and coughing from the dust, your horse galloped past the herd and has returned to a walk. The heat rises. The steppe is flat; *oqshuvoq* [Fergana wormwood] grows on both sides of the road; there is not a single tree to hide under or anything else to offer shade and rest. Yalanchag on the right and Iskovut ahead appear as if suspended in air.

Here and there appear fields of yellow wheat, *lutchak*,[16] its ears of grain nearly brown and lacking bristles. Three or four white spots flash somewhere ahead of you. These are *o'roqchi*, the sickle men, who have already started reaping wheat. Iskovut descended to the ground; it grows nearer; here you see the first dark green field, covered with sorghum, with leaves as broad as tropical sugarcane.

Then you see the low, pounded clay walls of *hayats*,[17] some of them run-down, protecting lucerne and other crops inside from cattle, with apricots, mulberry, or poplars planted along the walls.

And, finally, the kishlak itself starts. The walls are high with small gates and doorways.

Over there stands a row of slender Qo'qon poplars; on the left, an old, wide-branching peach tree with green, hard fruits has spread dusty branches over the fence; and next to them grows an apricot tree with a thick trunk and ripe orange fruit. Near the fence, you halted the horse under the branches, lifted yourself in the stirrup to reach for the nearest fruit, and pulled the branch too sharply; the beautiful overripe fruit fell, plopping on the ground and turning into a dirty flat bread. And here is the *rabot* (inn).

Thick elms surround a square pond about 2 or 3 sazhen long. A *supa*, an earthen platform similar to a stove bench[18] with blankets and carpets for sitting, is located under the trees. There are canopies and stables for protection from weather, and a high, rammed-earth wall surrounds it on three sides; from behind it come the sounds of a child crying and a women shouting. That is the *ichkari*, the internal yard, where the owner's family lives hidden from strangers' eyes. And here is the owner himself, dressed in a skullcap and a long robe-length shirt, a wide blue cotton belt circling his waist several times.

Smiling ingratiatingly, he greets you with the ordinary *salam*,[19] crossing his hands on his chest. He catches your horse's reins and quickly ties it up; then he invites you to sit on a felt rug. Adding another greeting, "xo'sh kelibsiz," which means something similar to our "welcome," and a polite question about your health, he runs into the ichkari for a *qumg'on* [copper pitcher] of tea and a tray with flat bread,[20] dried apricots, eggs, etc.

In his absence you were thirsty, so you scooped a cup of water from the pond, but it was mostly algae. In this respect, Iskovut is a disgusting place: water from the Padshaat flows here once every ten days and there are no springs nearby.

After rest and a snack, you bid farewell to the owner, who made a pretense of refusing payment, and you ride on.

Beyond Iskovut, the dust is simply unimaginable; it hangs in the air for 5 or 6 versts to Bulyk-basha and all the way to Naukent. That is where a developed[21] oasis begins, and it stretches along the wide ravine all the way to Namangan.

You crossed the springs by a bridge made from earth, with a permanent hole in the middle. You pass fields of drooping sorghum, cotton and maize, gardens and hayats.

From time to time you see vineyards with vines entwining large arches 7 feet tall, connected by poles. Here is Naukent, a small kishlak, where Khudoyor Khan's bek used to rule over the local people.[22] Houses here, like everywhere in Asia, are inside courtyards, and from the street one sees only rammed-earth walls with small gates or doorways. Here a *juvoz*, an ancient oil press, is squeaking; there, a small stall selling dried apricots; rice; and *nosvoy*, a type of tobacco similar to our snuff that the natives[23] put inside their cheek; flax or sesame oil in a bottle gourd with a narrow neck; and a heap of rubbish in the corner.

Here a small, noisy, native water mill runs tirelessly; here is a mosque, a large canopy inside the yard with a pond surrounded by elms, and then there are endless walls, high and low, with trees over them.

At every step are ariqs, small and large, with and without bridges, and in the distance all around are barren, yellowish hills.

Reaped wheat is standing in stacks, small or large; there are special places, *xirmon*, round, cleansed with running water, where this grain will be threshed. You come face-to-face with a long line of carts with dust-covered horses and cart drivers. They are carrying melons, already ripe, from Namangan and further on toward the [Syr] Darya [River]. Melons are transported to Iskovut, where they are rarely planted because of inadequate irrigation, and to Mamai, Nanay, and the foothills, where they cannot grow because of lack of heat.

Bread with apricots and bread with melons: this is, almost exclusively, the sedentary population's summer diet.

On your left, you see someone on the hill threshing barley or wheat. He spread part of the stack into an arshin-high layer over the xirmon; an eight- or nine-year-old boy on a tall bony horse rides around the xirmon dragging behind him a *val*, a triangular woven basket about 4 arshin wide; the val is loaded with weight, making it very heavy.

The closer you come to town, the more frequent vineyards become, and the crude dark blue fabric robes are quickly replaced by Russian chintz, *sumsama*, and adras.[24]

A young, sunburned Sart is plowing a small field, from which wheat was already harvested. He will plant carrots here, and they will ripen by early to mid-October. A couple of bony old bulls are slowly pulling a primitive native plow, paying no attention to the cane or the repeated cries "xo-osh, xosh, qol." Night is falling. The southern night's stuffy air gradually displaces the heat. You are entering Namangan, which is covered with gardens, dust, and the suffocating smoke of the evening meals being prepared everywhere.

To wish you good night would be a cruel joke. The road, the profound heat, and the doddering Kyrgyz horse have almost completely done you in; as soon as you lie down, you should fall fast asleep. But nothing of the sort. The terrible heat and myriad mosquitoes do not let you sleep, you, who just arrived from the cool mountain pastures.

*　*　*

Ways of life divide the native population of Fergana into two large groups: *sedentary* people, who live in the valley, and *nomads*, who live mainly in the mountains and the foothills, where besides herding cattle they also till the land, so they are more correctly called not nomads but seminomadic people. Their winter dwellings, located near the farmed land, are permanent, and in summer their auls return to the same mountain pastures year after year.

Nowadays, the majority are sedentary. For instance, Namangan district has 13,500 houses (sedentary) and only 3,000 Kyrgyz yurts, or movable felt houses.

In terms of race or tribe, Fergana's sedentary population, commonly called Sarts, consists of Uzbeks (or Turks) and Tajiks.[25]

Sart-Uzbeks, who speak a Turkic language, are descendants of formerly nomadic Uzbek lineages,[26] such as Kyrgyz, Bagysh, Kipchak, Karakalpak, Kurama, Ming, Yuz, Kyrk, and others. They settled at various times and adopted the agricultural practices of the local aborigines, the Tajiks. (We should note that for various reasons the sedentarization process is not finished and continues in the present time.) In the Fergana Valley, Sart-Uzbeks predominate numerically over the Tajiks. Tajiks, who speak a Persian dialect, live in comparatively few settlements (Kasan, Chust, Kamysh-Kurgan, Kanibadam, Isfara, Varukh, Sokh, and others), which are situated along the foot of the mountain ranges surrounding the valley, suggesting that today's agricultural oases originated from those points.

That aside, the only difference between the sedentary Uzbeks and Tajiks now is their language. Their religion, way of life, habits, and customs are so identical that henceforth we will refer to a sedentary Uzbek woman with the name "Sartianka"[27]—that is, with the term commonly used by the Russians living in Central Asia.

Having adopted Tajik agriculture, the Uzbek also adopted from Tajik the Persian names of different foods, names of household items, various instruments, tools, and construction terms, words for everything absent from the nomadic Uzbek way of life and lacking names in Uzbek or Turkic languages.

Many more Persian words entered the Sart (Turkic) language through the Persian literature that they adopted,[28] while the adoption of Islam introduced many Arabic words (mainly names of abstract concepts, judicial and theological terms, as well as most personal names).

Thus, in contemporary Sart (Turkic) language, almost half of the words are Persian and Arabic.

Through interacting with Tajiks, reading almost everything in Persian, boasting of their knowledge of this language and literature and, finally, mixing with Tajiks though marriage, Uzbeks, especially urban dwellers and those who were *mullah*s (literate), have significantly softened the rough pronunciation of their native language and partly corrupted it.

A Kyrgyz says *kymyldaidy* (waving); a Sart says *kymillyaidy*, and instead of the correct *nan* (bread), Sarts say *non*; instead of *chai*, *choy*; and so on.[29]

Agriculture is the main occupation of Fergana's sedentary natives.

The primary reasons for this are the following: first, the high profitability of local agricultural labor, due to the long growing season, high summer temperatures, and artificial irrigation; second, the absence of knowledge or conditions that could create widespread, profitable industries; third, the local population's comparative lack of elaborate needs, both because of climate and because of the lack of strong and progressive development of people's minds. This, in turn, results from the influence of religion and folk customs but also from geographic conditions separating this area and all Central Asia, by thousands of versts of sandy deserts, from the more civilized world. Actually, the will of historical forces brought a little bit of the latter, but it has contributed too little that could influence native life in the direction of progress. This is easily understandable. The elements that have been transferred here are not those that could act in this direction in an active and straightforward way. Their influence is, most of the time, indirect.

Such active influence could arise only from those elements that bring with them knowledge and capital, but this can be expected only when the colony becomes connected to the metropole by high-quality and vitally necessary routes of communication.

Religion should be thought of as the fourth reason for the prevalence of agriculture, or, to be more precise, the ideas it offers for this kind of labor. For instance, Sharia mentions that agriculturalists who live only from land and personally till it are called *ashraf ul-ashraf* (the most noble among the noble) if plowmen fulfill their moral obligations (*farz*) and pay Islamic tithes accurately.[30] In their *majlis* (gathering, council) they have the right to sit at the sultan's right hand beside the scholars and judges, while the administrative and military staff are seated on his left.

There is a light booklet titled *Risola-i dehqonchilik*, or "Agricultural risola" (*risola* means message, treatise). Besides agricultural instruction and moral norms (such as truthfulness, generosity, etc.) that farmers must live by, it explains that farming has divine origins; that the Archangel Gabriel made the first plow from the paradise tree, the *tubi*; that the first bulls were brought from paradise and the first whip was made from a bush called *kauran*; it also says that Archangel Gabriel made the first furrows himself and then handed the plow to the first prophet Adam; that farming is the best of all human activities because it best preserves human morality; and it is noble because the hand of the farmer yields food to feed both the rich and the poor, the weak and the strong, the low and the great.

The book itself is not only simple, but by the end it even becomes somewhat ignoble because the *ulomo* (scholars, theologians) who composed it neither forgot their own interests nor spared the God-fearing readers' feelings as they depicted various horrors of hell, such as turning those of evil intention into pigs after death. These are promised to those who refuse to give to them, the clergy, *haq-ullah* (a small portion of their harvest); nevertheless, the risola's importance is considerable.

Presently, when lifeways that used to be guided by Islam are being destroyed in front of us, something impossible to ignore unless you are really shortsighted, the risola's use has diminished significantly and it is no longer easy to find. However, not long ago, only a few years before the Russians came here, every respectable farmer cooked *plov*[31] and fed his household members and his workers with it before he cut the first furrow of spring. He also read the risola aloud or made someone read it; he rubbed his bull's horns with flax oil to protect them from various illnesses, and only after all that he would start work.

Be this as it may, farming still retains its leading role among the sedentary natives. It is so solid that almost no one, not even the wealthiest local merchants doing trade with Russia, has cut his ties with the land; such that the growth of personal capital leads to this result: to the extent that trade affairs grow, to the same degree the merchant also increases his landholdings.

We should mention that for the vast majority of the population, growth of capital does not change their way of life or improve their living conditions. There are small improvements in their everyday food, an extra servant, and a few more dependents residing in the house; a few more copper or porcelain dishes, pillows, carpets, and blankets; an extra silk shirt or robe (or quilted robe) for the wife. Only hospitality increases considerably, and even this is not always true, and that is all.

Even the many merchants who own tens of thousands in capital do not differ from the most ordinary farmer, whether in external appearance and dress or in manner of life.

Among people directly involved in agriculture—that is, who work the land with their own hands—it is unlikely that even half own private plots of land, at least plots of the size that would provide their owners with sufficient income to sustain life from their own produce.

Most agricultural workers till someone else's land as temporary, one-year-long workers, *chorikor* or *qo'shchi*, and some of them, *koranda*, have comparatively long-term rent contracts.[32]

Day workers in agriculture are employed only in suburban areas and in cities but never in kishlaks. Chorikors or qo'shchi usually offer their labor to the landowner in exchange for grain, a plow, and bulls or horses. [This chorikor] is responsible for the following work: plowing, watering and caring for the crops, threshing and final harvesting, as well as tending the working livestock. Near the cities, special workers carry out earthing up melons, sorghum, corn, and cotton, and in kishlaks, those tasks are done mainly by mutual assistance, *hashshar*. In both cases, these expenses are borne by the owner alone or are shared between him and the chorikor.

Harvesting is not included in the sharecropper's responsibilities but is carried out by hired harvesters.[33] The chorikor and the landowner pay them in kind, mainly in grain. Payment is made after the end of the harvest, and the harvesters always receive food during their work.

By the way, we want to point out that harvesters often come from afar, work for strangers or people they do not know, and leave at the end of the season. They come back for payment at the end of the summer or the beginning of the fall without having concluded any contracts or written agreements, but in spite of all of this, in the six years that we spent among these people, we did not encounter any cheating or defaulting on payment.

During the harvest, every harvester has the right to take one stack of hay for himself. At harvest's end everyone, but mainly the poor, can come and glean whatever stalks (*boshoq*, or *mashoq*) they find if the field is not fenced. These gleaners come to be called *boshoqchi* or *mashoqchi*.

A chorikor, especially if he has a family, lives at home and gets paid for his labor by receiving one-fourth of the wheat he harvests; one-fifth of the wheat that he receives goes to the harvesters and dues (tax). If it is sorghum or cotton, one-third goes to the chorikor and from that, one-fifth to the harvesters. In addition, during the growing season, the chorikor receives food from the landowner but only for himself and not for all of his family. Often, instead of meals, he receives a one-time, in-kind allowance in flour and grain (rice or sorghum).

A koranda (renter), who is not much different from a chorikor, usually lives on the land that he tills or in a dwelling provided by the owner or built by himself; often he ends up buying out his dwelling and becoming its owner.

If he receives grain and implements from the landowner, he works on the same conditions as a chorikor; if not, the harvest is divided between the koranda and the landowner equally after the harvesters receive their share and the dues are paid.

We should specify, however, that these conditions vary in different areas of Fergana depending on the profitability of the land, the supply of hired workers, and other factors; we have mentioned only average norms to avoid going into too much detail.

A daily wage in cities does not exceed 40 kopeks, and in kishlaks it varies between 10 and 20 kopeks.

In kishlaks that are close to cities, most people own only a garden plot; in the other villages, the percentage of the landless population (those owning nothing other than their house) decreases, but nonetheless, it appears that there is not a single kishlak anywhere without some who are landless, and their number keeps growing.

The amount of land that one person may own varies between ¼ *shanap* (shanap [or *tanap*] equals 400 square sazhen) up to 200–250 *desiatina*s. Land lots larger than 200 desiatinas are rare.[34]

(One native household in Namangan region owns 1,000 desiatinas, but this land is mostly fallow land—i.e., lands that cannot be irrigated because of inadequate water, and thus only a portion can be tilled every year; in this particular case it is only one-fifth of the total.)

Based on statistics from the organization of surveys and land demarcation conducted in 1876–1881, when the new tax system was introduced, the average per capita lot owned by the local Namangan population equals ½ desiatina [0.55 hectare]. Thus, the ratio of population to the arable land that can be cultivated with existing water supplies is not inappropriate; we can state that Fergana suffers from insufficient land rather than from the abundance of soil that is arable or usable for fields and forests.

Crop	Harvest from one desiatina (in puds)	PRICE PER PUD	
		Ruble	Kopek
Wheat	50.5	—	55
Barley	62.5	—	36
Rice	105.5	—	46
Sorghum	138.5	—	33
Cotton	58.5	—	90
Flax (seed)	28.5	—	65
Millet	41	—	27
Lucerne	300	—	12

Editor's note: A pud is a Russian measure of weight equal to 16 kilograms or 40 pounds. Thus, 50 puds per desiatina is about 800 kilograms per hectare. The average yield of grain in Russia in this period was between 29 and 39 puds per desiatina. Geroid Robinson, *Rural Russia under the Old Regime* (Berkeley: University of California Press, 1932), 98.

Land prices depend on the quality of the soil; on the altitude above sea level, and, thus, the possibility or impossibility of growing the more profitable crops, rice, sorghum, and cotton; on their distance from cities and other bazaar areas; on the relative flatness of the land, which makes planting easier; and on the amount of water available for irrigation. [Prices] vary between 6 and 400 rubles per desiatina.

Naturally, land profitability varies across Fergana; that is why we will demonstrate the average bazaar prices for the crops harvested in recent years in Namangan district, which we will consider as an average representative district, first, because of its soil, irrigation, and other conditions and, second, because we have more information about it than about the other districts of the province [see the table].

A 1-tanap (⅙-desiatina) garden provides an annual income of about 40 rubles; a 1-tanap vineyard, 20 rubles.

The reader may be interested in knowing the approximate gross income of the farmer. A farmer who farms alone (household head, his wife, and two to three children below working age), who owns enough land and a pair of oxen, manages to cultivate about 3 desiatinas of winter wheat, about 1½ desiatinas of sorghum, cotton, or maize, which can yield a gross income of 192 silver rubles, taking into consideration our average prices and the productivity of the soil. After deducting one-fifth of his income for taxes, he keeps 154 silver rubles. Drawing on the same assumptions, we find the chorikor who received land, grain, and tools from the landowner earning 43 silver rubles.

It is impressive to observe a Sart's ability to squeeze the maximum that the land can produce, using his financial means and his activities, especially in areas with dense population and expensive land. Not even the tiniest corner of land remains unworked. Every twig, every blade of grass, if it cannot either be eaten or sold, will be fed to cattle; and if unusable, burned. The economy is so elaborate that it goes far beyond the commonly accepted norms and turns into so-called *penkosnimatel'stvo* [milk skimming, highly intensive production]. It would be a good thing if this "skimming" were only the custom of the small and less able households, but we find it everywhere in agricultural practices and not only among the poor. It has become a distinctive feature of the Sart, of the local economy, and a popular habit. One might infer that this is the result, first, of an extreme deficiency of practical knowledge or of the possibility for exploiting other natural resources (salt, oil, iron, copper, etc.) or that it results from lack of resourcefulness or knowledge of basic arithmetic, which are all established by native ideas about wealth. These relationships are rather specific.

The word *yaxshi* means both "good" and "rich," which is not simply coincidence. For instance, for Muslims, hospitality is a cardinal virtue, and it is more feasible for those who are wealthier.

Religion advises slaughtering a ram or a goat during one of the three days of *Kurban* (celebrating the sacrifice of Abraham) and feeding the meat to the poor.[35]

Actually, the poor are rarely fed; instead, one feeds acquaintances, but in any case everyone who follows the religion slaughters a ram or a goat. He does it with his own hands, believing that this ram will help him cross *syrat*, a bridge as thin as a hair and as sharp as a sword; the sinners will fall from it into hell, and the righteous will cross it into paradise.[36] Women and children who desire to partake in this blessing hold on to the ram's legs while it is being slaughtered and butchered.

At the same time, only those (men and women) whose capital, after the deduction of debts, does not fall below 20 *tilla* (76 silver rubles) are allowed to slaughter a ram for Kurban.[37]

Thus, for the native, having good material conditions is one of the major means to be *good*, righteous, and pious.

Wealth and morality have always and everywhere been closely and naturally connected. The difference is that Sarts understand and accept this connection, while others refuse to understand it.

The primary supporting components for native agriculture are fattening livestock for slaughter; weaving *mata*, *qalami*, and other cotton fabrics; producing felts and lassos, as well as weaving crude woolen fabrics; cleaning cotton from cotton bolls and seeds and spinning thread; raising silkworms; driving carts; collecting the steppe grasses and shrubs for fuel in autumn and winter during the time free from farm work and selling them at the nearest bazaars; [doing]

day work in the nearest cities and towns; pressing flax and sesame oil; and, infrequently, fishing.

Hunting with rifles or otherwise is not popular among the agricultural population because the sedentary, farming population regards hunting as an occupation leading to impoverishment. As entertainment, hunting is known only among the wealthier classes of the native society, mainly among those formerly in service to the khan. (Nomads practice hunting for subsistence.)[38]

Talking about classes, we should point out that except for direct descendants of the khan's clan (who currently do not bear any social distinction) there are no noblemen or other privileged classes among the sedentary native population. There are *xo'ja*,[39] who present themselves as the descendants either of the Prophet or the first four caliphs; during the khan's rule they had certain privileges in taxes, but now they have lost those privileges. There are no distinctions between them and others, except for the fact that they [xo'jas] avoid marrying their daughters to [non-xo'jas]. (But they themselves [xo'ja men] marry the daughters of xo'ja or *qoracha*[40] without differentiation.) This is how high social status is defined among the native population: either by the position in [government] service that one occupies or by belonging to a line of scholars or, the most widespread, by the extent of their wealth.

As occupations, after farming come gardening and raising trees; drying fruits; and these types of production: weaving cotton, semi-silk, and silk fabrics; tanning leather; shoemaking; pottery making; blacksmithing; making knives, saddles, harnesses, and leather and dyeing (thread); making copper utensils; pouring the local cast-iron vessels, which is poorly developed; making gold and silver jewelry; carpentry; transportation; metalwork; making araba carts, plows, pitchforks, and spades; boiling *mum*, which is tar made from oil; making charcoal; and weaving things from bulrush. That is about all. Metal, glass, cloth, porcelain, a considerable amount of carpenter tools, cauldrons, nails, needles, thimbles, looking glasses, tea, sugar, most writing paper—all this is imported from Russia.[41]

There are no factories, plants, or any other large-scale industries here; all existing production is carried out by craftsmen and artisans.

Everything that is produced here is manufactured by individuals either at home or in special artisan workshops (*do'qon*), usually located adjacent to the house (weavers, araba carts, footwear, knives, utensils) and more rarely at the bazaar (blacksmiths, metalworkers, coppersmiths, silversmiths).

Most of the time, artisans who work in the same trade elect an *oqsoqol*, an elder, from among themselves, who acts as a dealer searching for orders or giving guarantees for various deals; he receives a monetary reward, called *sherikan*, when a deal is concluded and payments are made.

A blacksmith working for himself without an assistant earns from 20 to 40 kopeks per day; a dyer, from 40 to 60 kopeks; a weaver of cotton fabrics, from

15 to 30 kopeks; a weaver of silk fabrics, 20 to 40 kopeks; a tanner, 40 to 70 kopeks; a carpenter or whitewasher, 50 kopeks to 1 ruble; the *juvozkash* pressing oil, 15 to 30 kopeks.

In most workshops, the craftsman-owner (*xalifa, ustakor*) has several assistants (*nimker*) that he hires on various conditions: often weekly, from one bazaar day to the next, or monthly. Besides food, a nimker earns 40 kopeks to 1 ruble 20 kopeks per week. The craftsman's own weekly income varies by craft, between 2 and 4 rubles.

Trade is exactly the same, whether internal or external, import or export.

The commodities for internal trade are mainly those produced by the above-mentioned crafts. The most profitable trades are thought to be selling bread in the towns and meat in kishlaks.

Wheat yields profit due to the annual variation in prices. At the end of the summer and autumn, when the wheat from the new harvest has been threshed and the poor are willing to sell it because they need to pay the taxes or buy different things for the household, the traders buy it at lower prices and resell it at the end of the winter or in spring at a much higher price.

Despite the fact that religion disapproves of such occupations as butcher, midwife, barber, and some others and considers them to be *makruh*[42] (despicable, not approved), meat trade is extremely widespread: there is not a single kishlak lacking a butcher, qassob; and the latter prospers most in the most desolate, exclusively farmer-inhabited kishlaks with comparatively large arable lands.

Meat is sold at ordinary bazaar prices between mid-May and November, from the ripening of the barley to the end the farming season; meat is often paid for not in money but in grain, which the butcher usually values below the market price and values much lower in cases when the buyer purchases meat or fat on credit. Such trade with individuals does not allow for a large turnover of capital because there is rarely only one butcher in a kishlak, but throughout the summer a qassob earns a good deal of money.

(The average turnover capital of a kishlak butcher can vary between 50 and 200 rubles, and capital of less than 100 rubles manages to turn over about twice.)

Let us go to Nanay again, dear reader.

It is a hot summer afternoon at the beginning of August. We are approaching Nanay from the west, from the direction of Akhtam, moving along the flat, cultivated Biy-bag-dala (a steppe without gardens), where other than wheat fields and the small kishlak Ko'kyer situated at the very bank of the Padshaat, there is absolutely nothing.

Hills rise a verst away; on the right, the large, yellow, green, and gray Biy-bag-dala stretches with little Ko'kyer; and right in front of us, separated by the Padshaat's wide, rocky ravine, lies the dark green spot of Nanay covered with the thick foliage of apricots and willows, above which huge old poplars stick up here and there.

On the bank of the Padshaat, we are passing a xirmon with a pile of already air-dried wheat. On one side, there is *saman* (small chaff) and a horse harnessed to an araba full of grapes and melons. Two men are squatting near the grain and weighing it on native wooden scales, but instead of weights they use grapes, which are sold in Nanay for the same per weight price as wheat.

Two young Gypsy[43] girls are standing next to them and pushily inviting the somber owner of this xirmon to buy needles, thimbles, and thread, but the latter ignores them completely.

A *qalandar*,[44] sort of like a traveling monk, has appeared from somewhere and has said the usual greeting in such cases, "Xirmon to'lsun," may your xirmon be always full; he has recited various good wishes for the owner and received several handfuls of bran in return.

We take a rocky path down to the Padshaat and cross it at a shallow place, stepping on the rock-covered bottom; the horse trips all the time and splashes the rider in front with large drops of cold water.

Ascending a steep and little-traveled path, we find ourselves in a narrow, winding street with the omnipresent earthen walls, with children peeping from the gate doors, with ariqs and manure.

A whole flock of hens scatters in all directions from our horses, leaving the small arch in the middle of the street, where someone must have threshed several sheaves of wheat.

The wasteland on the right is covered with piles of manure and remains of some ruined walls. There is a forge on the left with bellows, hoes, and sickles hanging on its walls and a blacksmith inside dressed in a leather apron, who is absorbed in hammering the head off an old ketmon with a small iron hammer.

A heavyset, tall young man is riding toward us on a nimble, well-fed, two-year-old stallion loaded with four large sheaves of wheat, with a sickle bound to one of them.

In the middle of the street, in front of a gate door, a woman dressed in a white blouse with a white, crudely made muslin scarf thrown around her shoulders is threshing two sheaves of wheat. Being absorbed in work, she saw us only when we were next to her; she dropped the stick and rushed like crazy through the door of the gate, forgetting a tiny boy outside, who immediately burst into tears and cried. Here comes the *guzar*,[45] which serves the kishlak both as small bazaar and as a social club.

On the left, under tall old willows, there is a shop with sunshades and next to it a supa beside an ariq.[46] The inside of the store can be seen through the dissembled wooden doors: the front wall, covered with soot from smoke, has a

2-meter-long panel with long iron nails sticking out and parts of a dissected ram's body hanging on them. A butcher with a fat, sly face, dressed in a greasy robe, is waiting for the evening customers and, having nothing else to do, is gathering the wheat, piled in the corner on the earthen floor, into a sack.

A *satukchi*,[47] newly arrived from the city, has posted himself on the supa; under the willow, his sweating, narrow-chested horse carries an unwieldy baggage saddle; it has dragged its owner and a huge *xurjun*[48] made of thick cotton fabric and filled with various small everyday items.

The satukchi has spread a worn-out rug and has laid out the "worms" that will catch him "fish"—i.e., wheat. On the right, he has put several pieces of the local crude cotton fabrics: mata, qalami, and *alak* [smooth, hand-woven cotton cloth]. On the left, there are several arshins of pink chintz with large gaudy splotches, and in the middle, there is this multicolored trash that is always present on every bazaar day and not only at native bazaars.

Three tiny tin mirrors are leaning on a piece of mata and staring at the passersby; ten or twelve pieces of stinky cone-shaped Sart soap are lined up in front of them, and behind, closer to the edge, there is a mix of tin rings, several pieces of halvah and sugar, *saqich* (pine tar that women and children like to chew), wide and narrow *jiyak*,[49] needles, belts, buttons, beads, and other trash that is ogled by a whole crowd of grubby children. They watch the silent satukchi in awe and exchange their remarks in a whisper.

There are two stores opposite the butcher's, covered with similar sunshades. One is shut and locked. The other one is selling rice, flax oil, soap, nosvoy, and melons purchased from *arabakeshes* [cart drivers]; its owner, a young, slender Sart owner with a scanty beard, is sleeping at the door on a worn-out felt rug.

Five or six local elderly men are sitting under the sunshade of the empty store opposite the satukchi; from time to time, one or the other gives out a deep sigh and pronounces fragmented phrases in a low voice, "Allah!" or "Ya, Karim!" They have nothing to talk about and no interest in talking; it is their fasting period, *ro'za*;[50] they have not eaten or drunk since the early morning, so what kind of conversation can there be?

Two arabas filled with melons are approaching from Namangan; the tired arabakeshes, exhausted by hunger and thirst, halt their sweaty, dust-covered horses. They greet the elderly men with the drawling "As-salam alaykum!" and sit for a while without any reason on their out-of-breath horses, glancing with questioning eyes at the elderly men, who barely respond to them with "Alaykum as-salam," and at the empty street. Then they slowly dismount their horses and even more slowly unharness them and tie them under the willows.

The slender store owner who snored a while ago awakens and greets the newcomers with "Barak-allah, barak-allah" [Blessings of God] as he is leaving the sunshade of the do'qon with an expressionless face, still creased from pressing on a surface in sleep.

A woman passes by with a hurried, small pace, her head covered, according to the local custom not by a paranji but by a small child's robe. She slowly passed by the satukchi, glancing sideways at his goods, then resumed her fast, nimble gait, almost running, and was hidden beyond the corner of a mosque.

In about ten minutes, a heavyset, neatly dressed Sart in his forties appeared from around the same corner; he approached the satukchi in a slow, heavy gait, and after talking to him for a long time in a low voice, he untied the end of his long waist belt and poured several handfuls of wheat from it. The satukchi weighed the wheat, poured it into a sack, and gave a piece of soap to the man, who retreated in the same slow and heavy gait and disappeared round the corner of the mosque.

A good-looking young boy around twelve years of age, dressed in a dirty cotton shirt, walked into the butcher's store and handed him some wheat tied in an old cotton scarf. However, his interest was piqued more by the satukchi's movable store than his own purchase, and he was eyeing it all the time while the butcher weighed wheat, lingered over selecting a piece of meat to cut, and calculated how much to cut; then he made up his mind, cut a piece of meat quickly, wrapped it in the scarf, and handed it to the boy.

The number of people in the street increases. They are coming in from the fields either on foot or riding. Some are carrying sickles; others, ketmons; and others, bundles of stalks. Some walk past the butcher, others stop in, and some pause to chat with the elderly men.

One after another, customers bring grain to the butcher, to the arabakashes who brought melons, and to the lean shop owner.

Soon, there is a growing group around the elderly men and the cart with the melons; they are loudly talking while waiting for supper, about various Nanay and Namangan issues. One of the elderly men, who looked younger than the rest but had a long white beard, stood slowly, straightened his turban, took a long asa-musa cane that had been propped against the wall, and started walking toward the mosque in a dignified manner. Five or six elderly men arose, and three or four minutes later the evening air was filled with the drawling chants of the *azan*: "Allah akbar, allah akbar . . . !"[51]

A herd has arrived. A thick crowd of cows, calves, and goats, of all sorts and hues, most of them bony, flows between the stores and carts with melons.

The ram butchered today has been almost completely sold; half of the melons have been taken, and the other half will be driven tomorrow to xirmons.

The guzar empties out a bit. Everyone retreats to their homes; time for the next *namoz oqshom* [evening prayer] is approaching, after which the faithful can fill their hollow stomachs.

Tomorrow, more melons and grapes will arrive; the satukchi will spread his rubbish; the butcher will slaughter another ram; and various belts, scarves, xurjun, and feedbags will drag wheat to the guzar. This will repeat tomorrow and the day after tomorrow as long as various enticing things are brought in and the butcher slaughters cattle, which he will keep doing until late autumn when the farsighted heads of families will order their children strictly to stop secretly or openly carrying wheat to *muttaham* (parasites) or until the poorest have dragged most of their wheat, flax, and other products to him, after which begins a long season of winter and spring hunger.

Thus, much wheat is exchanged in trade transactions among farmers, who have a natural human wish to eat until they are stuffed at least several days in a year. There are obliging people who will bring all sorts of trashy goods exactly when the farmers have money in their hands in the form of the new wheat. Significantly, the farmer has a habit of thinking too little about the future and of the periodic hunger that he is as used to as the idea that summer is hot and winter will be cold, even extremely cold. Maybe it will be very cold, but if it is my fate to survive, I will survive somehow and will not croak either because of cold or hunger.

The great majority of people are engaged in petty trade and speculation. Everything can be traded or profiteered. Horses and various cattle are resold, as are small quantities of grain and cotton fabrics, and the prices on these rise and fall several times a year, and so on. Chintz, red bunting, and other fabrics are bought from wholesale traders and taken to bazaars around the area; traders whisk from one kishlak to another, from one bazaar to another, vowing, swearing, tricking, fooling the customers by selling short weight or mismeasuring fabric lengths so that they finally acquire a net profit of no more than 10 or 20 kopeks per day.

Most of these small traders are recruited from landless urban dwellers or kishlak residents who have somehow been driven off the land.

The largest turnover in internal trade, bringing some individuals up to several tens of thousands of rubles, is found in wheat sales and internal reselling of rams.

The product from slaughtered animals that is most valued by the natives is the fat and not the meat. Fat is for them one of the basic elements of any good meal, such as, for instance, plov, while meat is more an added decoration than a nutritional element.[52] In poor and middle-class farming households we almost never come across meat dishes—i.e., such dishes that have meat as their basic component.

There are several dishes in the folk cuisine, such as *qovurma* (small chunks of mutton fried in fat in a pot),[53] but such dishes are prepared for guests and never for the family meal.

Because of this attitude toward meat, the native requires the maximum fat from slaughtered livestock. The local fat-tailed sheep is the animal that meets these requirements best; a well-fed one produces as much fat as meat and, under especially favorable conditions, even more.

Thus, there is strong demand for sheep for slaughter, and for various reasons, Fergana cannot satisfy this demand by its own means. This sparked development of rather broad trading relations with the nomadic populations of Aulie-ata, Tokmak, Vernyi, and even with Western Siberian Kyrgyz.[54]

The main livestock paths lie across the mountains of Namangan district and at least fifty thousand head cross over them every year.

This trade, which evidently began long ago, was and still is almost exclusively barter. In exchange for rams, Fergana exports local cotton and semi-silk fabrics, some dried fruit, local footwear, padded blankets, and knives. Not more than a third or a fourth of the rams driven to Fergana are purchased for money in Semirechie or in Western Siberia.[55] Under favorable conditions this transaction leaves the native trader with at least 50 percent annual profit, while the number of rams brought by one person can vary from fifty to four thousand head.

Items that are generally exported are cotton and semi-silk fabrics to Semirechie and Western Siberia; silk and cotton to Russia; dried fruit to Semirechie, Siberia, and sometimes Orenburg; construction lumber (poplar) to Perovsk[56] and Kazalu; a small amount of furs to Russia.

Most of the internal trade is conducted on credit, and most of the time no receipts or other documents are written; the deal is struck verbally, but there are always witnesses present.[57] This preference for witnesses rather than a written document results from the fact that according to Muslim law, a document is authenticated not by the signature but by the stamp of the *qozi*[58] and is recognized as effective only when the litigant recognizes its authenticity and effectiveness or it is certified by two Muslim witnesses.

Bazaars, small shops, and caravanserais are where most goods in domestic trade are bought and sold.

Homes are very rarely places of concluding trade deals, since, first of all, religion requires that the traded goods should be present at the time of the deal, and, second, [religion] advises avoiding trade under conditions when one of the traders may be unaware of the existing bazaar prices, and, third, these deals should be concluded in the presence of two witnesses, who may not always be found at home.

For the same reasons, religion requires that trade should be conducted during the daytime, between dawn and sunset, which is when most bazaar stalls close.

In general, Islam, which is both a religion and a judicial and state code, regulates trade very strictly.

Only private property that can be observed, measured, or counted, that can be beneficial to the buyer and can be passed from hand to hand, can be an object of trade. Selling objects that are not present at the moment of sale is not permitted; wholesale goods cannot be sold without being measured; nor can standing wheat be sold; and so on. When a land lot, a house, a garden, or another piece of real estate is sold, neighbors, who in this instance are called *shapi* or *shafe*, are given first refusal; only if they refuse to buy it for the price announced does the right of purchase pass to strangers. The seller should himself point out the disadvantages of his goods and should avoid asking exorbitant prices.

When the deal is struck, witnesses should pose the question "Have you sold?" to the seller and "Have you bought?" to the buyer. A confirmation on both sides that must be expressed in the perfect tense completes the sale and purchase.

However, these as well as many other regulations of Islam are rarely followed nowadays, and if they are, it is outwardly, when it is beneficial for one of the sides.

In the past, under the rule of the khans, such religious regulations were followed more strictly, enforced with a rod.

This rod was of two kinds: material and moral. The *qozi-rais* [head judge] represented the former, and public opinion, the latter; above that, the qozi-rais dangled something like the sword of Damocles and above him a host of pedants and Pharisees [religious zealots], which we will discuss below.

Among the main responsibilities of the *rais* (a position that was eliminated when the Khanate was occupied by the Russians) was to observe the correctness of scales and other measurements, whether the town residents observed the fasts, daily prayers, or nomoz (there are five of them), and other rules of Muslim morality, as well as punishing those found guilty by caning, right on the spot.

This cornerstone held the edifice of exterior morality and good manners and an exterior respect paid to the foundations of the religion.

Once that stone was removed, when the rais was eliminated, part of the building began to fall apart. In the bazaars there was blatant mismeasuring and misweighing, pieces of fabric became shorter, while drinking, prostitution, and indifference toward religious customs have been on the rise.

We mentioned above that religion advised those doing trade to invite no fewer than two witnesses when completing a deal. This advice has been followed most strictly by the natives until today. This is not only in the case of the sale of a herd of rams, a large lot of fabric, a plot of land, a house, and so on. Two or three and sometimes even four witnesses are present during a sale of a horse, a cow, a calf, a ram, or a goat, playing the role of brokers setting the price and bringing the deal to a conclusion, and these brokers (*dallols*) receive sherikan, the size of which can range from one *chaqa* [small copper coin] to several rubles and even tens of rubles.

The habit of having witnesses is so widespread that often an exchange cannot take place simply because of their absence, the result of which is that the sides cannot come to a conclusion.

In every bazaar, especially the horse and sheep bazaar, you will always meet several suspicious-looking Sarts with predatory, hungry looks on their faces. They are scurrying in the crowd, searching for places where a deal is getting started, and they pop up from nowhere and interfere, literally pushing themselves between the haggling sides, persuading them to come to an agreement, to their own benefit because they may receive sherikan. They can even scold the parties if the haggling lasts too long. They join the hands of the hagglers and utter the traditional questions "Have you sold?" and "Have you bought?," and they receive an honorarium of 3 or 4 chaqa with a condescending air and move further to another calf or mare.

There are con artists for whom *dallolchilik* (the occupation of witnessing trade) has almost become a profession, or at least a source of auxiliary income. Sometimes it is both funny and sad to watch a Sart counting out several chaqa without really knowing whom and for what he is paying, but it cannot be denied that due to the above-mentioned Muslim regulations and folk habits of the natives that developed under the influence of Islam, a dallol provides a real service, especially in cases of necessity, when he cannot refuse to fulfill his obligations as a witness, even if uncompensated.[59]

Retail trade in meat, bread, vegetables, footwear, fabrics, and other items, for which prices are more or less known to the society, is conducted without intermediaries because otherwise it would be too cumbersome.

There are no native public credit institutions. All of such services are in private hands, mainly of Sart or Hindu moneylenders. There are five to ten, and sometimes more, of the latter in each local town, and they earn their living exclusively from moneylending.

The Koran is extremely disapproving of that profession, but life has its own way, and the moneylenders charge an enormous rate of interest, *sud*.[60]

Moneylending operations are mainly conducted in the form of money or grain; but very often, especially in the towns, lenders accept other things on pawn. Hindus operate only with money, and their rate is such that for each 16 *tanga* (equal to $3\frac{1}{5}$ rubles) they charge interest equal to 4 tanga (about 80 kopeks) for twenty weeks. Payments are made weekly, 1 tanga (20 kopeks) per week; thus, both the principal and the interest are paid out within twenty weeks.

The smallest interest that Sarts charge per 1 tilla (equal to $3\frac{4}{5}$ rubles) is $\frac{1}{2}$ tanga (10 kopeks) per month. For large loans given for a period of one year, for each 4 tilla the borrower returns 5, or for each borrowed 5 tilla, 6 are repaid.

There are loans without interest between relatives or acquaintances, but they are comparatively rare.

What is remarkable is that in the past, which those who are in their forties and fifties can remember, when most of the loans were made, it was the moneylender who gave a receipt to the borrower and not the other way round, the borrower to the moneylender.

Such receipts stated [that] so-and-so owes me, so-and-so, the following amount, and the interest and the time for repayment are such and such.

The receipt was kept by the borrower until the repayment was made to guarantee that he would not be charged more than he owed.

2 Religion and Clergy

BOTH THE SEDENTARY and the nomadic population of Fergana practice the Muslim religion, the Sunni strain, the sect of the *Hanafiya* or *Azami*.[1]

The Koran lies at the foundation of the Muslim religion, as is well known; it includes 114 chapters of different length, each of which consists of a larger or smaller number of verses.

Since the Koran was written by Magomet [Muhammad] at different times and undoubtedly under various impressions, there is often no logical connection between chapters or even among verses in a single chapter. At the same time, the names of the chapters are very strange and almost never correspond to the content of the chapters.

In addition, some of the later verses contradict the earlier ones, which forced the Prophet to qualify: "When We abolish some regulation and order it forgotten, We give another one, which is better or equal" (Koran, chapter 1, verse 100).

The extreme brevity of narration in the Koran serves to show why its application in life requires explaining to the masses many issues mentioned in it.

These explanations, offered by various representatives of the Muslim sciences, starting from the first caliphs, were recorded and later compiled into books that are currently known under the general name of *Sharia*, which can be translated from the Arabic as "the straight way."

The primary, foundational dogmas of the religion pronounced by the Koran are [these]:

1. Monotheism, rejecting the worship of idols and of the Trinity.
   "Do not accept any gods equal to God." (chapter 2, verse 20)
   "Your God is the one God: there is no god but He, compassionate, merciful." (chapter 2, verse 158)
   "O followers of the Book! Do not permit excess in your religion . . . the Messiah, Jesus son of Maria, is only an apostle of God, and is His Word sent down by Him to Maria, and is His Spirit; believe in God and His apostles, and say not, Trinity. . . . It is impossible that He should have children. . . ." (chapter 4, verse 169)[2]
   "It cannot happen that the Messiah considered it a debasement to be a slave to Him, in the same way that the angels approach Him." (chapter 4, verse 170)
2. Muhammad is the last and the supreme prophet. (Seal of the prophets).
   "Muhammad is not the father of any of you; he is only the apostle of God and the seal of the prophets." (chapter 33, verse 40)

"Before you (Muhammad) we did not give eternal life to any person; and so if you will die, then can it really be that they are without death?" (chapter 21, verse 36)

"I (Muhammad) am only a person like you; it is revealed to me that your God is the one God." (chapter 18, verse 110)

3. Recognizing the Koran as the final and the most perfect revelation of God while not denying such books as the Old Testament and the New Testament.

"This Book, there is no doubt, is guidance to the devout." (chapter 2, verse 1)

"Say: It (Koran) was sent down from on high by the One who knows the secrets of heaven and earth." (chapter 25, verse 7)

"We already gave Moses the Book; after him we sent other apostles; and then to Jesus, the son of Maria, we gave clear signs. . . ." (chapter 2, verse 81)

"In their footsteps we sent Jesus, son of Maria, verifying that prior to him there was the Law and We gave him the Gospel; in them is truth and light." (chapter 5, verse 50)

". . . gave him (Jesus) the Gospel; in the hearts of those who followed him We put kindness and mercy." (chapter 57, verse 27)

4. God rules the world and the destiny of man.

"Praise to God, Lord of the Worlds." (chapter 1, verse 1)

"No calamity takes place either on earth or among you if it has not been predestined in the Book before We create it. . . ." (chapter 57, verse 22)

"He is the One Who created you from clay and determined for each the term of life." (chapter 6, verse 2)

5. The existence of Angels and devil.

6. Resurrection from the dead and the Judgment Day.

"The trumpet will sound, so all those in the heavens and on the earth shall swoon, as if struck by lightning, except those whom God wishes to remain alive; then it shall sound another time, and they shall arise, looking all around them. The Earth will be lit with the light of your Lord, and the Book shall be laid down, and the prophets and the martyrs shall be brought up, and they will judge righteously. . . ." (chapter 39 [verses 68–69])[3]

7. The nonbelievers, who have not accepted Islam, cannot count on salvation.

"Unbelievers, in masses, shall be driven into hell, and when they approach it, its gates shall open." (chapter 39, verse 71)

8. Paradise and hell.

"Make those who believe and do good deeds glad with good news that for them will be gardens through which rivers flow. . . ." (chapter 2, verse 23)

"This is a sketch of heaven, which is promised to the devout. In it are rivers of water that has no stench; rivers of milk the flavor of which does not change; rivers of wine, pleasant to those who drink; rivers of honey, clarified. There, for them are fruits of all kinds and from their Lord forgiveness of sins. Is there anything similar to this for those who will be in the fire, who will be given boiling water to drink, which will torment their innards." (chapter 47 [verse 15])

"—drawing near to God. 12. They will be in gardens of delight. . . . 15. On thrones decorated with precious stones. . . . 17. Eternally youthful boys will carry around them urns and mugs, cups with drinks that will never stupefy or make drunk; 20. With fruits. . . . 21. With the meat of fowl, whatever they desire. 22. Black-eyed ones, large eyed, similar to protected pearls, 23. Will be rewarded to them for what they did earlier. . . . 27. They will be among the Lote-trees, which have no thorns, 28. among bananas on which hang fruit in rows; 29. in the shade that spreads broadly . . . 34. And it . . . was made by Us as a special creation: 35. for them We made to be virgins, 36. for husbands, kind ones, their equal in age. (chapter 36)

"They (the sinners) will be in a scorching wind and boiling water, in the shade of black smoke." (chapter 56 [verses 42–43])

"Their (sinners) abode will be hell. How torturous is their resting place." (chapter 3, verse 196)

Besides religious dogmas, the Koran includes moral rules and religious rituals (praying, ablution, etc.), a recitation of various duties placed on Muslims, as well as the main state regulations.

That is why to the extent that Islam is a religion, it is also a legal code; and in the books of Sharia are found directives for how the Muslim should behave in various matters, both in public and even in private life.

Evasion from these Sharia directives is *kufr*, disbelief, dishonesty, for which hell lies ahead in the future life, as we saw above. These are the reasons why the life of a Muslim is regulated even in its minutest detail by the multivolume foundation of Sharia.

Here is an example. Every even slightly respectable native not only avoids quick or angular movements, dancing and singing, whistling and other actions disapproved by religion, but even loud conversation. This became a mark of good form and entered the habits of all well-brought-up people, while the basis of this habit is the words of the Koran: "Let your bearing be modest. Speak in a quiet voice, because the most unpleasant of the voices is the voice of the ass" (chapter 31, verse 18).

The native goes to sleep facing the Sacred Mosque (*Kaaba*) because the Koran says, "Wherever you are, turn your face toward it. . . ." (chapter 2, verse 145).

It is clear that women's rights and lives are similarly dependent on Sharia; and since the Koran is the basis of their religion, we find it not irrelevant to reproduce a large portion of those verses that somehow deal with women.[4]

Chapter (2). The Cow

Verse 183. "During the nighttime of the fast, you are permitted copulation with your wives: they are your clothing, and you are their clothing. . . . From the dawn and until night maintain the fast; do not interact with them, preferring devout thought in the mosque."

Verse 220. "Do not marry the idolatresses until they believe. A believing female slave is better than an idolatress, even if she pleases you. Do not marry idolators until they believe; a believing slave is better than an idolator, even though he pleases you."

Verse 222. "They ask you about menstruation of wives. Say: this is their time of ailment; therefore stay away from wives during the time of menstruation, and do not draw close to them until they have become clean. And when they are clean, go into them as God has permitted to you."

Verse 223. "Your wives are a field for you: go into your field when you wish, but beforehand do that which is for the good of your souls (ablution)."

Verse 226. "Those who swear that they will not have any more marital relations with their wives should wait four months; if they turn to them again, then God is forgiving, merciful."

Verse 227. "But if they have resolved to divorce them, then God is hearing, knowing."

Verse 228. "Those who have been divorced should wait out three menstrual cycles by themselves; it is not permitted to them to hide that which God created in their wombs, if they believe in God and in the last day. Their husbands will show them greater justice by bringing them back to themselves, if they want to do what is good; but they, like the one on whom they depend, will show justice by agreeing to decency. Men are higher than them by the degree of their own honor. God is strong and wise."

Verse 229. "Divorce, repeated twice: either keep your wife with you with decency, or let her go from you with kindness. You are not permitted to take anything at all from that which you gave to them, except if both of you fear that you cannot uphold God's commands. If you fear that you both cannot fulfill God's commands, then it will not be a sin for you, if she gives him a payment for herself. Such are God's commands, and do not break them; those who break the commands of God, they are evildoers."

Verse 230. "If he divorces her, then afterward she is not permitted to him (she cannot marry him again) until she marries some other husband; and when that other divorces her, then there is no sin for both of them if they return to each other, if they plan to fulfill the commands of God."

Verse 231. "When you divorce wives and they reach their prescribed time, then either provide for them in a decent manner or let them go free in a decent manner. Do not hold them against their will, acting unjustly toward them. . . ."

Verse 232. "When you divorce wives and when they have reached the term that was designated for them, then do not prevent them from entering a marriage with their (new) husbands, after they have come to an agreement between themselves in a decent manner."

Verse 233. "Mothers should suckle their children for two whole years if someone wishes that this breast-feeding should be completed; and for the father this responsibility is to feed and dress them in a decent manner. Each one only is obliged to that which can be comfortably fulfilled: a mother should not suffer affliction because of her child; nor a father because of his child. The obligation is similar for heirs. If both of them, with mutual agreement and advice, wish to relieve the mother of breast-feeding, then there will be no sin for them. And if you wish to entrust your child to a wet nurse, then there will be no sin for you, as long as you pay sincerely for that which you obtain from her."

Verse 234. "If one of you dies and leaves a spouse, they should keep themselves in waiting for four months and ten days; when they reach the end of the term assigned to them, then it will not be a sin to you if they come to you by their own will: God sees all your actions."

Verse 235. "It will not be a sin for you if you offer marriage to these (divorced) women or hide that in your soul: God knows what you think about them; but do not enter into conversation with them secretly, excepting only when you will speak with them with kind conversation."

Verse 236. "Do not enter a marriage union before the prescribed timing for that has come. . . ."

Verse 237. "It will not be a sin for you if you divorce those wives with whom you have not been intimate or whom you did not give the determined amount for the marriage gift. Make provision for them, the wealthy according to his means and the poor according to his means, providing in decent measure, as is fitting for people who are charitable."

Verse 238. "And if you divorce them before you have been intimate with them and already have given them the determined amount for the marriage gift, then to them is half of that which you gave to them as the marriage gift, unless they (husbands) concede or will concede that which is in the hand of the one who made the marriage agreement. But if you concede, that would be nearer to righteousness. Do not neglect good relations among yourselves."

Verse 241. "Those of you who die and leave spouses behind should make an endowment for your spouses, needed for one year, without leaving the home. But if they leave, then you bear no blame for what they themselves do according to their own will."

Verse 282. "O you who believe! When you make loans for a fixed time to each other, then . . . call in two witnesses from the men among you; but if there are not two men, then let the witnesses be one man and two women, whoever you think is fit, so that if one of the two [women] errs, the second of the two [women] may remind the other."

Chapter (4). Women

Verse 1. "Honor God by whom you entreat each other, and honor the womb that carried you."

Verse 2. "Give orphans their property, and in it do not substitute the worthless for the good."

Verse 3. "If you fear that you will not maintain justice in relation to orphans, then marry among the orphans who are female as soon as they please you, two, three, four, but if you fear that you may not be equally just to all of them, then, only one, or her whom your hand possesses; this way it will be easier not to lean away from justice. With a kind disposition of the soul, give to wives their marriage gift; and if they want to grant something from it to you, then make use of those with pleasure, for your own good."

Verse 5. "Test the orphans until they reach the time to enter marriage; then if you find in them maturity of intellect, make over to them their property."

Verse 8. "To men is their own portion of what is left by their parents or close relatives; to women is their own portion of what is left by their parents or close relatives. . . ."

Verse 9. "When close relatives, orphans, and the poor are present at the division, then give them something for their living, and speaking with them, speak with a kind greeting."

Verse 12. "God commands you in relation to your children: The son's share is equal to the share of two daughters; if there are more than two wives, then a third to them of what is left of the inheritance after him; if there is one, then half goes to her. And to his parents, each of them, a sixth portion of the property that he leaves, if he has children; but if he has no children, then his heir will be his parents, and in this case, to his mother, a third. If he has brothers, then his mother (receives) a sixth portion of what remains after paying anything that he promised or after paying his debt."

Verse 13. "To you a half of that which your wife leaves if she has no children; but if she has children, then to you a fourth of what she left, after paying what she promised, no matter to whom, or after payment of debts."

Verse 14. "Likewise to them (wives) a fourth part of that which you leave if you have no children; but if you have children, then to them an eighth part of that which you leave, after paying of that which you promised, to whomever, or after payment of debts."

Verse 19. "If one of your wives commits an indecent act (adultery), then present from yourselves four witnesses about them; and if they bear witness, then keep them in your house until they reach their death; or God will provide for you some other way."

Verse 23. "Believers! It is not permitted for you to take the inheritance from a woman against her will, and also to prevent them from receiving the portion which you presented to them, unless only they commit openly some indecent act. Go around each other decently. . . ."

Verse 24. "If you want to exchange whichever spouse for another spouse and you gave the first a gift, do not take it back under any circumstances. Would you bring disgrace on yourself doing what is obviously unlawful?"

Verse 25. "And how can you take it after you have already started close relations with each other and when they entered into a firm union with you?"

Verse 26. "And do not enter marriage with those women, with whom your fathers entered marriage, because that is an indecent disgraceful deed; it is a bad deed."

Verse 27. "You are forbidden to enter marriage with your mothers, with your daughters, with your sisters; with your aunts from your father's side, with aunts from your mother's side; with daughters of your brother and with daughters of your sister; with your mothers that breast-fed you, with your milk sisters; with mothers of your wives; with your stepdaughters who live in your home, from your wives with whom you have entered spousal relations (but if you have not entered into such a relationship, then it will not be a sin for you to marry them); with wives of your sons who are of your own loins; and it is forbidden to have two sisters as wives together. . . ."[5]

Verse 28. "Forbidden is marrying women who are already married, with the exception of those whom your hands possess."

Verse 29. "Those among you who do not possess enough prosperity to be able to enter into marriage with the daughters of the believers who have been brought up under strict protection, then with those [women] who are in your possession, with your believing [female] servants . . . enter into marriage with them with permission of their families and give over to them a reward uprightly, as soon as they became honest, not of loose virtue, not having lovers."

Verse 30. "If after they have lived uprightly, they commit some indecency, then they shall suffer half of the punishment that one who has been well brought up under strict observation would suffer. . . ."

Verse 38. "Men stand above women, because God gave to the first preference over the second and because they make expenditures from their own property on them. The good ones [female] among them are obedient, and in their absence they are watchful for that which God guards; but those who are a danger to your righteousness, explain to them, separate them from your bed, give them a beating; and if they obey you, then do not be unjust in your treatment of them. . . ."

Verse 39. "If you fear a breach between the two, then appoint a judge from his relatives and a judge from her relatives; if they both want to make peace, then God will create agreement between them. . . ."

Verse 46. ". . . and if you are sick or on a journey, or when one of you came from a place of avoidance [a place for defecation], or when you were intimate with your wife and do not find water, then cleanse yourself with good dust. . . ."

Verse 123. "And those who do good, whether men or women, they will, if they are believers, enter into paradise and will not be offended at the great dimples of the date-palm stones."[6]

Verse 127. "If a wife sees oppression from her husband or his aversion to her, then it will not be a sin if they reconcile themselves by sincere peace; peace is a good deed."

Verse 128. "You cannot treat your wives all the same, even if you wish to do so; therefore do not attach to them all of your affection."

Verse 175. "If some man who has no children dies, but he has a sister, then to her half of the remaining inheritance. And he receives an inheritance after her, if she has no children. If they are two, then to both of them two-thirds of the remaining inheritance."

Chapter (5). The Dinner Table

Verse 7. "Permitted to you is marriage with the daughters of the believers who have been brought up under strict protection and with daughters (also brought up under strict protection) of those to whom were earlier given the Book (Christians and Jews), when you give them a reward, and you should strictly guard yourself, not being debauched, not taking lovers."

Verse 8. "Believers! When you want to perform prayer, then wash your face and your hands to the elbows and wipe your heads and your feet to the ankles."

Verse 42. "Cut off the hands of the thief (male and female), showing what they did, as an edification from God."

Chapter (23). The Believers

"Happy are the believers, (2) Who are humble in their prayers, (3) Who hold back from empty talk, (4) Who fulfill purifying charity, (5) Who are careful in relation to their sexual members, (6) limiting themselves with their wives and their slave women whom their right hand possessed. . . ."

Chapter (24). The Light

Verse 2. "Punish the fornicators [female and male] with physical punishment, giving each of them one hundred blows. Pity for them should not overcome you before the commandments of God, if you became believers in God and in the last day. Several people among the believers should be present at their punishment."

Verse 3. "The [male] fornicator should marry only a fornicatress, or idolatress; and the fornicatress should marry only a [male] fornicator or idolater. To the believers this is forbidden."

Verse 4. "Those who will accuse married women and who do not present four witnesses, sentence them to eighty blows, and never allow them to act as witnesses, as they are unfit people."

Verse 6. "Those who accuse their own wives, having no witnesses except for themselves, in witness he should make assurances to God four times, that he is just,"

Verse 7. "and on the fifth time, calling upon himself the curse of God if he lies."

Verse 8. "But she will free herself from punishment if she calls four times to God in witness that he is lying,"

Verse 9. "and the fifth time she calls on herself the wrath of God, if he is just."

Verse 23. "Those who accuse the honest wife, unconcerned about rumors of the believers, they are cursed in this and in the next world. . . ."

Verse 30. "Say to the believers that they turn their gaze down; that they might guard themselves from sensations of desire. . . ."

Verse 31. "And say to the believing women, that they should turn their gaze down; that they should guard themselves from sexual desire, showing only those of their ornaments that are external; they should throw over their bosom a covering; they should show their ornaments only to their husbands, their fathers, the fathers of their husbands, their sons, the sons of their husbands, their brothers, the sons of their brothers, the sons of their sisters, the wives, the slave women, the servants, to those who do not have a sexual awakening, to children who do not recognize a woman's nakedness yet; that they should not strike with their feet so that all of their hidden ornaments go on display."

Verse 32. "Allow the unmarried among you, your good servants (male) and women servants to enter marriage. . . ."

Verse 33. "And those who have not entered marriage should live chastely, until God enriches them from his generosity. . . . Do not force your slave women to debauchery in order to bring yourself gain in this world, when they also want to live honestly. . . ."

Verse 59. "To stranger women, those who do not expect to enter into marriage, they are not to blame if they remove their clothing, if they do not think by doing so to show off their ornaments."[7]

Chapter (33). The Clans

Verse 4. "He commanded that your spouses whom you divorce by calling them the spine of the mother would become mothers to you. . . ."[8]

Verse 33. "Always be in your own houses; do not boast before others of your ornaments. . . . Perform the prayer, giving purified charity from your property. . . ."

Verse 48. "Believers! When you marry believing wives and then divorce them before you lie down with them, then you should not force them to maintain the term that you reckon, but give them gifts and free them from yourself in a kind and seemly release."

Verse 49. "O Prophet! We permitted you to take as spouses those to whom you give a marital gift: slave women whom your hand possesses from among those spoils that God granted to you; daughters of your uncles and daughters of your aunts on the father's side; daughters of your uncles and daughters of your aunts on the mother's side. . . ."

Verse 55. "For them (women) it is no sin to uncover in the presence of their fathers and their sons, their brothers and the sons of their brothers, in the presence of the sons of their sisters, in the presence of their wives and their slaves."

Verse 59. "O Prophet! Say to your spouses, to your daughters, and to the wives of the believers: they should lower their covering closely around themselves: by such a lowering they should not be recognized, and therefore they will not be offended."

Verse 73. "God will punish the hypocritical men and the hypocritical women, polytheistic men and polytheistic women. . . ."

Chapter (46). The Sandhills

Verse 14. "Mankind we commanded to do good to his own parents. His mother carries him in her womb with difficulty and bears him with difficulty; her carrying him in her womb and breast-feeding him, it is thirty months."

Chapter (49). The Inner Rooms

Verse 4. "Among those who call to you loudly from the inner rooms, many of them are lacking in good judgment."

Verse 5. "But if they wait for you until you enter to them, that would be better for them. . . ."

Chapter (52). The Mountain

Verse 21. "To the believers and their progeny who follow after them in faith, we will give reunification with their offspring."

Chapter (60). The One Who Has Been Tested

Verse 11. "If one of your wives flees from you to the unbelievers, then you can take her back as spoils; and for such of their wives who flee from them to you, give to them exactly the same as what you used for the maintenance of them. . . ."

Chapter (65). Divorce of Spouses

Verse 1. "O Prophet! When you divorce wives, then divorce them for their prescribed term, and calculate that term truthfully. . . . Do not send them out of their homes; they should be made to leave only when they commit an open indecency."

Verse 2. "When they have reached their prescribed time, then you either sustain them decently, or part from them decently; choose as witnesses people among you who are just. . . ."

Verse 4. "To those of your wives who themselves are not expecting menstruation, but for you this is doubtful, to them a term of three months, and to them who have not yet had menstruation but rather a term of pregnancy, then they are permitted after their pregnancy."

Verse 6. "Give to them a dwelling there, where you live, according to your means; do not grieve them by giving them tight quarters. If they are pregnant, provide sustenance for them until the pregnancy is over. And if you take them as wet nurse to your children, then give them payment; consult with them and do what you consider the best."

Verse 7. "The one who has plenty should expend according to his means; and the one whose necessities of life are meager, let him expend according to what God provided for him."

The main guardians of the religion among the population are, of course, the clergy.[9] Among Muslims they are not ordained. Religious positions in the era of khans as well as nowadays were filled either by government appointment or by the choice of the people—i.e., the same as administrative positions, without any ordination or initiation from the highest religious leaders.

Everyone who is literate, who can read and write, bears the title of mullah, which in Arabic means teacher. Those who can only read are called *chala-mullah* by the natives (incomplete, imperfect mullah); such expressions as "a very mullah" or "not very mullah," "a big mullah," "a bad mullah," and others are often used.

People who, in addition to reading and writing, study the most important books that lay out explanations of dogma, religious rituals, and law are called by the term ulomo, scholar, theologian.

Thus, belonging to the status of clergy is a personal right, which is not hereditary and which depends on knowing Muslim sciences—i.e., the essence of Muslim theology (and law)—while one's relative position amid mullahs and ulomo depends primarily on the breadth of the individual's knowledge.[10]

In general, the local Muslim official clergy who directly participate in the public life of the population can be divided into four groups:

1. Mosque clergy.
2. Legal institutions.
3. Teachers for primary schools.
4. Professors of law and theology.

The mosque clergy consists of two people: *imom* and *azanchi* (the latter is also called *muezzin* or *sufi*).

Both are chosen, or more correctly, are hired by the citizens of the particular parish. In the past, imoms of the richest central mosques were appointed by the khans. Duties laid on the imom are to be present every day at all five namoz and reciting aloud those prayers that religion requires.

A few minutes before namoz, the azanchi calls out the azan, the call to prayer, and he sees to the cleanliness of the mosque.

In kishlaks, both imom and azanchi are paid in wheat. Usually, their payment amounts to a *shishak* (about 52 pounds) of wheat per year from each house. The imom gets three-fourths of the collected wheat, and the azanchi gets the rest. Wealthier households pay a bit more than the required norm. (The average number of households in a parish is twenty-five.)

The kishlak imom's annual monetary income varies between 15 and 30 rubles. These figures do not include additional income from weddings, funerals, prayers for the sick, etc.

In cities, the payments are made in cash, from 20 kopeks to 2 rubles from each house, depending on wealth. The azanchi receives one-fourth or one-fifth of the collected total, and, on top of that, he usually receives the hides of the goats and rams sacrificed during the holiday of Kurban. Each such hide is worth 1 tilla (3⅕ rubles), and he collects them annually. (Kishlaks have the same custom.) Causes for replacing an imom or azanchi are ordinary negligence, some act discrediting them as religious leaders, etc.

Removing and replacing them with a new person requires a common agreement of the community (usually, the same as the parish) or can be decided by respectable, influential elderly men.

The native legal institution that decides cases according to Sharia consists of three people: qozi, *a'lam*, and *mufti*.

The qozi is the first decision maker. His seal endorses and validates all the documents and court decisions.

The a'lam plays the role of assistant and adviser to the qozi; sometimes he replaces the latter during his illness, absence, or in other cases.

The mufti reports cases to the qozi and examines Sharia for articles that should be followed in a particular case. (Such an article of law is called *fatvo or patva*.)

In the past, the government appointed these positions; now they are elected. The number of qozis differs in towns depending on their size; in Namangan, for example, there are two. In the countryside, there is one per administrative district.

These days, the qozi's court deals with divorce cases and all other civil cases that do not exceed 100 rubles in silver, but only for the sedentary native population. (Cases over 100 rubles and appeals of decisions made by qozis are dealt with by the regional congress of the qozis.)[11]

The government does not pay qozis, muftis, and a'lams; they receive their remuneration from suitors and litigants or according to the price list adopted by the Russian administration or by mutual agreement.

Each mosque has a parish school, a *maktab*, where the boys of a given parish or quarter study reading and writing. The school building looks like a room that could fit ten to thirty children sitting close to each other with their legs tucked under them; it is usually built by the same person that built the mosque. (More rarely, these buildings are constructed on the public account.) Sometimes the school is located in a private house or in the mosque itself.

The school is set up, that is, a teacher is invited, with the agreement of either several influential people or the whole community (parish).

Either the imom or the azanchi of the mosque to which the school is attached is invited as teacher, or if he refuses to accept, cannot do it, or there is some other reason, then a different person.

In most cases, there is only one teacher. When there are too many students, the teacher can select assistants from the best, most knowledgeable senior students, approximately one assistant for ten students.

In the kishlaks located far from the city, where literate people are relatively few, the teacher or *domla* is paid fairly well and mostly in grain. He receives a set wage equal to no less than a *pud* of wheat per year for each student and in addition, occasional small gifts of money and food.

(A female teacher, *otin*, who teaches girls in her home in these kishlaks, also gets paid in wheat but half as much.)

In most cases in cities, the domla gets no pay. Each Thursday every students brings him a so-called *Payshanbalik* (*Payshanba* is Thursday), money, bread, and rice; its amount always depends on the wealth of the student's family. In addition, at the end of each stage of studying the domla receives a small gift from the parents, and annually, before the holiday Ramadan comes, schoolchildren walk around their community to sing praises, and they give everything they collect to the teacher. This custom is popular in kishlaks and is called *ramazanlik*. The domla composes verses for ramazanlik; his students learn them and declaim them in a sing-song voice. (In some areas, ramazanlik is sung only to their parents. There is the same custom for girls.) Here is an example of ramazanlik:

"The month of Ramazan has passed
The holiday of Ramazan has come
Give me a holiday gift
I will give it to my teacher
And God will reward you
For my studies, on the judgment day."

There used to be a similar custom of *navruzlik* (*navruz* is the New Year) performed in spring, when the new soil[12] appeared. This custom has become obsolete now.

The number of students at a school can be between five and thirty, in some rare cases up to forty boys, and their average age for starting school is about eight.

Studying is nonobligatory. All primary school students come there during the day and go back home.

The father or another senior relative brings the boy to school, and the latter brings a dish of plov or some other food to the teacher; he says something like, "Sir! We entrust our child to you. Teach him; beat him. Even if you kill him, we won't complain about it. The meat is yours; the bones are ours."

As a result, most of the teachers make broad use of this permission from the parents. We have seen boys (as well as girls) running away from school simply because they could not endure the extraordinary, constant beatings, especially on the head. There are teachers whose humane treatment of their students leaves nothing to be desired, but in general, beating is very widespread. Many people even are certain that without such measures, there will be no result [no learning]—i.e., essentially the same idea that was prevalent in our society until very recently. Once we tutored an adult Sart in arithmetic. Maliy turned out to be a fast learner, and things were going well, but in spite of this, this adult student seriously begged one of us to beat him from time to time, claiming that it would make his studies more efficient.

So, a young lad is brought to school. The first class starts with the teacher taking him by the hand and making him repeat the words of the first *sura* [chapter] of the Koran. Then, they move to the alphabet. Instead of an alphabet book, at least at first, they use a small wooden slate with pens or a white tin plate, where the teacher writes letters from the alphabet with a pen.

Learning the letters and memorizing the syllables take, on average, from three to six months.

The first book the student gets is the Koran in [the] Arabic language, which the teacher himself either barely knows or does not know at all.

It is obligatory that the Koran is read from cover to cover *à la* Gogol's Petrushka,[13] which takes several more months. Next always follows the reading (also mechanical) of *Chor Kitob*, which describes the rules of ablution, praying, fasting, and so on. It is written in Persian, which Uzbek students do not understand. (Arabic, Persian, and Turkic languages share the same alphabet, Arabic.)

Only a few lines are discussed every day, and the domla teaches only the correct pronunciation. When the student can read *Chor Kitob* fairly quickly, though without understanding any of its content, "Sabat-chikty" is said.[14] They are confirmed, and they turn to writing or to mechanical reading of other books, such as, for instance, *Khoja Hafez* (one of the Persian poets).

School studies last between two and five years. The classes take place daily, except Fridays and holidays.

Students come early in the morning, shortly after sunrise; they go home for breakfast an hour or two before noon; at noon they return and stay for another hour or two and sometimes till the evening. Sometimes, with the parents' agreement, they have summer holidays for a month or two.

In school, two students usually share one book or one writing tablet. In the most important part of the room (by the wall opposite the door) sit those who are reading *Chor Kitob*, *Khoja Hafez*, or other books; closer to the door the students who are reading the Koran, and, finally, nearest the door are those with tablets.[15]

All of them shout at the top of their voices the texts that their teacher assigned for memorization.

Sometimes the latter is absent during such a lesson. Having shown each student how to read the assigned lines of *Chor Kitob* or the Koran, or letters and syllables, and having pulled the dullards' ears, the domla leaves to go about his own business unrelated to his teaching job.

The majority of the students who finish a parish school enter ordinary occupations of the native population, including farming; some, who have learned to write fairly well, become book copyists earning between 10 and 40 kopeks a day[16] or become scribes, *mirza*, at institutions that do not require knowledge of arithmetic, which is not taught at a primary school.

A person who has finished the maktab's full course can become an imom at a mosque only if he has learned and can show evidence of his knowledge (provided that he has also reached adulthood): he has to know the first two books of

Mukhtasar ul-vikayie[17] (in Arabic) on the rules of ablution and prayer and be able to recite specific suras of the Koran by heart.

The minority, those who want to continue their education after the maktab, enter *madrasa*, the highest native school, which teaches Arabic language, theology, and law, making use of books that are written exclusively in Arabic.

Ilm-i feraiz, which comprises the rules of inheritance and similarly a short course of mathematics (the first four rules of arithmetic and a most unsatisfactory description of the ways of measuring the area of elementary geometric figures, necessary for measuring land), is studied separately and only by those who wish, and comparatively rarely, although the Prophet said, "Study the *feraiz*; it contains half of the human knowledge."[18]

Madrasas are found in all cities and also in most large bazaar kishlaks where the Khan's beks used to live, such as Yangi Qurg'on in Namangan district or in To'raqurg'on and Koson-Chust and others.

There is usually no more than one madrasa in a kishlak, with five to fifteen students.

In cities there are two different kinds of madrasas:

1. Small, located next to the parish mosque, with five to ten students attending, and
2. Large, independent madrasas with their own mosques located on their premises, with their own imoms, *waqf*s,[19] and between fifteen and one hundred students (rarely, such as the large madrasa of the city of Qo'qon, the number of students reaches two hundred).

The number of teachers or *mudarris*es may vary between one and ten, [and] in some cases up to twelve, depending on the madrasa's size and number of students.

The number of large madrasas varies in different cities.

There are four of them in Namangan; fourteen in Qo'qon.

Establishing a madrasa and supplying it with the necessary provisions are considered to be God-pleasing acts; that is why all of them were built from the private means by khans, hokims, and wealthy persons.

The person funding the construction of a madrasa usually also provides a considerable amount of land as a gift, which generates income used both by the teachers, mudarrises, and the students, mullahs (or *shogird*).[20]

Sometimes, in addition to land, a small amount of capital, a few hundred rubles, is also granted in the form of those books that are usually studied in the madrasa.

Sometimes the waqf that the institution possesses grows through donations from other, unrelated persons.

In the past, khans often dedicated their income from particular kishlaks to benefit a particular madrasa, which is why the income of some reached considerable proportions.

The founder of a madrasa usually compiles a document, a *shart-noma*, which states when and by whom the madrasa is built, how much land it is given and where that land is, and how the annual profits should be divided among the *mutawalli*[21] (the manager of the property), mudarrises, and three levels of students.

Sometimes this shart-noma mentions what books must be studied by each of the three levels of students, who has the right to serve as mutawalli or as imom of the mosque located on madrasa premises, etc.

A mutawalli receives between one-twentieth and one-tenth of the annual income from the waqf. The income of the mutawalli and the students varies depending on the amount of land that the institution owns.

The average waqf income for a mudarris is between 30 and 100, and, rarely, 200, rubles in silver per year. (Wealthy students and their parents also give gifts valued between 3 and 40 rubles after finishing the study of each separate book.)

A student of the highest level receives from 15 to 35 rubles annually; at the middle level, from 10 to 20; and the lower level, from 4 to 12 rubles. (These numbers are valid for madrasas whose waqfs are close to average. The wealthiest madrasa is the one in Marg'ilon.)

A large madrasa is built from fired brick; the roof, like the roofs of most of the native buildings, is flat and covered with earth. The main premises consist of a yard surrounded on all four sides by a tall wall, from 2 to 4 sazhen high, along the inside of which are built hujra, cells for the students and mudarrises, one to four people per cell; a *dars-xona*, which is a classroom that is bigger than a hujra; one or two sunscreens; and, finally, the mosque, *xonagah*.

Qo'qon's largest madrasas have hujras on two stories. The number of hujras in one madrasa can be between twenty and seventy.

The students and teachers spend most of their time in the madrasa itself, in classrooms, or in their hujras. Only those who are married go back home for the night but not every night (usually only on Thursdays and on bazaar days).

Classes are in session all the year round but not every day. The days of the week are divided into *tahsil* or study days (Saturday, Sunday, Monday, and Tuesday) and *ta'til* (Wednesday, Thursday, Friday), free days that are used for repeating lessons.

The students are divided into three levels:

1. *Adno* (the lowest),
2. *Avsat* (the middle), and
3. *A'lo* (the top).

Adno study these books, typically: *Kapiia, Sharkh-mulla, Shamsiia,* and *Mukhtasar al-Wiqaya,* staying at this level for about three years.[22]

Avsat study *Aqaid* [Beliefs] and *Tavsia* [Moral teachings] for about three to four years. A'lo study *Mullah Jalal, Mushkat-i Sharif,*[23] *Hidaya-i sharif* [The noble law], and others, remaining at the madrasa for various numbers of years, sometimes until they get the position of a mudarris, mufti, or a'lam and sometimes, not so rarely, for the rest of their life, which they dedicate to the study of theology, which along with Muslim law and philosophy is described in the books mentioned above.

We once asked an elderly Sart, a mirza, how long he had studied in madrasa.

The mirza responded that he had been there not too long, only seven years; he did not study theological books but only learned to write and learned twenty-two *siparas* from the Koran by heart. (Apart from being divided into chapters, the Koran is also subdivided into thirty siparas.)

In large madrasas that have several mudarrises, the students who study in the same year or who study the same book gather at their teacher's place. One student reads, and the rest follow the text in their books; the mudarris corrects the pronunciation and provides the necessary explanations and interpretations of the text.

Lectures of famous mudarrises are often attended by students of other madrasas or even outsiders and auditors; in the same way, there are mudarrises that do not belong to any madrasa and tutor privately, under various arrangements, both at a madrasa and in homes. (One such arrangement is accepting a fee for teaching this or that book.)

Since the student's level is directly related to receiving a larger or smaller share of income from the madrasa, his passage from one level to the next cannot simply be at his own choice.

Everyone who trusts in the adequacy of his own knowledge and preparation announces to the mudarris that he wishes to pass to the next level and undergoes an exam with him.

Bad students pass from one level to the next one very rarely, since their comrades will torture such a student with sneers and mockery about the inadequacy of his knowledge.

Long ago, mudarrises were invited by the students themselves; later they were appointed by khans; currently the situation is transitional, and mudarrises are either elected or appointed by an influential patron, such as the ulomo, native administrators, or others.

As far as how students enter a large madrasa with a waqf (usually after age fourteen or fifteen), it happens in a very peculiar way. The right to enter is mainly purchased with money. Almost all the large madrasas have cells for sale, *sashkyn.*[24] The thing is that after a madrasa is built, the cells, hujras, are sold to anyone who is interested, cheaply, usually between 3 and 8 rubles. (The money obtained from this sale goes to the mutawalli and is spent for the repair of the madrasa and other needs.)

The person who bought a hujra receives the eternal right to live in it, listen to the lessons of mudarrises, use the books bequeathed to the madrasa, if there are any, and receive, according to the conditions written in the shart-noma, part of waqf income, depending on his level as a student.

The owner of the hujra resells his right to one or more people when he leaves the madrasa.

Often the owner of the hujra sells the right to share his cell and along with that receives part of the income of the one who comes into this hujra.

Regarding those madrasas that do not have hujras for sale, students are usually admitted by the mudarisses.

There is no common table. Food is bought and prepared separately in each cell. The cell's two or three inhabitants usually do not form a cooperative.

The food is very bad and insufficient: tea, bread, dry and raw fruit, and very rarely plov or another nutritious dish. The latter is often prepared in a hujra, in a small, almost plaything-sized pot, once a week.

By his elaborate politeness bordering on servility, the habit of lowering his eyes, speaking quietly and eating little; and in particular, if there is a specific beggar's tidiness in his clothes, in his habit of injecting speech with numerous Arabic and Persian words, by his somewhat unhealthy complexion and a whiteness of hand unusual for his race: these are how it is always easy to recognize a person who has spent many years of his life at a madrasa, lacking personal means sufficient for a tolerable living.

Having started to describe the native Muslim clergy, and having said everything that is possible within the limits of this work about the mosque preachers, judges, and teachers in the basic native school, we cannot silently pass over *eshon*s, *qori*s, and *duo-xon*s.[25]

In ancient times, or more accurately, in the past, the titles eshon and pir meant people who were known for their strict, ascetic way of life and strict moral rules. Not bound by the five namoz required for each Muslim and month-long fasting, such men of faith took up obligations for voluntary fasts, reciting sections of the Koran throughout the day, multiple repetitions of some prayer, or chanting the names of God and other similar penances.

Gaining popularity among the population, eshons acquired followers, *murid*s.

What formed was something similar to monastic orders, although the members did not leave their ordinary private occupations, or their families, etc.; they gathered only to perform public prayers and have talks with their spiritual guides.

Currently, among previous eshons who are now thought of as saints, the natives most respect the memory of these ancient Bukhara eshons: Khazret-i-Shirin-Kulial, Khazret-i-Baba-i-Agalyk, Khazret-i-shakh-i-Dzhan, Khazret-i-Pat-Abad, and Khazret-i-Divan-i-Bagaveddin. (Khazret means saint.)[26] Becoming a murid to this or that eshon was and is still accompanied by the following ritual. The eshon takes the new murid by his right hand and asks him: Does he repent of the sins he has committed? Would he refrain from them in the future? Would he follow the rules set by the religion in his future life? And so on.

Naturally, the answers are positive. The eshon recites a prayer and immediately enjoins some kind of penance on the new murid, for instance, reciting some short prayer several hundred times a day or repeating the name of God, *Allah*.

The most zealous murids who have gone through a lengthy period of trial and obedience received from their eshon an *irshod* (a testimonial), a document or a patent certifying that so-and-so has undergone trial with so-and-so and has strengthened himself in the rules of faith so that now he can be a mentor (*xalifa*) and that he takes the responsibility to enjoin a particular penance or perform a particular rite throughout his life.

Eshons grew in numbers through such initiations and spread across Muslim lands. Currently, there are three and sometimes four eshons in each Namangan quarter; however, there are only a few who are deeply respected and have many murids, and their impact is receding every year. In the recent past, there were eshons (such as Katta Xo'ja Eshon in Namangan) who made a fortune on voluntary contributions from their murids.

Such examples are hard to find now. Reasons for the collapse of the eshons' influence might be thought of as, first, a gradually spreading indifference toward religious matters; second, an excessive propagation of eshons, as a result of which people who compromise the title can easily infiltrate; third, the fact that current eshons cannot be called religious mentors since their role is mostly limited to mere representation at common prayer, while their way of life has become far from ascetic; and fourth, the position of eshons among their own murids has become extremely dubious, sometimes due to their demands for contributions.

One can often hear news that such and such eshon has gone off to hunt for new murids.

Murids of a male eshon are usually men. Women have their own women eshons, but they are not numerous, probably because the ulomo treat women eshons with disapproval.

Muslims consider reading the Koran and, even more, knowing it by heart, a soul-saving act. Muhammad recommends that every Muslim read this book as often as possible, and for those who cannot read, he advises asking someone who does know to read it.

These circumstances led to the formation of a whole division of so-called qori who know the whole Koran by heart (there are many blind people among them) as well as *qori xona*, premises for such qori.

A qori xona is usually built for a very small number of people and under the same conditions as a mosque, a parish school, or a madrasa; and in most cases the qori who lives there takes on the responsibility of reciting part of the Koran daily for the peace and salvation of the founder's soul.

The same qori can sometimes read prayers for the sick, but the latter job is mainly performed by the so-called duo-xon. Duo-xons read prayers for the sick not from the Koran but from their own special books on that subject that are compiled from selections of extremely varied books, but often they have cabalistic content.

We cannot say that duo-xons are treated with great respect, but still, we find that all layers of native society appeal to them all the time.

In cities, the vast majority of patients are women. In Namangan, there used to be a duo-xon who specialized on reciting prayers against sterility and other female ailments, but his immutable requirement was that each woman had to come alone.

These are the main functions of the native Muslim clergy. We only have to add that every somewhat educated, God-fearing but not very knowledgeable native turns to a scribe in every instance when he is not sure how to act, asking him about the best way to act and what religion recommends. The native does so because he is deeply convinced that among Sharia's many rules, there must be an answer that he seeks. And this answer is always found.

A mouse fell into a pot. The pot obviously is unclean since everyone knows that a mouse is unclean, desecrated, *harom*. What should be done? If you eat from this pot, you will be defiled, but it is hard to throw it away because it costs money, and money is scarce.

People go to the scribe. "What shall we do?" The scribe searches his books and answers thus: "If a mouse, dog, or another unclean creature falls into a pot and defiles it, you should heat it three times, wash it three times, and dry it three times; it will become clean, *halol*."

In the native's view, Sharia solves so many small dilemmas of everyday life that there are no questions that Sharia cannot resolve. He believes in it and adds an additional belief: a book, if it is of ancient origin and if it is the work of one of the famous people in the Muslim world, cannot lie; everything it says must be true. That is the reason why new books, and books unrelated to theology and law, are held in some contempt, in comparison with old books.[27]

That helps the reader understand how negligible scientific knowledge is, not only among the general population but also among literate people.

Knowledge of mathematics does not go beyond basic rules of arithmetic, which are known to a small number of people. Even among the most educated people, we have never met one who has the least scientific impression about fractions.

Knowledge of anatomy includes the fact that animals have a brain, a heart, a liver, blood vessels, guts, and lungs, etc., but the interactions among all of these are unknown to any local Sart doctor.

The only exception is historical knowledge, but that is limited to the history of the East.

Medicine flourishes but only in the sense that thousands of the most ridiculous pieces of advice are given, and a whole array of the most bizarre stuff is taken, rubbed, or applied on a daily basis, some of which is not so harmless.

Most of the medical books are published in Bombay, and almost all are in Persian; they are very much alike and are brought directly from India. Local medical books are written in the local Uzbek language, but they are rare and their content is no different from the Bombay ones.

One such book is right in front of us, and we will offer you several excerpts from it in Russian in order to introduce the reader to the current state of local medical knowledge.

The book is called *Shifa-i kulub*, which can be translated as *Treating the Heart*; but since the Sart concept of the heart is equivalent to the Russian concepts of *insides*, it would be more correct to translate the title as *Treating Internal Illnesses*.

Like all the Muslim books including even collections of anecdotes, *Shifa-i kulub* starts with the words "Bismillah ar-rahman ar-rahim," [meaning] "In the name of God, the Compassionate, the Merciful." (This is the phrase that opens the Koran, and it is pronounced at the beginning of every deed.) The book proceeds to explain the heavenly origin of medicine, after which there are thirty-five chapters dealing with treating various illnesses. Here are some excerpts:

Chapter 1 . . . Headache. Boil the flowers of mallow and thistle and rub this infusion on your soles, or below your knee, staying calm. . . .

Chapter 5 . . . Earache. If it comes from the outflow of bile, the signs of disease are yellow color of the face and eyes. The remedy is an infusion of violet. . . .

Chapter 8 . . . Chapped lips. If resulting from bile, the signs of illness are bitterness in the mouth, dry lips, and dry tongue. The remedy is to take a laxative (to reduce the bile) and to rub the lips with saffron ointment.

Chapter 9 . . . Swollen gums. The symptoms are if it results from blood, the gums will ache constantly and cracks in the mouth will appear; if it results from gall, there will be a bitter taste in the mouth; if it results from phlegm, the swelling is whitish in color and soft. The remedy is according to the cause: if first cause, blood should be let, and if there are other causes, use the laxative appropriate to each particular cause. . . .

Chapter 11 . . . If you have worms in your bosom, gargle your throat with a mixture of 10 *zolotniks*[28] of sugar boiled in a tea cup of water and 5 zolotniks of salt boiled in the same amount of water. . . .

Chapter 12 . . . Lung ulcers. Symptoms: constant fever, coughing that expels pus; if one separates the pus from the saliva and throws it into fire, it produces a foul smell, and it sinks in water. The remedy is to drink donkey milk and add barley juice to food.

Chapter 25 . . . Complete male impotence. The cause is that *ab-mani* [Persian, semen] turns from liquid to solid. The remedy is to add caraway seeds and ginger to food and eat chicken meat.

Chapter 26 . . . For barrenness, eat hare's tongue.

An introduction to another similar book says that all elements, like illnesses, as well as remedies for these illnesses, are divided into *hot* and *cold*.

Since food and drink can affect the state of a human organism, they should be treated as medications, too, and should also be divided into hot (*issiq*) and cold (*sovuq*).[29]

Medicines used by native doctors are extremely varied. Flowers and roots of all kinds, from both native and foreign plants; alum; vitriols; dried snakes and lizards; boiled, baked, and dried vegetables and fruit; lime; sulfuric acid; mercury; wax; and honey brought here from Semirechye, etc.

Mostly, these are prescribed in combinations.

One of the most popular medicines is *mumiyo*.[30] We do not know exactly how this mumiyo is prepared and from what; we only know that it is usually of yellow or reddish color, [with an] unpleasant and bitter taste; it is sold in the bazaar at about 20 kopeks for a piece of a size of a pea, and it is recommended to be taken internally for cuts, strained limbs, bone fractures, and many other illnesses.

Most of the Sarts think that mumiyo is prepared in China (or Tibet) in two ways: either from the juice of some indigenous plant or from human fat. As far as the second way of preparing it, each person describes it differently. Some mention the Chinese who died; others are more inclined to think that the Chinese catch and fatten people with a predilection for obesity. Whatever the reality is, public opinion supports the idea that mumiyo is prepared from human fat, insisting on this so strongly and firmly that there was even an investigation of a most unusual character a few years ago in one district of the province, since the native village authorities suspected that a murder had taken place in order to prepare mumiyo.

For the whooping cough, which is called *ko'k yutal* (blue cough) in Sart language and which both of our sons suffered from in Qo'qon province, we were advised to use the following treatments: (1) plant five blue dolls into the ground; (2) attach several feathers of the roller bird (*ko'k-qarga*)[31] to the sick person; (3) tie several blue rags on a *mazar*, the grave of a saint; (4) feed the sick person with eggs that have been dyed blue; (5) ask the first person passing by on a gray horse (*ko'k ot*) dressed in a blue or gray robe (*ko'k tun*) what remedy he would recommend for whooping cough. Do whatever he says.

3   Houses and Utensils

THE MAIN CONSTRUCTION materials for all the native buildings are clay (to be precise, loess)[1] and wood, mainly poplar and willow. Clay forms the walls of buildings and enclosures; wood makes poles, props, beams, doors, window frames, and roofs.

The building materials made of clay are (1) dried bricks; (2) *guvala*, elliptic globs about 6 *vershok*[2] long and 4 vershok in diameter; they are made of thick clay, mixing in *saman* (fine-chopped straw), and they dry in the sun in the same way as the dried brick; [and] (3) *loy*, a soup of clay with or without saman.

Fired bricks are used very rarely, mainly in the construction of public buildings such as madrasas, caravanserais, etc., and almost never in the construction of private homes (except for their foundations).

The walls, *devol*, usually narrow toward the top. They are rarely made of bricks, which are used mostly in the construction of niches and fireplaces; much more often, the walls are constructed of guvala, which are laid in rows intersected by clay mud, loy.

The so-called *paxsa-devol*, a rammed-earth wall, is also widespread.

Such a wall, rarely more than 1 arshin thick, is constructed in layers, *paxsa*, 1 to 1½ arshin high, beaten down from a thick clay material prepared a day in advance.

Since the layers of the paxsa-devol always crack in a vertical direction when they dry out, the next layer is not placed until the previous one dries sufficiently and cracks a bit, to prevent the formation of vertical cracks going through several layers.

After the walls of a room are built, the internal sides of two parallel walls are laid with rafter plates (*sarrov*) on vertical posts so that the top edge of the sarrov is about ½ arshin lower than the wall's top. Beams are placed on the rafter plates about 1 arshin from each other, and over them, sticks (*vassa*, lathwork); bulrush wickerwork is placed over them; then a layer of bulrush, saman, and dry weeds; then a layer of soil 1½ vershok thick, which is covered with loy, making the surface of the roof slant slightly toward one side or the other. Small wooden gutters for rainwater are installed along the edges of the roof.

If a house is built with private rooms, they are plastered coarsely first so that all the posts holding the rafter plates are concealed by the plaster. Niches between ¼ and ½ arshin, as well as windows and the fireplace, are made in the spaces between the posts.

Holes for the doors and windows are left during construction of the walls, but jambs are plastered later.

The fireplace, usually about 1 arshin deep, is built in the wall with a smaller part of it sticking out. The chimney is straight and without dampers or any other devices to close off its flue.

Dual-pitched roofs, *shipangs*, that are sometimes constructed over small buildings in Qo'qon and Marg'ilon are more rare here, as are domelike roofs, *gumboz*. The latter [domes] are mainly built with fired brick, less often from raw brick, over native bathhouses, mosques, and cemetery chapels, mazars [tombs] built over the grave of local saints and other honored people in the community.

Religion forbids local women to appear uncovered in front of unrelated men and advises that they should not even be able to hear her voice. Such a religious statute must have an impact on the general character of the home and space within it.

Whenever a family has financial means, the yard is divided into two completely isolated halves: the outer, male, is the *tashqari*; and the internal, female and family oriented, is the ichkari.

Among the poorest families that lack the means to construct almost double the buildings or those whose lots are too small, we find no such a division of the household into tashqari and ichkari. In these cases, in order to meet the demands of religion, natives orient their buildings so that when the front gate leading to the street is open, a woman who is going from a room into the courtyard cannot be seen by passersby. For this purpose, frequently a wall as tall as a person is built inside the door or the front gates, blocking most of the courtyard from a stranger's gaze. Such courtyards can be found both in cities and in kishlaks but more frequently in the latter.

The courtyard is almost never large; in towns, where land is expensive, the tashqari and ichkari of even the wealthiest takes up not more than 10 × 15 or 15 × 20 sazhen of land.[3]

The courtyard is always surrounded by a wall on all sides, and the living quarters and other household structures are built with their backside attached to this wall so that windows almost never face the street. All communication with the street is conducted from the external courtyard, the tashqari, through a door or gates that are about twice as wide as a door; that is why horsemen dismount the horse in the street and arabas cannot enter the yard and are always parked in the street. Often there is a small shaded gatehouse, the *darvoza-xona*, built inside the gates.

In the external courtyard, arranged in any order, are found (1) mehmon-xona, a room or a space for male guests; it consists of a room with curtains and, if the owner is wealthy, two rooms and a curtain between them; [and] (2) a stable usually covered by a canopy with hayracks along the walls.

Less frequently, the stable is a square building covered by a roof with a small hole in it, about 2 or 3 arshin, and hayracks along the walls, similar to the ordinary stables covered with canopy. Separate stalls are almost never found.

Apart from these constructions, essential elements of every well-furnished courtyard are several trees, one or two supas under the tree or by the wall, a small ariq, and if the yard is more spacious, a pool or *hovuz* measuring 1 to 4 square sazhen, and one or two rows of flowers: African marigolds, asters, daisies, basil, cockscomb, and shrubs.[4]

A supa is a clay (earthen) platform ½ to 1 arshin high and 3 to 5 arshin long. In summer, the native rarely stays inside a room, except in the worst heat. If he is not busy in the field, in the store, in the workshop, or at work, and if the supa is shaded and not in the sun, he sits, eats, works, and sleeps on it.[5]

Generally, the tashqari is kept relatively clean, and wealthy people who have servants keep it extremely tidy. It is swept daily, and in the summer it is sprinkled with water at least twice a day, in the morning and in the evening.[6]

Stables in wealthy houses are also kept very clean, and in summer, if the stable is covered, the horses are led out and are tied to high wooden poles for the night.

The mehmon-xona rarely consists of only one single room. In most cases, next to it, or attached to its front facade, is a porch room of about 4 to 7 arshin in width, with the same sort of flat earthen roof as on all other native buildings.[7] Sometimes there is also a *jigit xona*,[8] which is a room for male servants, and *osh-xona* or kitchen, a tiny room with a hearth or a fireplace for those cases when the food should not be prepared by women in the ichkari but should be prepared in the tashqari by the male servants.[9] The dimensions of an average mehmon-xona do not exceed 5 to 6 arshin in width, 7 to 9 arshin in length, and 4 to 5 arshin in height.

The entrance door is usually a double door and a bit lower than an average human height; as a result everyone enters stooping slightly, and from there, when entering the room, each newcomer makes a small bow, followed by the customary greeting "As-salam-alaykum," set by the religion.[10]

The two halves of the door move in jambs plastered over on the outside of the wall, not on hinges but on legs, short ledges of the door that fit into sockets made in the threshold and lintel. The door fits the jamb very loosely; there are large gaps, thanks to which in winter the temperature inside the room differs little from the temperature in the courtyard. Even more than the doors, the windows and fireplaces with straight flues that never close contribute to this condition.

There are usually one or two windows in the mehmon-xona. They are the same size as the doors; the bottom of the window is only 1 or 2 vershok from the floor of the room (because the native needs light in the lower part of the room since he does not know furniture and usually sits, works, and eats on the floor);

the shutters follow the model of the front door. Frames, if they are present, look like thin wooden gratings; paper is glued over them for the winter.

Wealthy people plaster the inside of the mehmon-xona with white alabaster; small and large niches are made in the walls, which are decorated, like the fireplace, with delicate patterns in plaster; the ceiling and the top wooden cornices of the walls are decorated with bright paints (the main colors are red, blue, yellow, and green), leaf gold, and fine, sometimes very beautiful and intricate carving. Most of the patterns are in Arab taste.

The fireplace is always beside or near the door. The floor is earthen and very level. Two cavities are made in it: one is square, about 1½ arshin per side and ¼ arshin deep, and located near the door; galoshes are left in this cavity. The other one is smaller but deeper, located almost in the center of the room, built to hold coals for heating in winter. The floor of the room, except for the two cavities for galoshes and coal, is covered first with bulrush mats and on top of them felt rugs or, more rarely and only among wealthy people, carpets.

On top of the felt rugs or carpets, near the cavity for the coal, which especially in winter becomes the room's focus and its most comfortable place, are laid two or three *to'shak*, narrow, cotton-stuffed blankets or mattresses made of Russian cotton or native silk fabrics.

In wealthy homes, a large wall niche houses a pile of quilted blankets and thick, stuffed pillows; these quilts and pillows are used by the guests staying in mehmon-xona for the night. A European should use them very carefully and with caution; otherwise by the morning he may start feeling various insects slowly crawling on his body; these insects are as intrinsic to the native way of life as ablutions, namoz, salam when acquaintances meet, etc.

After everything that we have seen for ourselves and occasionally suffered, we wonder whether there is any Sart whose undergarments do not host so-called *bit* [lice], which the native treats with more kindness than a flea. He definitely hates the latter. It is fast moving, often uncatchable, and bothers him mainly on hot summer nights, when he is viciously attacked by mosquitoes and gnats.

In a niche near the fireplace stands the *choydush*, a copper vessel in biblical form, and beside it one or two *piyola*, small porcelain or glazed clay cups that resemble our slop basin.[11] The choydush is used to boil water and brew tea, and the piyola is used as our glass or teacup.

If not more than four or five are drinking, they each drink, one after the next, from one and the same piyola; first it is filled from the choydush for one and then refilled for the next.

They usually drink tea without sugar, although wealthy homes serve a small plate with lumps of it as part of the so-called *dasturxon*.

Dasturxon means a tablecloth, but natives use the same word to mean everything that is offered to a guest.

According to native etiquette, after a guest arrives and lengthy greetings and inquiries about health[12] are exchanged, a dasturxon, a wide cloth made of colorful cotton or semi-silk fabric, is spread before the guest; it is often covered with oil, since wiping one's hands with it is customary, and washing it is considered a waste of time. On the dasturxon is placed a tray (copper or painted iron) with flat bread, raisins, and pistachios; the wealthier also serve several small plates with lumps of sugar, fruit drops, candy, halvah, and other sweet things (in summer, fruit is served instead of sweet things), and tea is always served, but it is usually of poor quality, the so-called *oq quruq* [white, dried out].

One of those present breaks several flat breads into pieces by hand and sets them down, always with the top side facing upward; the opposite is a sin.

It is extremely impolite to take a bite from a whole flat bread, just as rude as sitting cross-legged, *chordana*. All well-bred natives seat themselves in the following way: first they go down on their knees, which should be slightly spread, and then lower their buttocks onto their heels, leaning their body slightly forward.

When the flat bread is broken into pieces and the pieces are arranged on the tray, the guest is invited to eat with a gesture of a hand and with words "Mirvan bo'ling" or "Marhamat qiling, nonga qarang" ("Please do me the kindness of turning your glance to the bread").[13]

The guest should be the first to start the repast, and etiquette requires him to eat at least a small piece of bread first. After this, he can drink tea, eat fruit, etc. At the beginning of the meal, everyone says, either in a whisper or in a low voice, "Bismillah al-rahman al-rahim," meaning "In the name of God, the Merciful, the Compassionate."[14]

The entrance to the ichkari is built somewhere on the side opposite the mehmon-xona. It is usually an open corridor perpendicular to the entrance formed by the rammed-earth walls; it is slightly taller than a person's height and usually has a single door or gate.

Thus, the ichkari's interior is always invisible to the external courtyard.

The size of the ichkari is either the same as the tashqari or smaller.

In the ichkari are found dwelling rooms; a kitchen, which in wealthy homes is separated from the living quarters; a small pantry, *hazina-xona*; a barn, *mol-xona*, and sometimes a stable and a small granary. The *badraf* (the latrine) is usually located somewhere among nonresidential buildings (or inside the stable); the pit is usually dug very deep, up to 2 or 3 sazhen; the excrement loses most of its liquid to the lower layers of the soil (usually porous conglomerate), condenses, and grows in volume very slowly. Due to the depth of the hole, even in the hottest time of the year, almost no smell is noticed, and certainly no ammonia smell, especially because the badraf (which has an earthen floor and a wooden covering only over the hole with a layer of clay on top) is always very tidy.

The barn is usually built in such a way that one of its walls adjoins either the street or the garden (or the vegetable garden), if the house has one. Through that wall a hole is made, such that a spade with manure would easily fit through. Manure is thrown either into the garden or into the street, where it stays for years in conical piles against the exterior, street-side walls of houses and buildings. That is why apart from dasturxons and the underwear of the natives, the streets of kishlaks and even cities are the dirtiest spots here.

The internal courtyard, like the outer one, has two or three trees and sometimes grapevines, an ariq, and, if space permits, a supa. The condition of the ichkari is generally dirtier than the condition of the external, model, showy tashqari.

The number of rooms in the ichkari varies, corresponding to the size and the means of the family. When possible, teenage children sleep separately from the parents, and when there are several wives, the native tries to provide each one with a separate room.[15] But since only a few wealthy people, mostly in cities, take advantage of the right to have several wives, the number of internal rooms is usually limited to two. Poor families have only one.

The arrangement and furnishing of these rooms in the middle-class families are the same as for the mehmon-xona, with the only difference that they are rarely decorated with alabaster or have painted ceiling beams. Poor people often have no windows in the rooms in the ichkari, and a hole in the roof substitutes for them; the door is small and single; the floor is covered with felt rugs, but only for half of the room. The whole family sleeps side by side on these felt rugs.

The arrangement of the ichkari dwelling room differs from that of the mehmon-xona only in having a larger hole for the galoshes, and in one of its corners, usually on the side away from the door, closer to the fireplace, there is a deep hole, widening toward the bottom, called the *obrez*, covered over with a sandstone with a small hole in the middle or an iron grating or with a wooden plank with wide gaps. Water used for ablutions is poured into this hole.

In one of the large niches that runs from the ceiling to the floor, and that is usually built opposite the entrance door, stands a *sandiq* [trunk], usually made by Russians, tin bound. Sometimes it is replaced by a small cabinet installed snugly in the lower part of this niche. It is used to keep the bedding, clothing, cloth rags, some dishes, and other household junk or else sweet things, pots with fat and oil, etc. Blankets and pillows are stored on top of the trunk in the daytime.

In one of the corners, usually near the trunk, there is a stick, usually 1 sazhen long, fixed (horizontally at head's height) between two adjoining walls; it is used to hang the hostess's silk shirts, sleeveless vests, and robes as a sort of decoration. Also serving as decorations, distributed among the niches, are copper and painted tin trays; choydush; porcelain teapots and cups, often made by Gardner manufactures,[16] with pink and blue flowers; gaudy Russian small and medium boxes with women's jewelry; locally produced tin candleholders with a wide base and tallow candle ends; occasionally, a little crystal vase appears and a Russian vial made of blue glass that used to contain a silver nitrate solution and is now used as a snuff box. From time to time, the hostess spills a pinch of a finely ground dark green nosvoy into the palm of her left hand and places it between her cheek and gum. Keeping it there for about five minutes, she spits it out. If this is happening inside, the lady spits either into the hole for the coal (*otashdon*) in the middle of the room, or she lifts the edge of the felt rug and spits under it. Outside, she spits randomly anywhere, and if an inexperienced European happens to see the spittle half an hour later, he may think that it came from a bird that was feeding on greens.

In wealthy families, in winter, when the temperature outside and inside does not differ much, heating takes place thus. A pile of well-burned coals is placed into the otashdon; a small platform, a *sandal*, stands over them [the pit and coals] and is covered with one or two quilts. They sit near the sandal with their feet under the blanket. Of course, only their legs are warmed.

Most winter days and nights are spent near the sandal; people work near it doing everything that can be done in such a position, putting their food on top of the sandal, and they sleep near it, too.

If the sandal does not go out completely and turn cold by the morning, it is very comfortable and pleasant to sleep near it, because you can let the warm air reach your knees or your waist or your neck by lifting the edge of the blanket. Your head stays comparatively cold and is always fresh in the morning; but on the other hand, it is easy to catch a cold.

One cannot help wondering how the natives manage not to catch colds and die in the hundreds because of staying near the sandal all day. A Sart woman will pile fresh coals under the sandal and warm her bare feet; she heats them almost to the point that her skin cracks; then she gets up, puts galoshes on her bare feet, and goes out into the yard, stays there for half an hour or a full hour, then comes back into the room and seats herself again near the sandal, heats her feet again, goes out again; and this is happening on a daily basis, all the time, and without any serious immediate consequences. Of course, there are cases of rheumatism and colds but not as many as you would expect when the basic rules of hygiene are violated so commonly.[17]

A sandal is a rare thing in poor families since coal is expensive, so they usually warm themselves near the fireplace, *o'choq*.[18]

Bedding is oriented with the head toward north or west, less frequently toward south, and never toward east. Going to bed in a new place, the native first figures out where the *qibla* is, the direction toward the Holy Mosque,[19] since in the Koran, it is said, "Wherever you are, turn your faces toward it . . ." (chapter 2, verse 145). First, a blanket folded in two[20] is laid out, and at its head is placed either a flat pillow (*quroq*) [patchwork], sewn from pieces of various fabrics, or a cylindrical pillow (*bo'lish*), made of red bunting, chintz, or a local semi-silk fabric.

A sheet, *choyshab*, is used very rarely; it is usually made of light-colored chintz with a small pattern.

The second blanket is used to cover oneself up; more often, however, especially in cold weather, the person puts half of the blanket under himself and wraps himself in the other half.

*   *   *

All food except bread is prepared in a cauldron.[21] Fuel consists mainly of weeds, cotton-plant stalks, thin grapevines that are pruned every year, etc.

A Sart protects artificially planted, cultivated trees and rarely uses their bark or branches as wood. Charcoal is prepared mainly in wild mountain forests.

Dough is mixed in a large clay bowl, *tog'ora*, about an arshin in diameter. It is kneaded on a white raw goat hide called *surpa*; it is wrapped in the surpa and covered over with something additional; it rises for two to four hours, depending on the temperature of the air. (Usually the surpa is left hanging somewhere on a peg, because there is a folk belief that, otherwise, one would never bring in money.)

Bread, round and flat and formed in various sizes, is baked in a special oven called tanur or tandir. Tandirs are built by special artisans called *tanurchi* in the following way: clay is mixed with horse or cattle hair purchased from tanners and formed into a thick dough, which is kneaded into thin layers about ½ inch thick, 1½ arshin wide, and 2 to 2½ arshin long.

The layer, rolled out and carefully leveled, is left in the sun for about one and one-half hours to firm it up a bit. Then it is carefully bent along the length, turning it into a cylinder with one of its ends somewhat narrower; the seam is smeared over with clay and on the narrower end is placed a band made of the same material as the tandir itself.

A tandir is used for baking bread in the following way: An elevation, the top of which is just above waist level, is constructed from globs of guvala next to one of the walls of the yard. The tandir is placed horizontally on this chairlike structure so that its wide orifice would fit tightly to the wall and the narrow one, fastened by the band, is facing out. Then the surface of the whole structure is plastered with clay, and near the wall the top of the tandir is punctured so that the smoke can escape through a small hole, which then is covered with a glob of clay, a stone, or something similar after it is heated.[22]

Most of the kitchen crockery is made of clay; some is made of copper, cast iron, or wood.

Large bowls, tog'ora, each about an arshin in diameter, are used for mixing dough, fermenting milk if the household has a lot of it, washing rice for plov, and so on; smaller bowls, *kosa*, are used to serve liquid food; *xurmacha*, medium-size bowls with handles for preserving milk, hanging them by the handles from the ceiling or by some pegs hammered into the wall, to protect the milk from mice; piyola, teacups; dishes, *toboq* (or *tavak*) that are always round: all of these dishes are crockery, slipware (*sopol*), or glazed (*chin, china*).

Jugs for water, *ko'za* (they also may hold grape molasses and other liquids as well as oil and fat), come with wide and narrow mouths and a wide range of sizes; also there are small and big amphorae, kiln fired but not slipware. The reader knows the shape of these jugs and amphorae well from pictures of biblical stories.

There are copper and cast-iron jugs, qumg'on, of the same type for boiling water; washbowls, *oftaba*,[23] and teapots, choydush. The latter are almost always made of copper.

The spoons are wooden, very roughly made and gaudily colored with long, thin handles and a tip not at the front but on the left side.

Wooden bowls and dishes (walnut or willow) are little used by the sedentary population.

Noodles, dough for pies, and other similar things are prepared on a board (*osh-taxta*) that is about 6 vershok wide and 1 arshin long. The osh-taxta's surface is slightly convex, and it stands on four tiny legs.[24]

In poor families, grain such as rice, millet, and sorghum is pounded out at home in large wooden mortars, *ug'ir* [mortar] or *keli* [pestle]. The pestle is also made of wood, as thick as an arm and 1½ to 2 arshin long; it gets wider in the middle and has a hole through it, from which are formed two handles. This task falls to women. Usually, grain is ground by the *objuvoz*, a mill driven by water.

Tallow candles are used either by wealthy people or by those who are engaged in reading, writing, and other similar kinds of work. Everyone else lights a night lamp, *chiroq*, with flax oil or sesame oil. A clay or cast-iron lamp is placed in a cast-iron or wooden holder, *chiroq poy*. The wick is spun from cotton. The oil is kept either in gourds or in *kiima*, very strong pitchers manufactured from *kunjara*, oilseed hulls.

Almost every well-off person in the cities has a garden, and the rich have more than one. If the family does not live in the center of the city, its garden is usually next to the house. Otherwise, their garden is somewhere near the city.

In both cases, the garden's area is rarely larger than 1 desiatina, and its arrangement resembles both an orchard and a vegetable garden. There are almost no paths. Along the rammed-earth wall is a row or two of mulberry trees, poplars, and a few fruit-bearing trees, such as cherries, apples, or plums.

Most of the internal space of the garden is planted with grapevines, and pomegranate bushes are spread far apart.

Local grapes have long vines. The vines are planted in parallel rows about 4 to 5 arshin apart. Arches are constructed out of dried willow switches with their ends stuck in the ground between the two rows of grapes; these arches are a bit higher than the average human height. The arches are connected either with thin switches or straps made of bulrushes; the latter are tied to vines, and if the vineyard is already mature, it creates a covered arbor or a corridor with walls and roof formed by the small vines and leaves. If there are several such corridors, their side walls are adjoined.

The rest of the garden is planted every year with melons, pumpkins, watermelons, carrots, and onions and sometimes with several rows of maize.

Fruit trees are usually planted in disorderly fashion along the sides of the vineyard, between the rows of vegetables or along the sides of the ariq passing through the garden.

If the garden is not too small, then somewhere near the entrance there may be a pool, with an area of 1½ to 2 sazhen, surrounded by willows or plane trees. Here, in the shade of the trees, there is a supa or two.

Sometimes a strong rope net is constructed over part of the pool; it is used for sitting in the daytime and for sleeping at night, over the freshness coming from the water.

If the garden is located next to the house, there are no buildings in it. Otherwise, there can be one or two rooms for the family, depending on its financial means, and a small stable for horses.

Wealthy people's *dacha* homes are like their urban houses.[25]

Gardens are comparatively rare in kishlaks, but almost every house has a hayat, something like a vegetable garden, planted with melons, pumpkins, maize, and lucerne. Around the walls of either a vegetable garden or hayat there are one or two rows of trees, usually mulberry trees. Their leaves are used to feed silkworms.

In some areas in Marg'ilon, Qo'qon, and Namangan regions, where there are large fields of melons, natives and their whole families move to the melon plantations, living in huts built of sticks. They usually move there in May—i.e., when melons start to form.

4 Woman's Appearance and Her Clothing

Native women are predominantly of middling height or short. Tall ones can be seen more often in kishlaks than in cities. Because of nutritional conditions, which we will dwell on later, the native girl develops quite slowly, but she is given in marriage, on average, at age thirteen or fourteen; so after getting married, the young woman continues to grow for a long time and sometimes considerably. There is a belief or a conviction that the more she likes her husband, the more and faster she grows.

There are quite a few plump women. Most of them are predisposed to being chubby and put on weight at a mature age, when they come into good living conditions. Plumpness is an indispensable condition of beauty; a woman with a curvy figure and a good complexion is often called a beauty even if she has ugly features. Women usually start filling out around age nineteen or twenty but usually after the birth of the first child.

Their build is rarely regular. Most have disproportionately long torsos, which are often considerably disguised by the fall of their outer dress; in the absence of large, well-developed breasts, the torso is extremely and equally flat in the front and in the back. Because of these shortcomings of their build, native woman would rarely look attractive in European dress.

The majority of the subjects, whether plump or lean, have wide hips. There are frequent cases of death during childbirth, but considering the complete absence of scientific knowledge of midwifery, we think that the reason for most of these is not a natural narrowness of the pelvis but more likely is the wrong position of the child and other pregnancy pathologies originating from the unsatisfactory hygienic conditions surrounding the pregnant woman and the birthing mother. Our opinion is based on the fact that, first, death often happens not during childbirth but after, and, second, cases of death are more frequent in winter. Unfortunately, there are no statistics of that sort or about rates of birth and mortality, so we cannot state anything with certainty but can only suggest a possibility.

The shape of the head is usually irregular. The back of the head is frequently wide and flat. We think this is because for a year the infant is kept lying flat in a *beshik* [cradle] with a thin padded mattress or pillow placed between its wooden bottom and the infant's head. The cotton mats quickly loses springiness, and the pillow becomes so hard that it cannot help making an impact on the correct development of the back of the head. There are almost no high, large foreheads among adults, or they are extremely rare, but women disguise this shortcoming very elaborately, though not always consciously, with a *durracha* [small scarf], which we will speak about later. Skin color is mostly dark with a great variety of tones, including the so-called spectrum of an unpolished boot.[1] White and tender skin can be seen comparatively rarely; such faces are called *paxta-dek*, like cotton, and are unconditionally preferred to others unless the hair color is too light. Women with light brown hair are rare; blondes and redheads are extremely rare and are completely scorned by the natives. Gray eyes, which are also rare, are disapproved as well. Most people have brown or black eyes.

Pale, sickly, or gaunt faces are rare and can be seen mainly among the inhabitants of the central parts of large cities, especially Qo'qon and Marg'ilon, where unhealthy hygienic conditions prevail. Ruddiness is frequent among the young native women.

All faces can be divided into three main types: Mongol, Persian, and mixed.

The first two are, obviously, familiar to the reader, so we will not speak of them. The mixed type, originating from mixing Mongoloid and Persian types, is prevalent among the sedentary Sart population. Faces of this type are round, and female faces are often very flat. The distance between the eyes is rather large. Facial features are irregular in most cases. The upper lip is often thinner than the lower one; it often disappears or goes into vertical lines when the person is silent and gives the face a malicious expression. Brown eyes prevail, and the eyebrows are often not so well and beautifully shaped as among others. This type, more often than others, goes with plumpness, soft and light complexion, and lighter hair colors. Narrow, upward-slanting eyes, the so-called *bit-ko'z*, are rather rare. Most people have large, slightly protruding ears.

Because of the vast variety of types, it would be difficult to offer some general idea about the prevailing expressions of female faces. However, scrutinizing the latter, one cannot help noticing that on the faces of female natives from all strata, energy prevails over apathy. An apathetic expression is often seen among men but is much rarer among women. Mostly one notices a sly, roguish, penetrating, or thoughtful facial expression or look in the eyes.

The front teeth, even and strong, would retain their whiteness for a long time, if many of the native women did not have a habit of dyeing them with black dye, *tishqoli*, which stays on the teeth for a long time. Teeth frequently have cavities, both among men and women. Mostly the molars suffer. Perhaps the main reason for these ailments is eating hot food in the frosty weather in winter.[2] The reason we believe this is that, generally, men and women treat their teeth with great care; for instance, they do not break nuts or pistachios with their teeth or cut thread with them, etc. Second, they very rarely eat such products as sugar, candies, and so on, since most of them do not have money to buy them.

A birthmark is considered to be one of the best facial adornments. The verbal expression *xoldor*, having a birthmark, is almost equal to the word "beautiful." Freckles are rather rare and are mainly found among women with lighter or reddish hair.

Hair is mostly thick and long but almost always wiry; soft hair is extremely rare not only among women but among girls as well. Until they give birth to their first or second child, young urban women braid their hair at the back of the head into four or eight plaits; that is why a young woman here may be called *beshkokil* (five braids). [Older] married women usually wear their hair in two braids.

The hair is always parted in the middle. In Namangan, it is carefully arranged to flow along the top part of the forehead in two large festoons. In Qo'qon, many fashionable women leave a lock over each ear. The ends of the braids are always tied with a string made of twisted cotton; there is a belief that if the ends are left free, the hair will fall out in the hot summer wind, *garm-sel*. False plaits, *ulama*, usually made from one's own fallen hair, are very popular.

In the morning, after getting out of bed, a Sart woman simply smooths her hair with the palm of her hand and covers it with the obligatory scarf; it would be indecent and even sinful not to wear it. It is especially sinful for a woman to be present without a headscarf in a room with the Koran, as well as during Koran recitation, and many of them even sleep in a scarf, tying it tightly around their head. Hair is combed only on days when it is washed, which is usually once a week on Fridays, less frequently on Thursdays or Sundays. It is against custom to wash one's hair on Tuesday (which is considered to be a difficult day) and on bazaar days. The hair is loosened, combed, and rubbed with *qatiq*, sour boiled milk; then combed again with a small, dense, wooden comb; rinsed with warm water in winter or cold water in summer; and then pressed out, twisted into a bunch over the middle of the center of the forehead, and left to dry for about half an hour, then combed and braided. This operation is followed strictly by all women not only in Fergana but all over the Turkestan region. Soap is never used for washing one's hair. In winter, if qatiq is unavailable, it is replaced with curds saved specifically for this purpose, dissolved with water or raw eggs. Bull's or cow's bile is considered one of the best means for strengthening and improving hair growth.

Especially in cities, most women who are muscular or chubby have wrists that are small and exquisite. Their nails are convex and oblong. Their feet are, on the contrary, rather large, or, to be precise, long, with a low instep and long, flat toes. Most have well-developed breasts. There is a belief that a woman with undeveloped breasts has little capability for bearing children.

Маргеланъ. Сартянки на своей половинѣ.

Women at a gathering for tea and music, Marg'ilon, Fergana Valley, late 1880s. Similar to the Nalivkins' descriptions, the room features niches and a trunk with bedding piled on top. The woman seated left wears a koynak made of atlas, resist-dyed silk, in a bold, multicolored pattern. The photo is signed by the photographer, Orden, whose notes read, on the left, "Margelan', Sart women, women's half (of the house), No. 1500," and on the right, "guests, dastarkhan, entertaining. F. Orden." Source: MAE RAS No. 255-126, image ID 3588125, Peter the Great Museum of Anthropology and Ethnography (Kunstkamera), St. Petersburg, Russia.

Among the most widespread deformities, we can mention goiters, *buqoq*, which can be gigantic in size and which are seen mainly in Qo'qon and Marg'ilon regions; there are also large scars on the face and hands from the so-called *Sart illness* and pockmarks. Vaccinations against smallpox are very rare among the native population; there is an annual epidemic of smallpox (*chechak*) both in the cities and in kishlaks, which leaves pockmarks on faces, leucomas in eyes, and probably carries off a considerable number of young children. The Russian administration has made some attempts to introduce vaccinations among the native population, setting up a Sart vaccinator in every regional and provincial hospital, who receives support and vaccines from the land fund, but progress is very slow despite the fact that vaccination for smallpox is not at all a new thing among the Sarts. There are native Sarts with vaccination scars in the palm, usually near the thumb.[3]

The cut and appearance of native female clothing have mainly been influenced by the climate, the way of life, and religion. The long, hot summer that lasts about half a year, the habit of sitting on the floor with folded legs, and the need to mount a horse from time to time, forced women to give almost all elements of their clothing the form that least hinders movement, while religion demanded that when she goes into the street, a stranger's eye should not see anything except her outerwear, which should not be so bright as to attract the male gaze.

Trousers (*ishton*) are very wide from waist to knee and narrow toward the ankle or foot, while still easily allowing the foot through. The bottom is decorated with brightly colored bands, jiyak, and the trouser waist is tied with a tape (*ishton-bog'*). Girls are dressed in trousers from the age of two or three. Adults must wear them, and failing to do so is considered a sin or indecent behavior, which is why this clothing element is called *lozim*, Arabic for necessary. Wealthy women wear trousers made of bunting, bright chintz, semi-silk adras, or thin silk; the poor, from coarse local cotton fabric, usually white with bunting, chintz, or semi-silk sewn on to the bottom quarter or half. A shirt, serving both the roles of undershirt and pinafore or dress, is worn over the trousers.

The shirt, *qo'ynak or qo'ylak*, is always made very wide and long, even down to the ankles, with wide sleeves falling below knee level. During dancing, these long sleeves are used in the same way as Russian women use a scarf, and they are also used as a handkerchief in everyday life; however, the latter use as a handkerchief is limited; the nose is only brushed but never blown into sleeves. The neck is cut in two ways: either horizontally above the shoulders or vertically down to the waist. In both cases, the edges are bordered with wide, patterned bands, jiyak. If the neck is cut vertically, keys to a chest or pendants made of beads or corals are tied to the fringelike lower ends of the jiyak. Shirts with horizontal necks, *mullocha-qo'ynak*, are worn only by young women; if the latter is breast-feeding, then special slits are cut over the breasts, which are not made in ordinary female shirts with vertical necks.

(The name mullocha-qo'ynak originated from the fact that initially only literate men, mullahs, wore this style shirt. Children of both sexes and adolescent girls wear the same type of shirts. Illiterate men wear *yaktak*, shirts that resemble a robe. Recently, fashionable Sart women began wearing wide, turndown, Tatar collars.)

Female shirts are sewn from all sorts of fabrics. In kishlaks, the ones worn every day are made of coarse white or striped blue native cotton fabric; festive ones, from bunting or chintz, less frequently, from thin silk or thin atlas, iparkak.[4] In cities, shirts made from native fabrics are seen less frequently, worn only by the poorest strata of the population. Better-off urban women and girls wear shirts made of multicolored or patterned bunting, bright-colored cottons with large patterns, and from brilliantine.[5] Silk shirts are worn either on holidays or for paying visits. Older women, over thirty or thirty-five, wear both cotton and silk shirts in dark colors: dark blue, purple, two-colored with shimmer (*kabutar*, the color of a dove's breast), etc. A dark blue color corresponds to our black and is considered the color of mourning. Summer shirts are often made of local white or colored muslin, crude and of low quality. (In some areas, married women do not hem the edge of the shirt but only baste it, since there is a belief that a woman who wears a hemmed shirt will suffer from barrenness.)

Women in Osh, Fergana Valley, late nineteenth century (photographer unknown). The woman on the left wears a paranji (veiling robe) covered by a chachvon (horsehair face veil); the two women in the middle wear robes with excessively long sleeves over qo'ynak (shirts/dresses) made from atlas, embroidered do'ppi (skullcaps), and large earrings; the woman second from right has dyed her eyebrows with usma; and the woman on the right wears a robe with a turned-down Tatar collar. The caption below the image reads, "Fergana Oblast'. Female types." Source: MAE RAS No. 512-142, image ID 3595879, Peter the Great Museum of Anthropology and Ethnography (Kunstkamera), St. Petersburg, Russia.

We mentioned above that it is sinful to walk around with uncovered head. A woman's guardian angel departs if she eats food without a scarf on her head. The scarf, white or red, muslin or, in rare cases, from bunting, is usually square, with sides 1½ arshin in length; it is folded diagonally and made into a scarf that is placed on or tied around the head. In the first case, the edges of the scarf are put behind the ears and the ends fall over the chest. In the second case, the scarf is wrapped around the head, covering the top of the forehead, and its ends hang at the back.

When a woman leaves the house or goes on a visit, she puts over that large scarf, *ro'mol*, another one (durracha) that covers her forehead; this scarf is small, always patterned, and brightly colored; it is folded several times into a strip and tied as a headband.

In summer, the clothes worn by women at home consist of trousers, shirt, and a scarf; when she goes into the yard, she puts galoshes over her bare feet. During the cold season, the wealthy ones put on soft boots[6] with galoshes; the poor ones wear galoshes over their bare feet or soft boots without galoshes all year round. Sometimes, one can see a woman wearing white cotton stockings instead of soft leather boots and galoshes. In the past, about thirty years ago, most women wore such stockings, but this has been abandoned now. It is improper to walk in the street in [Russian-style] boots, which are worn by most of today's prostitutes. Russian lace-up ankle boots, the sacred dream of many local fashionable women, who may have seen them somewhere by chance, are just entering the fashion and are rarely seen.

When planning to leave the house but still in the internal yard, a woman throws over herself a *chimbet*,[7] a thick net made of black horsehair covering her face and chest, and then, over the chimbet, she covers her head with a paranji,[8] a long robe made of gray or dark blue cotton or sometimes semi-silk fabric. The lower edge of the paranji reaches her ankles or the ground; the ends of her long sleeves, hanging behind her back and connected at the bottom with a thread, often drag on the ground. Decency requires that none of her colorful clothes be visible from under the paranji, but this law is almost never observed, especially now.[9] From the way she wears her paranji, natives can tell which town a woman comes from. For instance, in Namangan the top edge of the paranji is always placed low over the forehead, and the lower edge of the chimbet is allowed to hang from under the paranji; in Qo'qon, it is the other way round; the top edge of paranji is placed in the middle of the top of the head, and the bottom edges, held by hand, cover the lower part of the chimbet.

In kishlaks that are far from cities, the paranji is seen rarely and only among the wealthy women. Instead, an ordinary robe is thrown over the head in the same way as a paranji. In many areas, kishlak women are accustomed to covering their head with a child's robe instead of their own, and usually the opening of one of the sleeves is put over the head.

In cold weather, two shirts may be worn instead of one, and the outer shirt is usually newer and fancier than the under one.

Over this, women usually wear a quilted robe of the same cut as men's. It is not customary for a woman to wear it with a sash. (Red bunting sashes 6 to 8 arshin in length are very popular among native women of easy virtue.)

While traveling or doing work, such as laundry, women use a folded scarf as a belt. A blue sash is a sign of mourning, and she wears it at home as a belt while lamenting the deceased or during visits to the grave on the second, third, and fortieth day. A woman's robe is made of chintz, patterned bunting, or semi-silk adras; less frequently, of light silk or atlaslike iparkak. Silk and semi-silk robes mostly have a chintz lining, while chintz and bunting robes usually have a white lining made of coarse cotton fabric or from the native gauze fabric. Wealthy women have recently started replacing the robe with a tunic made of semi-silk fabric, but since it is made locally and without any cotton padding or with a very thin layer of it, it is often worn under a robe if the weather is cold.

Old women in towns and all the married women in kishlaks can still be seen wearing an old-fashioned *munsak*, a robe with short, elbow-length, very wide sleeves.

Fur coats of the same cut as the ordinary native robe, made of sheepskin, fox, or wildcat, edged with beaver, marten, or otter, can be seen only on the wealthiest women.

Everyday trousers and shirts are changed and washed very rarely. Well-off people do that once every two weeks. Poorer people change them only when they reach a degree of filth called *shakar-kir*,[10] which varies depending on the wearer's way of life, the time of the year, etc. The destitute wear shirts and trousers without changing them until they fray, fall apart, and turn into rags. Laundry is done using water boiled in a pot, which may be the family's only large pot, with potash or *tsushtan*,[11] a plant from which potash is made. The laundry is scrubbed either in a small washtub or a large clay bowl, tog'ora. Soap, which comes in cone-shaped pieces 2½ vershok high, is used very sparingly, not more than two pieces for the whole family's laundry, which is the reason why the latter is never well washed. (One piece usually costs 3 to 5 silver kopeks.)

Having rinsed the laundry in cold water, the woman[12] always twists in the same way: she holds the shirt at the shoulder with her right hand and twists it with her left, away from herself. The laundry is left to dry in the sun and then stretched by hand. Pressing and ironing are not done and are mostly unknown. In cold wintertime, laundry is either not done or done very rarely on warmer, sunny days.

Every woman who has even the least means, in addition to the underclothing and dress she is wearing, has one or two more silk shirts and robes, and wealthier ones have quite a few; they don one before going visiting. These shirts, which are almost never washed, can be used for a very long time; we have often seen Sart women's shirts that have served for ten or twelve years but still looked like festive clothes. Such shirts are never worn at home; as soon as one returns from a visit, she removes them and stores them in a chest, which is why they last so long. If in cities we often meet large groups of women wearing silk shirts and robes, that does not necessarily mean they are wealthy, since most of the fashion lovers may wear out only two or three such silk shirts in a lifetime; one is a gift (from husband or parents) when she gets married; another one or two she acquires by means that we will mention later. Having arrived home and taken off the top silk shirt, she is still wearing a dirty, worn-out chintz one. She puts on a similar-looking chintz robe, and her staple food is *go'ja*, a porridge made of sorghum, or *mosh-xurda*, a mix of rice and lentils,[13] and she eats plov with microscopic additions of meat once a week on Thursday nights. Women in wealthy families have many festive, fancy clothes for going out, but in spite of that, their housewear, including dress and underwear, is mostly dirty and untidy. Wearing a new dress or robe, a Sart woman sits down on the ground, leans on a clay wall, wipes dishes with her sleeve, etc. It is understandable that such an attitude toward one's underclothes and dress does not keep them clean for long, and thanks to infrequent washing or other cleaning, clothing almost always looks dirty and soiled.

New clothes are made for each of the two holidays, Ramadan and Kurban.[14] Women receive them from their husbands; less frequently, they make them themselves or receive them from rich relatives. These clothes vary a lot in quantity and cost. Wealthy women get a full set of clothes; others get a robe and a shirt; some get only a robe or a shirt, a scarf, or soft boots with galoshes, etc. Festive new clothes are worn during the whole period of the holiday without taking them off, and, unless this is a silk shirt, they are worn as daily clothes afterward. Oftentimes, especially among the poorest kishlak population, we saw instances when for lack of means, a woman's new holiday clothing was an arshin of chintz, used to add new sleeves to her worn-out shirt, which would show from under the sleeves of her robe.

Two or three days before the holiday, new shirts, robes, soft boots, galoshes, boots, and skullcaps appear in the streets, since newly received clothes are usually donned immediately. So many tears flow, so much swearing comes out, and so many divorces are planned among the poor during the two or three days before holidays, especially on the day of the so-called *arafa*, the evening before the holiday!

Almost all the bazaar stores are open. People rush back and forth everywhere. The streets nearest the bazaar become visibly lively. Pedestrians and horsemen, with happy, celebratory faces, carry around various purchases. A gray-haired, respectable Sart tugs a ram with a short lasso; his small son pushes it from behind. Another one dressed in a new robes and skullcap carries a bundle with chintz and bunting. His wife and daughter will spend the evening and the whole day tomorrow making new clothes for the holiday. Baibacha, the son of a wealthy merchant, rides a horse, holding a pile of chintz, bunting, and ticking on his saddlebow.

A holy fool, devona, demandingly begs for alms for the coming holiday. Village Sarts in carts and on horses, with their purchases of chintz, galoshes, and dresses in their hands, rush about and scatter toward home. Women with children in hand and adolescents hurry to various sides, carrying bundles that are wrapped in tablecloths on their heads. In these bundles are plov, flat bread, chintz, dresses, and a small mirror. Before the holiday, the women deliver these presents to their *quda*, whose daughters and sisters they sought as wives for their sons and brothers.

A long, loud wail comes from one of the yards. A girl of twelve is squatting, with her face in her hands and elbows on her hips, wailing so that the whole quarter can hear her. Her father has not bought her anything for the holiday, while she expected at least a scarf.

Further, by a small gate, a Sart dressed in an old skullcap and a worn-out striped chintz robe is squatting; he is watching passersby, perhaps thoughtfully or with amusement. In the ichkari, his wife is cursing him. She must have been busy spinning thread, but she stopped her work, sat down in another corner of the yard, took off her headscarf, and ignoring the baby crying in the beshik, curses her husband with all the worst words she knows. She expected to get a new shirt from her husband and galoshes with soft boots, but the only thing he has brought her from the bazaar was a white lacy scarf and cheap, low-quality galoshes.

She is scolding him and saying that she has decided to go to the qozi after the holiday and get a divorce. At that moment, a young neighbor woman comes in wearing a crisp new chintz shirt.

The cursing woman pauses for a moment and suddenly starts wailing. The guest sits down next to the wailer. "A? Nima yiglab o'turibsiz?" (Why are you crying?) The wailing continues. "What has happened to you?" The woman[15] thrusts the galoshes that her husband has brought and, without stirring from her place, wailing and cursing, starts explaining her misfortune. "Die! May the earth take you! What a present you have brought me for the holiday! While you promised me a shirt, you said you'd buy galoshes and soft boots. Let the holidays pass, and I will go to the qozi for a divorce. Why should I live with him; what sort of life is this if he cannot buy a shirt for his wife for the holiday: I will get a divorce. I will leave him."

If up until now she has lived with her husband tolerably, it is possible that her decision to divorce will pass with the holidays; if not, during the whole period of *Hayit*,[16] their small house will be full of cursing and scolding, and after the holiday she will go with her husband to the qozi. If the situation is in her favor, she will leave her partner and marry someone else by the winter.

On average, in a year, a woman from a modest family, whether urban or kishlak, wears out two shirts and pants, two robes, two pairs of galoshes, one pair of soft boots that she does not wear all the time, and two scarves. A chimbet and paranji last several years. So her family's annual expenditure on clothes can be on average 12–17 silver rubles.[17] (The lower figure is an average for the kishlak, where soft boots are worn rarely and where the chintz is replaced by crude local native fabrics for everyday wear; the higher figure is for the city.) A shirt made of native fabric costs between 80 kopeks and 1⅕ rubles; from chintz, requiring about 10 arshin, 1½ rubles to 2 rubles; cotton pants, about 80 kopeks; soft boots, 1 ruble; a pair of galoshes, from 1 to 1½ rubles; a robe, from 1½ rubles to 3 rubles; a scarf, 1 ruble. These figures increase considerably for wealthy families since they do not use the native cotton fabrics, which they replace with Russian cottons, bunting, and ticking; festive and dressy clothing for women, especially in towns, is almost always made of semi-silk or silk fabrics. (A shirt made of thin atlas, iparkak, costs about 7 rubles; a semi-silk robe or tunic is about 6 rubles silver; a nice semi-silk paranji, about 11 rubles.)

If a woman has her own property that generates revenue, she almost always buys her clothes with her own means. We knew one not very wealthy peasant family in the Qo'qon region. The woman was married to her second husband; she had several children and some property that she inherited from her first husband: a small land lot that generated profit that she used to dress herself and her children from the first marriage.

If the woman has no property, her husband buys her clothes. In poor families, she earns the money that she needs by her own labor, doing such things as spinning thread, raising silkworms, cleaning cotton from seeds and pods,[18] and in cities, baking bread for sale, sewing blankets and robes, etc. Wealthy families in some kishlaks of the Namangan region that practice cover cropping[19] often produce a special independent crop of one of the kinds of grain that requires very little attention (no mounding), for instance, barley, wheat, or flax. The crop from that field is given to the woman; she sells it and spends the money buying herself the clothes she wants, not receiving any other subsidy from her husband, sometimes not even presents for holidays. Since this money is often not enough, the woman steals grain from her husband, secretly sells it, and spends the money; often this requires cooperation with the children, who often have a closer relationship with their mother than their father, since the power of the latter oppresses everyone equally. Interestingly, although they hide this pilfering from husbands, women do not think of it as a secret among female friends or even mere acquaintances. Telling one of the authors about her deception, one Sart woman asked her how much she steals from her husband and always treated her negative answers with disbelief.

The concept of fashion must have appeared fairly recently. Details of female dress changed in the past, but the reason for the previous changes was not striving for elegance but toward more practicality and comfort. Thus, cotton lusterless stockings were changed for soft boots, a munsak with short wide sleeves and usually without a collar for an ordinary robe with a stick-up collar and long sleeves.

Currently, both women's and men's attitudes toward dress are changing or have changed; among urban residents we see the ambition to make clothes from fashionable fabrics, with some deviations from the main forms of folk costume. For a short time in the later [18]70s, among the native fashion lovers and merchant youths who mixed with the Russians and people from Tashkent, native boots with extremely high, thin heels and robes with turndown collars were extremely popular; at about the same time, women began wearing tunics instead of robes. Later, galoshes with wide toes, robes sewn by machine, and underclothing made from chintz rather than from native cotton fabrics became fashionable among men. In the streets, women were increasingly wearing shirts of fashionable colors.

Goods have arrived from Russia. A batch of chintz that has a novel pattern has come. A rumor spreads around the town that *yangi chikkan chit*, the newly arrived chintz, is being sold at the bazaar. It is displayed in the most prominent place in the stalls selling the best goods and is sold not for 18 or 20 kopeks per arshin but for 30 kopeks, at first. Naturally, it excites appetites even more, and shirts made from this chintz become a mirage arousing the imaginations of those who are more inclined to self-adornment. For a while, such a yangi chikkan chit was chintz with a sparse pattern of red zigzags on white; then it was replaced by a cotton and wool fabric with a small flowery pattern, etc. The fashion for headscarves among women is similar. Formerly, white muslin scarves with silk edges called *duro'ya* were extremely popular; then they were replaced by red muslin scarves with large white and yellow flowers; then the simple white muslin ones returned, and now these are pushed out by white or colorful silk ones produced in Bukhara. Along with this, the turndown Tatar collar for women's shirts spread through all the cities, and we have also noticed an unconquerable desire for ankle boots among women, but they are somewhat afraid of wearing them in the street, first, because they look like the soled boots that are worn only by prostitutes and, second, one faces possible accusations of disrespect toward religion.

The Sart woman, especially a young one, like the woman of any other race, loves dressing up in fashionable clothes, but here self-adornment not only is inspired by personal and subjective stimuli and desire but is also based on religious beliefs. Sharia (see Tornau[20]) advises a woman to take care of her appearance so that she pleases her husband and recommends using such things as blush, skin whitener, *usma* (to color eyebrows), beauty spots (*xol*), locks of hair, etc. Thus, for the native woman, taking care of her looks is to some extent a moral duty that she can drop only when she reaches the age, common for most peoples we know of, when excessive care about one's appearance is considered funny and ridiculous.

Skin whitener is prepared from rice or from eggshells, while rouge (*fuchsine*), beauty spots, and false locks are rarely used in Fergana. Painting eyebrows with usma and eyelashes with kohl is much more widespread. The most beautiful eyebrows are considered clearly delineated, wide brows that extend across the space above the nose. That is why usma is painted in a broad stroke from the outer end of one brow to the outer end of the other brow. The result is very clumsy and garish, but the opposite, elegantly painted eyebrows, are very rare.

Usma is a cruciferous plant cultivated by the natives. When it is fresh, one uses hands to squeeze a dark green, slightly purplish juice from its leaves; the end of a thin wooden stick or match with a cotton ball wrapped around it is dipped into the juice, and one's eyebrows are colored several times. The area that was dyed becomes almost black after a while and stays like this for a long time, because women, except for the most affluent, rarely wash their faces.

The dye can be made from dried usma, for which the leaves are wrapped in a piece of cotton and chewed for several minutes till the dye gets diluted by saliva.

Usma juice is considered good for the growth of eyebrows.

Painting toes and fingernail, as well as palms, seems to be losing popularity; decorated palms can be seen only on festive days and in certain cities.[21] Locally produced perfume does not have a nice fragrance and is not much used.

Sart women's primary adornments, aside from dyed eyebrows and eyelashes, are rings, earrings, bracelets, beads, corals, silver amulets, and other locally produced pendants. Recently, large European cufflinks have become popular among women who wear shirts with Tatar collars. These decorations, except for rings and simple inexpensive earrings, are almost never worn at home.

Small pearls that are used as the eye in rings and pendants on earrings, as well as small, low-quality corals or precious stones, are imported from India, Bukhara, and partly from Russia.

Turquoise is mostly fake, and stones are often replaced by simple colored glass. The most widely worn are silver rings with fake turquoise, corals, colored glass, small pearls, or sometimes amber, which is a great rarity here. The price of such rings can be between 30 kopeks and 5 silver rubles. Gold rings, bracelets, and earrings are rare and can be seen only on the most affluent women. Earrings are usually in the form of large, thin rings made of silver wire that can easily be opened up without hinges. These get additional attachments from small pearls, corals, beads, and small gilded silver trinkets. The length of such trinkets can sometimes reach up to ¼ arshin, and many torn ears testify to their weight.

When the earrings are extremely heavy, the woman attaches them not to the earlobe but to her hair behind the ear or the front edge of the scarf adjacent to the ear. The cost of ordinary silver earrings is between 40 kopeks and 4 rubles. Silver bracelets priced between 2 rubles and 8 rubles in silver are made with blackening,[22] gilding, or small, fake turquoise. The most widespread necklaces are from coral. One zolotnik[23] of the latter (usually small and of low quality) is sold from 30 to 1 ruble 40 kopeks.

A coral necklace is often made like a net with the bottom of it hanging as low as the waist; sometimes corals are interspersed with large polished silver beads. Large and small, blackened or gilded amulets, *tumar*, usually triangular in form, are attached either near the shoulder or over the shoulder blade. So-called *chach-popuk*, tassels from twisted black silk, with heads decorated with silver and sometimes with beads and other trinkets, are often attached to braids on long strings. In kishlaks, such chach-popuks are often replaced either by large glass beads or by a simple stone with a hole drilled in the middle. Naturally, such a stone serves not only as a decoration; it is also tied to the braid so that it will wave around less.

Wearing a large earring in the nose, which is widespread among the women and young girls in some parts of the Central Asia, is not known in Fergana. Wearing such earrings can be seen here only among native Jewish women, who are very few.[24]

The cheapest and most beloved decorations for Sart women, both adults and girls, are flowers, especially roses, but, unfortunately, they decorate themselves extremely gracelessly. The flower is usually stuck behind the left ear; in less frequent cases, two flowers with long stems are fixed in the hair: the ends of the stems placed near the ears dangle on both sides of the face.

In spring, almost every Sart has a flower stuck behind his skullcap next to the ear or temple. In springtime, girls braid into their hair thin strips of bark with small leaves and catkins that they carefully peel off the branches of the willow.

5   Occupations and Food

Islam recognizes staying at home and working hard as the best deeds for a woman. A pious, hardworking Sart man is called sufi (pure, godly), and a house-wifely woman is *mastura* (homebody),[1] but very few young women can qualify for this description.[2] Having observed men and women for several years, we have come to the conclusion that there is a huge difference between them when they are the same age. A woman up to twenty-five or thirty years of age usually has little interest in housework or any other labor. If she is not forced to work by poverty or a husband's pressure, she would not lift her finger and would run around visiting others, strumming a *dutor* [two-stringed lute], pounding a tambourine, and gossiping; the most she can do is sew a new dress for herself. The man is the other way round; before thirty to thirty-five, he is extremely hardworking, serious, and ambitious. In many families, he takes on the heaviest load in agriculture, crafts, and trade starting at age ten or twelve, while the majority of girls who are soon to be brides can do almost nothing. However, when they become mature, the roles of an average man and woman change. He often becomes deficient in energy and sedentary, even lazy; she, on the contrary, does not lose her energy and ambition until a very advanced age and, with very rare exceptions, becomes very energetic, good at homemaking, and hardworking. We see old gray-haired women who spend the whole day on their feet, never stop working, baking bread or sewing or weaving or preparing food, *moki dek yurubti*, running back and forth like a weaver's shuttle.

We are not trying to explain this purely physiological fact, but we think that aside from the climatic, nutritional, and other arguments that play an important role here, we should consider the way of life of both one and the other or, to be more precise, the ways of expending their energy before they age.

Exceptions toward the hardworking side exist, of course, especially among the kishlak farming population, but they are rare among the well-off. In the kish-laks, [working hard] originates from constant need and not from personal incli-nation toward labor. In general, a kishlak woman is much more active than an urban one, and the wives who are the best masters of household work are chosen by Sarts from the Kyrgyz or other nomadic groups, where women and teenage girls perform all the housework, including tending cattle, setting up the yurts, etc.

However, despite the obvious practical benefit of such marriages, they are comparatively rare since by long-standing tradition, Kyrgyz *qalin*,[3] or payment for one of their daughters, is much higher than qalin for a Sart girl, and therefore very few can marry a Kyrgyz [girl]. That is first, and, second, among most Sarts, taking a bride from distant lands is not accepted. Both Sart men and women are used to living and dying where they were born. The notion of *musafir* (a stranger, a foreigner, a person who lives apart from his motherland) is related to an extremely grim and simultaneously very childish notion of having no relatives and, because of that, being allegedly helpless. This scares the bride and her parents, which is why marriage arrangements with someone from afar are made extremely reluctantly.[4]

In the domestic sphere, a Sart woman acts as a housewife and a worker only to the extent that this is properly linked to the main religious statutes, which recognize her husband as the head of the family and offer to her, as a woman, avoidance of strangers' eyes. The husband must earn the money and bring food; the wife must prepare it and make clothes.[5]

Based on these regulations, a woman's responsibilities are primarily those that she can do inside the ichkari. That is why her main activities are preparing food, milking the cows, sweeping the internal yard, spinning, sewing, and feeding silkworms with leaves brought by the man, who also brings water, wood, and feed for cattle that are kept in the barn of the internal yard.

Men always carry out activities such as trading, buying, and selling, since it is considered improper for a woman to go to the bazaar. She still goes there, but rarely, and only when there is no one else who could do it for her. A woman usually conducts her personal transactions through middlemen, mainly her husband and other relatives.

We knew one wealthy woman who was widowed and remarried to one of her workers, a very deft and smart man, whom she trusted deeply; she transferred into his hands the transacting of all of her trade and other business.

Cases when an educated wife helps her husband in keeping trade accounts and other written records are very rare, because there are very few women who can write and do figures.

In families where husband and wife live in mutual agreement, the husband usually consults the wife about things he wants to do or at least informs her about his decision.[6] If there are several wives, the husband usually asks the advice of the first, senior wife. Several times we have been asked either to lend money or to participate in a commercial company, a trade, or agricultural enterprise. If the husband agreed, we would ask him whether his wife also agreed; if he refused, he was asked not to hurry but to discuss it with his wife, since she may find the offer interesting or beneficial.

It should be noted, however, that such a rule exists mainly among the agricultural population, whose moral world in all respects can be called the most appealing compared to other classes and groups of the native population.

Our discussions of women's occupations and work will concern only the kishlak population and the class of modest urban residents, since the woman from a family of the wealthy merchants or affluent former khan's servicemen does very little except for sewing and embroidering.

Among these [rich] families, dirty household jobs are performed either by female servants, *oqsoch*, or female slaves, *joriya*. Female servants are usually homeless widows who have reached an age when there is little hope to remarry. They usually live in the family and get food and clothes; if they are paid money, which is rare, it is very little, usually not more than 10 rubles per year. (Oqsoch means white hair.)

Before the arrival of Russians in Fergana, almost all the wealthy families had male slaves (*kul*) and female slaves (joriya). Both male and female, all of them Dungans,[7] were brought here as children from Kulja and Kashgar, where they had been bought by the local traders who conducted business in those cities, or had been taken captive or had been bought directly from parents. In Fergana, a slave boy cost from 70 to 100 rubles, and a girl from 50 to 80 in silver.

With the Russian arrival, abolition of slavery was proclaimed. Most male slaves abandoned their former owners, but almost all female slaves stayed in their places, either because they had married other workers or servants of their former owners or they were too young to start their own independent life. Some of them did not want to leave since they had a decent living where they were. Such Dungan women are still called joriya.

In wealthy families where a wife has been taken from the poor class, her mother or distant relative frequently fulfills the duties of a female servant, oqsoch, and her position is no different from the condition of an ordinary servant.

The daughter mistreats and commands such a mother-servant, totally ignoring the existence of any other relationship than that between lady and servant. We have often heard mothers talking about marrying their daughters off to a rich husband. She asks the bride to forget that she [the mother] used to beat and scold her, and she always expresses the worry that her rich daughter will not allow her to cross the threshold of her house. We knew a case when a daughter who married a wealthy man and took her mother as a servant not only mistreated her mercilessly, constantly scolding for bad service, but even beat her.

We will talk about preparing food later and in great detail, so we would like here to describe other female occupations, mainly spinning thread and cleaning cotton from seeds and pods.

The bolls of the native cotton do not crack open well, so when the crops are harvested, they are cut from the bushes intact and sent to market.

After cleaning, the cotton fiber weighs only one-fourth of the initial weight; half of the weight comes from seeds, *chigit*, and a quarter, from pods. Chigit are added to flax seed for pressing oil, and most of the pods are burned in the cooking fire. Cotton is removed from the pods by hand, and chigit are removed with the help of a special wooden device, *chig'iriq*, which operates by having two rollers pressing against each other, with spiral cutting. Cotton is pressed between the rollers, and the seeds are cut off and fall down. Before seeds are removed, the cotton is carefully dried in the sun. In a week or six days, a woman cleans no more than ½ *chorak* (2 puds[8] and 25 pounds) of cotton bolls. This amount can produce 2 *chaksa* (26 pounds)[9] of cotton fiber and 4 chaksa of chigit [seeds]. Currently, for example, ½ chorak of crude cotton in its bolls (go'za) sells for 2 rubles 40 kopeks; 2 chaksa of cotton cost 3 r. 60 k.; and 4 chaksa of chigit, about 40 kopeks. The average weekly income of a woman engaged only in cleaning cotton may be 1½ rubles, but only when the woman has helpers among children, whose responsibility is to remove the cotton from the pods. Besides, it is a rare woman who can work without resting, since her hand and shoulder grow numb from rotating the handle of the chigi'riq. (Such cleaned cotton is partially used for local needs: bedding, robes, etc.; but it is mainly purchased by traders at the bazaar at cheap rates and taken to Russia.)

Thread is spun from the best, whitest cotton. The cotton designated for processing into thread is beaten with thin reeds and then formed into layers, each layer being about a finger thick, ¼ arshin wide, and several arshin long. Then each layer is rolled lengthwise into a ball. The spinning of thread itself is carried out on a spindle moved by a small, wooden, hand-turned spinning wheel, *charx*. The thread is twisted from small cylinders of cotton rolled by hand. These cylinders, about ¼ arshin long and a finger thick, are formed from previously broken cotton fiber.

The thread that is needed for sewing underwear and clothes is usually spun at home. All the yarn that is produced for sale goes for weaving white or colorful locally produced fabrics. (Weaving here is an exclusively male job; in some Karakalpak and other seminomadic families, women weave only crude woolen fabrics.) By spinning, a woman can earn 40 to 80 silver kopeks per week; in most cases the yarn produced during the week, or in six days,[10] is sold at the following bazaar,[11] since the money earned this way is needed for food, since the poor, especially urban, population never has any reserves. Besides, it is best to buy food on bazaar days because otherwise it will have to be bought from small traders along the road at higher prices.

During cold winters, women's work, such as cleaning cotton and spinning thread, ceases, first, because there is no place to dry cotton; second, most dwellings are so cold that it is impossible to work there for very long; and third, there is no demand for yarn at the bazaars because weavers, whose workshops are as cold as other buildings, are on strike. The prices for yarn fall so much and so rapidly that at the start of the winter a woman taking thread to the bazaar may sell it for the same price for which she bought the crude cotton a week ago. There are women who survive exclusively and only on this kind of labor. We knew one old woman like that. She spun yarn, and her husband, a sixty-year-old man, sold *halvah* [a sweet] on the street; he took it on commission, earning about 10 kopeks per day. You can imagine the situation of such people during the weavers' work stoppage when cold winters come, when they need wood and hot food, and when all the foodstuffs become much more expensive. We knew another such family. There was an old woman, more than fifty years of age. She had a daughter, age twelve, and a tiny yard in one of the most crowded quarters of Namangan. They lived by cleaning cotton and spinning thread, and it stands to reason they were always hungry. The old woman began growing weak. She saw that things were bad. She married her daughter to a homeless wage worker and took him into her house; he earned on average about 20 kopeks per day, but he had a hernia and turned out to be a halfwit. The very cold winter of 1881–82, which everyone remembers, arrived. Temperatures dropped below minus 20 degrees Celsius. All were without work. The daughter was already fourteen. Hunger and cold pushed her toward the worst. The girl's virginity was sold for 4 silver rubles. Then things got better for them; the idiot died, and the former nominal wife became a secret prostitute.

We knew other families like this, but we are afraid to bore the reader, and also if we start describing everyone, we risk taking too much time, while we must move on with our work.

Breeding silkworms and feeding them is the favorite occupation among women of all ages but also among young girls, although it is labor intensive. Its attraction comes from the fact that, if successful, it is the most profitable of all women's work.

At the end of May or the beginning of June, cocoons that had been laid out for that purpose somewhere in the middle of the room on the damp earthen floor, transform into butterflies. They are mated, placing a male and a female one together into a small fabric sack that is hung somewhere in the room on a stick. The female lays eggs in it, and the butterflies are thrown away. The eggs are pre-served until spring and kept from cold. Some people put them deep into the snow in the middle of the winter and leave them there for a day, believing that this can protect the future worms from getting sick. In March, when the first buds ap-pear on mulberry trees, women launch artificial incubation of the eggs; the latter are suspended in small sacks under the armpit, breasts, or around the waist and warmed with the body's heat for fifteen to twenty days.

At the same time, eggs weighing 1 *paisa*[12] (about 6 zolotniks) are sold at the bazaar for 20 to 40 kopeks. As soon as worms appear from all the eggs in the sacks, they are laid out in a small flat basket covered with a rag, and the basket is also covered either with a towel folded several times or with a thin padded blanket. The cover serves to protect the young worms in the basket from the light, changes of temperature, and such enemies as ants and sparrows. The baskets with worms are kept in a room or under a sunshade. At the same time, the first leaves appear on mulberry trees; they are collected, cut finely, and sprinkled over the worms twice a day, in the morning and in the evening. (As soon as the worms hatch, there are baskets of them sold at the bazaar.) Eight to ten days after hatching, the worms fall asleep and sleep for two days. There are four such sleeping periods, about ten days apart. As the worms grow, they are moved from small baskets to large ones, and the leaves are cut into larger chunks until, after the second sleeping period, they are given uncut leaves. After the third sleep, when the worms reach about 2½ inches in length, they are transferred from the baskets to a plank bed created from sticks and brushwood, built in a dark room. During that time, the worms are fed with whole branches of mulberry leaves, spread out over the plank bed. After the fourth sleep, bunches of large dry stalks are placed around the plank bed and along the walls of the room; the worms crawl down over them and start making cocoons. The latter appear about fifty days after the worms hatch. In the first half of May, bazaars are literally heaping with cocoons. Large baskets and bundles are carried from everywhere. Everyone is in a hurry to sell his cocoons as fast as he can before they dry up and lose some of their weight.

At that time, a chaksa of them (13 pounds) costs from 1 ruble 60 k. to 2 rubles 80 k. at the bazaar. The color of cocoons varies from white to bright orange, but the cocoons are sorted at the bazaar not by color but by durability. A good cocoon, squeezed in one's hand, should not cave in to pressure. Buyers spread them (the cocoons) in the sun right away to prevent the butterflies from coming out, which would tear the cocoon, and only the intact ones can be used. Cocoons preserved for household needs, like the ones separated for sale, are unwound by specialists who have formed a special guild in cities.

One paisa (6 zolotniks) of eggs that cost from 20 to 40 silver kopeks produces 30–50 pounds of cocoons, the price of which varies between 3 rubles and 11 rubles 20 kopeks; the net profit, if one has access to free leaves, is between 2 rubles 60 and 11 silver rubles. One family can use between ½ and 20 paisa for production. Since there are not many people who can get by using only leaves from their own mulberry trees, there is a lively trade in mulberry branches during the feeding time, and the price of these can sometimes skyrocket, making the whole business not only unprofitable but even lossmaking for those who need to feed the worms with mulberry leaves. Often, groups are set up. The owner of a large number of mulberry trees provides the leaves and half of the eggs, while the others [provide] the second half of the eggs and the labor. Cocoons are divided equally.

Here is one example. One poorer Namangan family, consisting of a husband, wife, and an eleven-year-old son, set off to Chartak, a settlement situated about 12 versts from the city, where the family entered such a group; the total number of eggs was equal to 20 paisa. When the worms grew up, the father and the son could barely deliver enough branches. The weight of the cocoons was 10½ puds. Each side got 38 silver rubles. The profit was acknowledged to be more than satisfactory. (Three people worked for two full months on it.) Feeding the worms, when carried out using not one's own leaves but purchased ones, is, along with holiday clothing, the cause of endless quarrels among husbands and wives. The wife demands more leaves and hustles the husband to bring them from the bazaar or the orchards outside the city. The husband scolds her for forcing him out of the house and spending money for some worms, which may or may not bring any profit. "May you die if you don't bring me leaves!" scolds the wife. "May you die! What am I going to do without them? The worms will die; my labor will be lost. It's all because of you. Go, faster, go!"

"I am fed up with you and your worms; it is all useless, just a waste of money; no good will come out of it!" "If you don't go, I will take your robe to the pawnshop; I will go for the leaves myself." "You will? Before you pawn my robe, I will trade all your worms." They reach the point of starting a fistfight before the husband finally puts on his robe and goes to get the leaves or, to be precise, to get mulberry branches. Sarts say that there was one year, thirteen to fifteen years ago, when for some reason the price for the mulberry twigs soared. They claim that it was the year when the number of divorces was the highest, and there have never been as many divorces as in that memorable and hapless summer.

Local women sew very badly and carelessly. Most of them sew using only running stiches for everything; felling and machine stitches (*baxya*) can be found only on silk shirts. Bottoms of female shirts are not hemmed but only whip-stitched. Ordering a robe or bedding to be sewn can cost about 20 kopeks.

Women who specialize in sewing robes and bedding sold at bazaars cannot produce more than one robe or blanket per day.

The embroidery of silk skullcaps, scarves, and belts is more durable and exquisite than any other sewing. Skullcaps embroidered all over with delicate, elaborate patterns are very widespread. The most popular pattern is flowers and leaves of various colors and shapes. Usually, such a skullcap costs no more than 1 ruble 50 kopeks, and it takes the woman at least four or five days of work. Making skullcaps is almost never a specialization; this is usually done between other things. For instance, spinning thread on Friday is considered sinful, and that is why many women sew skullcaps on that day.

As far as embroidering scarves or belts, there are women who specialize in that. Such a woman earns usually about 80 silver kopeks per week (the floss and the silk for the scarf costs about 40 k., and the embroidered duro'ya is sold for 1 ruble 20 k.).

Women's participation in agricultural work is negligible. She participates, together with children, only in picking melons and cotton bolls, and a woman from a poor family also collects boshoq, stems left on the field after harvesting.

In some areas, women also harvest lentils, *mosh* [mung beans], and *yasmiq* (the latter is a kind of flat red lentil). We have never seen women with a sickle or behind a plow and only once have seen a woman removing dung from the yard into the hayat (vegetable garden) near the house, carrying a pallet together with her husband; this case was observed in Nanay, where the majority of women, half of them Kyrgyz, do not hide from other villagers.

A Sart woman who is working in the field and sees a stranger passing by pulls a scarf over her head so that her face is covered, or if that is uncomfortable, she grudgingly squats and turns her face in the opposite direction.

Sarts do not force their women to do difficult or dirty work, so they rarely can be seen helping their husbands build rammed-earth walls or similar activities and only among the poorest kishlak people, where women are more used to work than in the cities; and when they work, it is usually in the internal courtyard. In some kishlaks of the Namangan region located near the mountains (Nanay, Ko'kyer, Qizil-yozi, Axtam), where the nearest bazaars are too far away, tandirs for baking bread are made at home, and women in poor families sometimes help men doing this work. However, it is men who set up the tandir. When a woman participates in such work, she usually does it voluntarily. We have never heard of a husband who would pressure his wife to do this work, which is outside the common range of women's activities. We believe that the main reason for this is a very strong habit set in everyone's mind to live as is customary (*rasmiy*), and the basis for that, as the reader knows, is Islam.

As we mentioned above, most women, not only those who are wealthy but even the poor ones, who have husbands and adult sons (above ten to twelve years old) avoid going to the bazaar because it is considered improper. However, on a bazaar day, there are plenty of women there.

In a lane, deserted on an ordinary day but very crowded with horsemen and passersby on a bazaar day, stands a group of several dozen women, wearing gray and blue shabby, ragged paranjis and carrying skeins of yarn in their hands. A small, bent old woman in a similar worn-out paranji is clinging to the wall, squatting; on her knees she holds a wide flat basket with flat bread covered with a shabby, soiled, red dasturxon [tablecloth]; you can discover that she is an old woman by looking at her wrinkled, dry hands with crooked fingers. A young man passes by her with a similar basket, screaming at the top of his voice, "Issiq" (hot) and attracting buyers. The old woman is sitting silently because she cannot even talk loudly in the street, let alone shout; it would be sinful and shameful; she is a woman, *zaif-kishi, zaif* (which in Arabic means weak, helpless). Passing by, you cannot help pondering that this expressive term, zaif, is a perfect description of this gray-haired, bent old woman; she is zaif. It is quite possible that she will be sitting here, in the dirty street, all day, and only by the end of the evening will she sell all twenty flat breads, earning something like 10 to 15 and, at most, 20 kopeks of net profit.

If she had a teenage son, she would have stayed home and sent him to the bazaar, but she definitely has nobody to send. Maybe her daughter married and then died; perhaps her son went to Tashkent as a day laborer and disappeared there. She had a husband who died a few years ago, leaving her a tiny house and yard, where she lives from hand to mouth, obtaining a decent meal very rarely, mostly when visiting others for funerals and holidays, where she is treated as a beggar. Only Allah knows how she manages not to die from hunger. Truly, Allah is great and his deeds are wondrous. He is *akbar* (great); he is *rahman* (merciful), he is *hu* (the living one); he gave her strength to teach her body to survive on one flat bread and several cups of what she calls "tea" per day and which is, in reality, a mix of some herbs that only she knows. You can judge yourself what would have happened to her without Allah.

But reader, let us walk further along the bazaar; why should we stand here, in front of this old woman?

It is terribly crowded. Here is a row with skullcaps. Typically here, the stalls are small, their fronts open; lines of skullcaps of different colors are displayed on a felt rug spread on the ground, multicolored, black, red, blue, and purple, embroidered with flowers. The sellers are ceremonious and tidy; crowds are standing near every stall. Boys are picking their noses and looking at red skullcaps; further on, tea, sugar, trays, and china teapots. Next come the textile stalls. At the crossroads, by the stalls, sit several women in embroidered scarves and sashes. Here comes a well-dressed Sart woman walking her fast-paced, smooth gait, as if flowing along the stalls with chintzes and looking around shyly. She is very young. She was given in marriage a year ago. Today, getting permission to go see her mother, she slipped away to the bazaar; she was dying to take a look at the chintzes and the stalls of the attors[13] selling buttons, trim tapes, looking glasses, cufflinks, and other shiny trifles. If only you knew how her heart is beating because she is afraid of running into her father or husband, who would recognize her by the galoshes that they bought her recently and her paranji. She wanted to borrow someone else's but could not find anyone's and finally went out bravely. Let us follow her, turning right past chintzes, colorful scarves, light silks, atlases, and other fabrics and walking toward the attors. The mischievous girl has crossed the street and is looking at beads, so we will stop by that stall. In front, among the beads, coral necklaces, buttons, vials, boxes with sulfur, alum, and bits of fabrics, sits a handsome young Sart. He is focusing his gaze to the side, trying not to look at the old woman who has been standing in front of him for a long time but, having grown tired, has squatted. "So, will you take it?" comes from the shabby chimbet, made of [horse]hair and discolored with time. The Sart does not respond and looks in another direction. "Really, I bought it last year for 40 kopeks per zolotnik. Give me at least 30 k." "Only 20; I won't give more." "My God, my God! What should I do? Give me at least 25." "Well, go, I said I won't give you more; why are you bargaining?" "Take it, take it, if you don't want to add anything," and the hand with corals reaches out toward the Sart.

Do I need to tell you, reader, what is going on here? Should I tell you that this morning the corals were taken from her daughter, how the girl cried at losing her only treasure, which her late father gave her a year ago for a holiday? Should I explain why this is being done? Of course not. It is too dreary. Let us leave this place. Here is a choy-xona at the corner. Several fashionably dressed *boybacha*s (young merchants) are sitting on a carpet there. There is a tray with flat breads, pistachios, and raisins. An attractive bachcha[14] pours tea from a copper choydush into a cup and takes it to one person after another. The bachcha flirts and makes eyes at everyone. They take the cup from him after forcing him to touch it with his lips. One of the men scrutinizes the crowd, squinting his eyes, and slowly, pretending to adjust his robe, presses his right hand to the left side of this chest. He has recognized one of the courtesans he is familiar with, and he sends her a *khushamat*.[15] She quickly passes by wearing a dressy light gray paranji that sparkles in the sun and carefully looks back toward the choy-xona. And there in the crowd walks a slim, sullen Sart, muttering to himself. He paused, ignoring the people that keep pushing him from all sides, took out several copper and silver coins from a leather pouch hanging from the belt near his left hip, placed them in his hand, looked over them, counted them, poked each one with the pointing finger of his right hand, looked around without a purpose, put the money back into the pouch, and went further. He is a weaver. He just sold the fabric he has produced in a week and received 1 ruble of net profit, so he is now walking to the *kappon*, bread bazaar. For this money, he is supposed to buy a piece of meat, fat, several pounds of rice, lentils and flour, carrots, onions, and wood; and his wife will have to worry about how all of this will suffice for them and their two children for a week.

The bazaar is so excellent and informative! It has all the life, or at least the life drama, so lively and truthfully presented that you can never see anything like that on any theatrical stage because the art of theater does not permit such types as we can see here onstage.

Here, we can see everything: pieces of bright atlas, old shabby paranjis, merchants dealing with tens and hundreds of thousands, weavers who earn 1 ruble per week, a decked-out disobedient girl who ran away from home to see the bazaar, and the old woman selling flat breads, and many, many other things!

From half a verst or a verst away, we can hear the noise of the bazaar. Come closer. You will start distinguishing some discordant sounds. Enter the bazaar, mix with the crowd, and open your eyes and ears, and you will hear a whole opera. You will hear the soft and liquid laugh of an inattentive merchant; the cracked, weak cry of an old woman crushed by poverty; and the combat of two poor men passionately bargaining over a minuscule difference in price and refusing to back off since the difference in price is equal to one and a half flat breads, which would feed a hungry man for a whole day.

The local bazaar is a huge anatomy theater, in which the masterful hand of life demonstrates to everyone present all the failures and sores of local humanity.

Thus, only a woman of the poorest strata directly participates in earning a living; and the family relies exclusively on her labor only when there is no man in the family, which can be caused by widowhood or her husband's temporary absence, which can sometimes last for a long time, up to several years. We knew a woman with three small children was deserted by her husband. This woman lived in the kishlak and was forced to earn a living for herself and her children.

In cases when a husband leaves the family for work or travels for trade, if he is in any way a decent person, he leaves a reserve of grain, flour, and some small amount of money for the family. We knew a wealthy merchant family, whose trade amounted to 20,000 to 40,000 rubles, whose husband, going to buy rams in Semirechie or Western Siberia, left his family with reserves of fat, flour, rice, and other things and in addition about 15 to 20 silver rubles. Sometimes, no money was left at all, on the proposition that some would be received from their debtors.

There are other cases as well. The husband may be a live-in worker. His wife, living in the same kishlak or city but receiving no financial support from him for a long time, goes to the qozi. The qozi orders the husband to pay a weekly allowance to the wife equal to 40 silver kopeks, an amount that has been set by a long-term folk custom, ignoring the fact that when this custom was established, a pud [16 kilos] of wheat cost from 10 to 15 kopeks, and now the same pud costs from 50 to 80 silver kopeks.

To give you the best idea of the nutrition of the natives, we would like to make a list of dishes that are staples, most commonly served.

The native's favorite national food is plov, which is considered the best food and, to a certain degree, aristocratic; a plov dish is often given as a present exchanged among relatives or acquaintances on the eve of Ramadan and Kurban. At the same time, this dish is one of the most expensive, and poor people cannot eat it very often.

Among the not-well-off urban people, it is usually cooked once a week, on Thursday evenings.

Plov is prepared in various ways; we will explain only one way of making it, which is very widespread. First of all, a soup with mutton is prepared in a cauldron. The soup is poured from the cauldron into a bowl; carrots, onions, and the pieces of meat taken out of the soup are fried in a considerable amount of fat. Then everything, not excluding the soup, is mixed with rice and boiled in the cauldron until it turns into a solid porridge; the cauldron is covered for several minutes with a large, upside-down clay pot, and plov is ready.

It is heaped up onto a platter, and on top are placed cut-up pieces of meat. One of the meal's participants divides the meat into small pieces by hand or knife.

Shavla—a liquid plov or, to be precise, a rice gruel cooked with fat, carrots, onions, and small pieces of mutton.

Sho'rva—a mutton soup or a soup with any other meat, pepper, onion, carrots, turnip, or pumpkin, and sometimes with qatiq [qatiq, sour milk or yogurt].

Kulchatoi—a soup made of small pieces of meat, rice, onion, and sour milk.[16]

Mastava—a soup made of finely cut pieces of meat, rice, onion, and sour milk.

Chuchvara are dumplings. The filling can be made of onions or a small quantity of meat.

Such meat dishes as qovurma, bits of mutton fried with fat; *hasip*, sausages made of mutton and liver; and *qazi*, horsemeat sausages, are prepared only in the wealthiest homes.

Shir-guruch is a milk-based rice porridge. Go'ja, a liquid gruel made of jugara (sorghum) or from millet (less often from corn or barley) with some qatiq, is the staple food, especially in kishlaks, not only of the poor, vulnerable population but of wealthy families as well. We knew a family of regional administrators who cooked go'ja every day and whose food rarely was varied with mastava, shavla, pumpkin turnovers, or turnovers with lucerne leaves.[17]

Un-osh (a flour-based dish) is noodles boiled in water without meat with the addition of qatiq.

Xo'rda is a liquid porridge made of rice boiled in water with the addition of qatiq.

Mosh-guruch is a liquid porridge made of rice (guruch) and lentils (mosh) [mung beans] boiled in water with turnip, carrots, onions, peppers, and qatiq (or meat).

Atala is a flour-based jelly-looking gruel. Flour is fried with fat and then watered down.

Shir-kadu (milk and pumpkin) is a gruel based on milk with pumpkin and rice.

Having enumerated all the widespread staple dishes, we cannot help mentioning another one, so-called *sumalak*, a dish similar to a watered-down jelly, made of malt. Cooking sumalak here has the same ritualistic character as pancakes have in Russia. It is always boiled in early spring, using the flour and malt, for which wheat is artificially sprouted.

Mainly young girls and women are invited for sumalak; most of them bring along some malt and flour. They gather in the evening. Old women boil sumalak through the night and recite prayers over the cauldron, and the young people, women and girls, treat themselves with plov, raisins, nuts, and other things. If a male stranger comes, women and girls who have gathered for sumalak do not hide.

In the morning, they leave, having eaten sumalak and taking some of it back home in bowls. Often these gatherings are used to look for brides or meet lovers.

This is how we explain the origin of this holiday. Reserves of wheat for bread are put into holes in the ground for the winter, which are called *o'ra*. If the wheat is not dug out on time, then it starts sprouting. It is certain that in the past such germination was not unusual, until the means of storage were improved a bit (although this happens these days, too). When wheat is taken out, it has germinated. They tried to make flour out of it, but it turned into something sweet tasting. They added water and tried the dish, and they liked it. Then they invited their neighbors, and the neighbors liked it, too; in addition, spring is the hungriest time of the year here. So this is how sumalak developed into a custom here.[18]

Tea is the most widespread drink here. There are two ways to make it: either water is boiled in tea pots—i.e., the same way as in Russia—or it is boiled in cauldrons with milk, butter, salt, and pepper. In the latter case, it is called *shir-choy*.[19] Such drinks as vodka, grape wine, and *bo'za*, a sort of beer or fermented drink made from millet, are prosecuted by religion; nonetheless, they are openly used by the natives and in growing frequency from year to year, which has given birth to rumors that Russians introduced drunkenness.

In reality, this is not true. First, bo'za is a local drink, and not a single native would deny its previous considerable use, especially by the nomadic population. Second, not only natives but even many Russians know that even before the latter had arrived in Fergana, secret preparation of fruit vodka and grape wine was widespread among the local Jews, so the Russian administration in many Fergana towns applied significant effort to stop this production, if not completely, then in part. And where there was production, there also were demand and users. Third, it is known that Alim-khan and Madali-khan were awful drunkards, which is described in the native books on the history of Qo'qon Khanate.

Finally, in the fourth place, if we look Sultan Babur's memoir, written about four hundred years ago, on almost every page of the second half, we can read descriptions of the famous sultan drinking with his courtiers.[20] It is obvious that secret drinking, hidden from the sticks and whips of the qozi-rais, has been around for much longer than a century. It is also obvious that if the Russians are guilty of expanding the circle of openly drinking Sarts, they can be accused only of not beating drunks with sticks.

In summers, for most urbanites and also in kishlaks, the staple foods are bread, fruit, and sour milk; the amount of meat in the meals increases a little only in those kishlaks where arable lands are considerable and where from the time wheat ripens until autumn, peasants and butchers trade grain for meat and fat.

In winter, among poor families, food for women and children grows worse for several reasons, including this main cause. Poor men from kishlaks and cities form groups, *jo'ra*, ten to fifteen people in each; and each contributes 3 to 7 rubles. They elect a team member, *jo'raboshi*, in whose house they meet daily.[21]

Using the group's money, they prepare meat, rice, vegetables, and fuel. If the group has enough money, it hires a dancer, a bachcha, for the winter; it also stocks up tea, raisins, and pistachios. (Sometimes wealthy young men participate in the jo'ra.) The cook is either chosen for the whole winter, or cooking is done in turns.

They get together in the evenings. Plov is prepared, and the time waiting for it is spent doing *chaq-chaq*, idle talk and exchanging jokes; songs are sung, and the bachcha dances. Sometimes they stay until after midnight. Married men return to their homes, and bachelors remain for the night. In these cases, the husband or father loses interest in the quality of the home meals that he does not eat, and consequently the quality of food for the rest of the family decreases considerably. To fully understand the importance of jo'ra, we should bear in mind that the [male] Sart is a person of the street and of social life. We cannot say that he does not love his family; in the same streets we see men who are not busy with work but are taking care of children. He loves his family to an obvious degree; he loves his children very much and spoils them when he can; but that does not interfere with his attraction to the street life. The street is his club; it has people, life, conversations, news. But in winter it is either cold or dirty, and he still needs company; that is why he goes to his jo'ra. The only ones who stay home are the righteous sufi and the rich man, who is himself visited by many people, because his house is, in reality, a jo'ra.

Food is improved, or, more precisely, diversified, only on holidays, Kurban and Ramadan, and during the fasting period, ro'za, since religion regulates only the time of eating and not the diversity of the food that is eaten.[22]

Every day, the evening breaking of the fast, *iftar*, takes place soon after sunset, after the namoz *aksham* [evening prayer]. It is customary among the natives to eat a small pinch of salt, drink *airan* (qatiq mixed with water), and then eat bread and fruit, after which they are served with one of the dishes listed above.

In the first two weeks of the month-long fast, the bodies of those who strictly observe the religious demands grow so weak that by the end of ro'za the stomach becomes incapable of taking any significant amount of food. However, not everyone is so zealous. The wife eats in secret, away from her husband and children; the husband eats in secret from his wife and children; neighbor hides from neighbor; and so on and so forth. They fast and make sour faces *pour fair les apparences*. By the way, religion excuses the sick and the traveler from fasting, and we knew cases of Sarts traveling during the fast specifically for that reason.

A woman may skip fasting when breast-feeding. Women should not fast in the six weeks after giving birth and during menstruation.[23]

In cities they drink tea with bread in the morning, and tea is often replaced with herbs in poor families, but we cannot specify the herbs since it is impossible to identify them (their scientific names); in kishlaks, some kind of gruel is prepared in the mornings; sometimes it is warmed-up leftovers from last night.

In the daytime, around noon, bread or the leftovers from the morning food are consumed; in cities, at this time of day especially in winter, they make xo'rda, mosh-guruch, or some other gruel.

In the evening, around sunset, or a bit later than that in winters, they prepare shavla or another stew with meat whenever possible or even plov.

Poor people eat the unvarying go'ja, atala, or something similar in the evenings.

Plov is prepared in the daytime only for guests. The family eats plov when they are together, all at the same time, and children are served in separate dishes. Family members eat other foods in separate bowls and often at different times. If the whole family is eating together, the hostess fills her bowl last and serves the first bowl either to her husband or the eldest in the family.

It is hard for us to evaluate the average appetite of the general sedentary population of Fergana; it would be more valid for us to describe the facts that we have been able to observe. Among men, appetite is more energetic in general than among women. (Kyrgyz women, on the contrary, are much more gluttonous than men and are always ready to eat anything as long it is not haram, unclean.) Among men, the most considerable amounts of food can be consumed by (1) cart drivers, arabakeshes, who move in columns, and are accustomed to eating very well from having formed groups; at least they are used to eating better than they do at home; (2) wealthy merchants who engage in trade that requires frequent travel; and (3) all those doing heavy labor. The lowest appetite is characteristic of men who spent a long time in madrasa and who had very limited means of existence during that time.

The appetite of kishlak women is higher than that of town women; it is higher among the wealthy classes than the poor, whose stomachs have gotten used to eating less.

At the same time, eating very small quantities of food has been one of the signs of coquettish behavior among almost all the refined young women and girls. Such a girl is said to be eating *chimchilap*, in nibbles, like a sparrow.

We would like to add here that Sarts almost never treat constipation as a pathological state and that thick consistence of excrements is considered normal, while the liquid state of the latter is treated with great concern.

The amount of food consumed by the natives daily is also a matter of interest, but we can turn here to only anecdotal facts and stipulate that we would be considering only the poor strata of the population since a wealthy person who eats plov not once but several times a week has considerable amounts of meat, fat, rice, flour, tea, and even dried fruit at his disposal; he is of lesser interest to us for a number of reasons, including that the wealthy make up a small share of the population.

A kishlak family of average wealth with five to seven people consumes the following amount of food per day: not more than two or three flat breads (about 1–1½ pounds) per person; more flat breads are consumed by men working in the field or doing other heavy work. In the mornings, the preparation of un-osh or go'ja requires 3 to 4 pounds of flour plus six or seven glasses of qatiq, or 6 to 7 pounds of sorghum plus six to seven glasses of qatiq. In the evenings, either go'ja is prepared again from the same amount of ingredients or mosh-guruch, which requires about 3 to 4 pounds of rice, about 1 to 2 pounds of lentils [mung beans], and several glasses of qatiq (or 1 to 2 pounds of finely cut meat). The same-size family preparing plov uses about 6 to 7 pounds of rice, between 1½ and 3 pounds of fat, and the same amount of meat.

According to the official data of Namangan district, the following amounts are harvested here every year:

Wheat—about 1,666,400 puds
Rice (unhulled)—662,400 puds
Jugara (sorghum) and millet—1,333,560 puds

Let us assume that all this is eaten on the spot. Estimating the population of Namangan district at one hundred thousand, we will get the following amounts [per capita] per year:

Wheat—16.6 puds [256 kilograms]
Rice—6.6 puds [105 kilograms]
Sorghum, etc.—13.3 [213 kilograms]

Bearing in mind that the distribution of vital staple products and other things here, like everywhere else, is unequal, we should come to the conclusion that there are poor people here whose nutrition is much lower than these values. And we do find them, in reality. For instance, we knew a Sart in Yangi-Qurg'on kishlak (Namangan district) who survived through the winter, three months, with his wife and little son, on 5 or 6 puds of wheat, eating atala every single day.[24]

We could bring many similar examples of this, but it would be superfluous, since the reader can figure out on his own fairly well how people who earn from 40 kopeks to 1 ruble and 20 kopeks per week can feed themselves.

As another illustration of everything said above about the nutrition of the natives, we can add a few words about the food for domestic dogs, which in this respect have nothing in common with either Russian dogs or other dogs all over the world. Very rarely do local dogs here get food leftovers and bits of bread, so they have to search out daily food on their own. If a Sart throws a bone to his dog, he has not only picked off all the meat from the outside but also has broken it and sucked out all the marrow before he throws it away. The bone gets to the dog only after it has been meticulously picked. Do we need to mention that the dog attacks the bone with avarice, but what it can squeeze out of this bone is hard to tell; we only know that it breaks smaller bones and devours them.

Once a Sart saw us giving milk to the dog and was indignant about it. He said we should not be giving such an expensive food product to the dog. In the first place, it is sinful; and second, its eyes can crack and run if it drinks milk. The Sart does not feed his dog partly because of a long-term habit and partly because he has nothing to give; but he is not satisfied with such an explanation, and he wants to absolve himself, saying that the dog's eyes will crack and run. How he came to that conclusion is hard to tell, but it is obvious that he has adopted this belief and spreads it around; his instructional tone makes him believe in what he is saying even more while it also convinces others. So nobody gives milk to dogs.[25]

Not only are bones picked clean, but the bowl is similarly cleaned after plov or any other dish has been eaten, using the left side of the right hand's index finger, and sometimes it is even licked with the tongue.

So a Sart dog always lives in hunger; but hunger, as we all know, is not an aunt but teaches one to make pies.[26] It has not taught the Sart dog to make pies but has taught it to live on fruit, ears of corn, and even human excrement. Not only are dogs here commonly seen eating fallen apricots, but there are cases when a dog scrambles up a mulberry tree and eats the berries. We are afraid that this would be treated with disbelief, but we can point to kishlaks where these cases are repeated often. There are mountain or foothill kishlaks of Chust district, where mulberry trees are cultivated mainly for their berries, which are used in the production of molasses, *shirna* or *shinni*, and *tut-malkan* [*tolqon*], which is a sort of mulberry-based flour.

Distant maize fields have to be protected from wild boars, and in kishlaks they do not know what to do with the many dogs that attack and destroy the maize grown in vegetable gardens.

Kyrgyz villages, which do not have outhouses, surprise everyone by the total absence of human excrement, which is eaten by dogs.

6 The Woman, Her Character, Habits, Knowledge, and Behavior toward the People around Her

In general, the native woman's character should be described as lively and extremely merry; naturally, she experiences grief and melancholy from time to time, but she never indulges in them for too long. Even in extremely rough material and moral situations, she is never averse to chatting, laughing, singing a song. Especially when she is young, she sings or hums almost constantly. It is true that occasionally she lets herself get teary eyes, but this tearfulness is always false, insincere, and she uses it as a tool to achieve her goals.

All her movements are quick, sometimes jerky but almost never awkward. From a very early age a girl controls her movements, trying to make them similar to the local standard of propriety. That is the reason why not only most of a woman's movements but most of her mannerisms are far from being simple or natural. For instance, she loves to walk fast, but respectability based on religion bans her from moving her legs too fast while walking, waving her arms, etc. (Koran, chapter 24, verse 31). That is why her gait has acquired a very special character. She moves her feet very quickly, making tiny steps, while not only her hands but her head and shoulders remain almost motionless or move very little. There is a similar imprint of moderation in her moral "I" as well. Not only the woman but even a ten- or twelve-year-old girl who receives a present that she loves extremely does not express this admiration; often she does not even express gratitude for it. She expresses gratitude only if the present is given as alms or financial assistance. If this is a dress, shoes, or an ornament, the highest degree of her gratitude would be to put it on right away, which would mean that she loved it. (The same is customary among men.) If the present cannot be put on, she shows it to the people around, accompanying it with gestures and a smile so sweet that one of our most experienced coquettes would envy it. We would like to note that many Sart women and girls have reached perfection in expressing their feelings with lips and eyebrows. When she wants to ask a question, she silently raises her brows slightly upward and does it so adroitly that any other question from her becomes unnecessary, because her whole face becomes a perfect expression of a question mark.

Similar to her attitude toward joy is her attitude to grief; it can overwhelm and engulf her but not for long. Cases when grief devastates the person for a very long time are rare among women as well as men. It is possible that after some sort of a catastrophe a woman would cry and wail for a long time among her friends and acquaintances, but this would be wailing without tears, an affected wailing; it is not the kind of grief that erases all other thoughts except for thoughts about itself, the kind of grief that follows the person everywhere and never leaves him, even in sleep. There is only one case when a Sart woman openly expresses her feelings of grief freely: when wailing for the deceased. But even here, perhaps more than in other cases, tearing her hair, scratching her face, and the most in-human, fierce wail is nothing but an ordinary, everyday comic act, which cannot be skipped as it is impossible to skip crying when she marries. Even here, when mourning the deceased, you will hardly ever see a face distraught with grief and quiet tears. Soon the reader will understand this even better when we talk about the meaning of kin relations, the moral meaning of which is extremely weak, if not completely nonexistent.

Very rarely have we seen a native woman who is crying. If she runs into deep trouble, she comes asking for advice or help, and, at most, a few tears will fill her eyes; but she will keen and wail from morning till night. She does not cry even when her husband beats her; she either wails without tears or scolds;[1] even her complaining is closer to anger or frustration than tears.

One of the characteristic features of the native woman is her talkativeness and extreme sociability, closely connected with her ability to adapt rapidly to her surroundings, and her habit of calling things by their names.

As far as the latter is concerned, all parts of the body as well as the organic bodily functions are called by their ordinary folk names. Softened terms or meta-phorical names are used only in the most sophisticated society that has some relationship to literature.

For a Sart woman, spending several hours alone and silent, even while work-ing, is the torture of Tantal;[2] this is far beyond her capacities. That is why if she is not surrounded by teenage children with whom she can exchange some words, she always waits for someone to visit her, and if no one comes, she leaves the house, if only for a quarter of an hour or even for five minutes, to stop by the nearest neighbor, chat, and gossip with her. Thus, a woman is very rarely alone; either someone is visiting her, or she is leaving the house to visit someone. If she leaves for a long time, she sometimes takes her work with her; even more often, when she pays a visit to one of her acquaintances, she helps her with sew-ing, spinning, cleaning, and beating out cotton fiber or something else. Often people who know each other are invited to get together with the purpose of help-ing. The invitees respond to such invitations with pleasure because, first, such invitations usually come from wealthy people and one can always expect to be treated to plov, flat bread, and tea; second, she can talk about or listen to all sorts of things, including the juiciest gossip, to her heart's content, sing songs, play the tambourine, etc. Once several women get together, the conversation never stops; there are endless stories about all the latest events, such as weddings, quarrels with their husbands, divorces, visits to lovers, and so on; the conversation is filled with sayings, proverbs, puns, and jokes, often even tales and playful anecdotes, which they all enjoy a lot. The skill of conversation, of retorting smartly in response to a question or a remark, and defeating a challenger in a verbal duel is considered a virtue; a woman with such a skill is treated with certain caution, especially if she never misses a chance to mock or bad-mouth another, who may not be able to respond in the same way.

We often came across women who astounded us not only by their ability to speak well but also in their high degree of eloquence in expressing their thoughts, in the sense of carrying on speech that is just as beautiful as it is logical. Most of the time, these were wives of khan's servicemen, who have seen a lot in their lifetime and have encountered diverse aspects of native life.

Because of this extreme sociability and the custom of not regarding what happens in family life as a secret, as dirt that should not be carried outside the hut to strangers, women who meet each other for the first time in their lives feel like they have known each other for a long time within two or three hours.[3] If the liking is mutual, one meeting is enough for the women to call each other *o'rtoq*, friend.

Apart from such events as death, wakes, weddings, divorces, and so on, the favorite topics of conversation among women are quarrels with husbands, news about pregnancies and the number of children, the nature and timing of menstruation, and even their sexual intercourse with husbands.

In the latter case, the usual question is "Have you done ablution recently?" Addressing the other person with "ty" [informal, singular "you"] is not widespread even among the closest acquaintances either in the top or bottom layers of society.[4]

Family dirt, which Russian families are required by the Domostroi to hide from strangers, by contrast here is shared in the streets both by men and women.[5] That is why, despite the seeming isolation of women, hiding themselves from the gaze of the stranger and walking under chimbet and paranji, family life is never secret from neighbors or acquaintances; on the contrary, it is familiar to them not only in every possible material but also moral detail. Often, when a husband insults and beats his wife, she shouts, "Voy-dod!" (*karaul*).[6] Anyone hearing this cry is permitted, even obliged, to enter the courtyard and do what is possible toward reconciliation. The role of the reconciler is sacred; bringing the enemies to reconciliation is a soul-saving act, repaid in the afterlife, so nobody avoids this role.[7]

The habit or practice of making her family life public is a shield protecting the native woman from the tyranny of her husband. Despite all the rules offered to him by the religion and the law, the degree of a husband's tyranny here is much lower than in Europe. Tyranny can be practiced here only if the material conditions make it impossible for the woman to use her right to divorce. When we introduce the latter to our readers later, they will better understand that in some respects the Muslim woman's situation is better and the range of her personal rights is wider than it is for women of European peoples. We will discuss this in more detail later, and now we want to return to the talkativeness of the native women, a feature that is as typical to them as their love to bad-mouth, gossip, and engage in verbal dueling and is much more widespread among women than among men.

A female guest of a higher status than the hostess never hesitates to make a critical remark about the cleanness in the rooms and so on; in most cases, this is said in hints but with an obvious wish to put someone down. If a country woman and a sharp-tongued urban woman show up together in this society, the former may be literally crushed. In her presence a conversation will begin about how kishlak life is dirty, how rarely they eat plov there, how crude their speech is, etc.

Because of that and due to the inherently quick temper of native women, there are many quarrels, and occasionally there are quarrels that begin as a verbal duel or disagreement and escalate nearly to a fistfight. This can extend to offers to wallop one of her new female friends or to rearrange her hairstyle, things that can be heard very frequently.

As much as a Sart woman likes verbal duels and gossiping, she is afraid of mockery and gossip. She does not hide the conditions of her family life and her relations with her husband or other members of the family, but she avoids talking about herself, fearing she will compromise herself in some way. A woman notorious for her merry living and various adventures, who treats men in an openly vulgar way, acts like such a puritan that even an experienced person would not dare suspect her of any vice. Gossiping about the intimate adventures of her friends and acquaintances, she would never say anything about herself; nor would she confess even to a friend that she has a lover. So if you want to make an inquiry about her personal behavior, you need to ask one of her friends.

Lying, flattery, and exaggerations are so widespread and address so many aspects of life that little by little everyone acquires the habit of disbelieving everyone or at least treating all information very cautiously.

A Sart man has very similar inclinations. His past has taught him to tell the truth only when he is convinced that it will be to his benefit; if not, even if there is a slight doubt about the benefits or in cases where there is no gain, he either avoids the answer or lies, not always successfully. In 1879, for some reason the administration demanded information on the number of elementary native schools and students. At that time, we lived in a kishlak, in a thoroughly Sart manner, and had gained the thorough trust of the other villagers. When the order to provide the above-mentioned information was received, the head of the province came to us and insisted on getting our advice on what he should do, since we were familiar with Russian methods of order: in the report, should he present larger or smaller numbers of schools and students? He did not know how this information would be used, and that was enough for him not to even consider the idea of reporting real figures.

Let us give you another example. Two Sarts got into a fight; of course, they fought not in the Russian style (*à la russe*); that is, they fought without knocking out teeth, smashing cheekbones, and other physical harm but in an orderly Sart way. This is how this fight occurred: first, they quarreled about something and one insulted the other's mother; the second one returned the insult to his mother and added his daughter; then they insulted everyone, the father, grandfather, and the grave of the great-grandfather and again the mother, ending with the turban and skullcap. Then, becoming very heated, they grabbed each other's collars, began shouting even louder, tore each other's shirts, and the less nimble got a couple of blows that left him with a black eye and a scratch across his left cheek. Paying the price of losing a shirt, getting a black eye and a scratched cheek, a Sart considers himself not only a loser but also insulted. He screams, "Voi-dod!" A crowd gathers around the fighting men: only a few incite them; the majority try to pacify them.

Having freed himself from the rival who managed to send him off with a farewell blow to the head, the defeated man starts to wail like a woman and begs the people to witness the injustice done to him. Feeling blood running down, he smears it all over his face, sometimes tearing his scratch open wider so that it bleeds more, which is necessary to make the impression that he needs, and rearranges his clothes in as big a mess as possible. Then, thoroughly disguised, he goes to the administration asking for justice. Half an hour later, people at the bazaar start talking about a terrible fight in the street: "Juda o'rush bo'ldi!"[8] (We should mention that fights like this are not frequent and happen only among the lowest class of the population. The well-raised Sart behaves in a proper way when on the street or in public and does not compromise his reputation even with such acts as superfluous fast walking or riding, loud talking, singing, whistling, etc.)

Several female friends are sitting together. One of them, the most sharp witted, starts telling others about how her husband beat her some days ago. "'Play a dutor!' he would say. And I would say, 'I won't.' 'Play, I say!' 'No. I won't.' 'I will hit you if you won't.' 'I won't still.' So he started beating me with a whip and went on and on, but I was silent; then he tied me to a pole and continued beating, and I was still silent. My whole back is black and blue; take a look." She shows her back;

there is nothing there. "Oh, he beat me two weeks ago; they must have healed; but it was pretty awful then; I was blue all over; it was scary to see!"

Boasting comes in various ways: imaginary stoicism toward fictional beatings, imaginary closeness to important people, and various arts and skills including culinary. For instance, recently one Sart woman bragged in our presence that she could cook three different dishes without taking the pot off the stove and would be able to clean it right on the stove with the help of a ladle.

Women brag about their clothes, their wealth, and the position their husbands occupy, etc. In other words, a Sart woman cannot be rebuked that she is behind other women in any way. Sart women, like others, make an effort to conceal their age. Five or six years after being married at age fourteen, she frequently claims to be sixteen or seventeen at the most.

Begging and stealing are extremely widespread among the lower-class, poor strata of native society, and stealing is more widespread than begging since being called a beggar, *gadoi*, is considered shameful, while stealing is more difficult to prove. Beggars make pleas only to wealthy people, but they steal without differentiation. It should be noted that women's pilfering is usually small and happens only in homes. At the bazaar, you can often see an open stall with all the goods spread out and the owner gone on a quick errand. No one among the Sarts will touch anything. This is a habit that has remained since the time of the khan's rule, when thieves had their hand cut off. Pilfering from homes, which can be done much more easily, is frequent. Often things are stolen from those who would have given them away with pleasure had they been asked. We encountered such cases directly, more than once.

Several years ago a woman who had long received our assistance arrived from her kishlak, probably to ask for more help, but before addressing us, she used our absence from the room to reach into the drawer of the desk from which she saw us taking money. By chance, one of us disturbed her but did not let on that we noticed her intent. She was not ashamed at all, went to the kitchen, and, when everyone left for a moment, filled a sack with various provisions but was caught red-handed by the servants.

When we lived in the kishlak, small dishes, harnesses, bread, and pieces of fabric frequently disappeared.

However, nowhere is pilfering spread as widely among women as among the Kyrgyz. In the fall, when felt rugs are made (this work is usually done by women), wealthy families call all the aul women to help them make the felt. In this case, two or three members of the family are present near these women guarding the wool. But even such guarding does not always help: every dexterous woman manages to hide several rolls of wool in her wide pants and take it home.

Poor people have a similar attitude toward their debts and other duties. While most of the native trade is done on credit and one almost never hears about any deception, small transactions and debts, especially among the urban population, can lead not only to quarrels or fights like the one we described above but also to court cases that can last for a long time because debtors go into hiding. Hiding is a direct consequence of the times of the former khans, when each *bekstvo* (province) was a separate vassal state, and it was unsafe to enter it without the protection of your own bek or an appropriate gesture toward the local bek. This hiding can sometimes be extremely comical.

A simple creditor who does not like appealing to court or administration authorities considers his debtor completely uncatchable even when the debtor hides somewhere 20 to 30 versts away; he has no time to go there. He considers the debtor "caught" when he encounters him in the street face-to-face. "I can never meet him," he complains to his acquaintances. But then by chance he found him in the bazaar; he catches his debtor by the flap of his robe as the custom requires; twisting it in the same was as wet laundry is twisted and firmly grasping both of his arms, the creditor proposes that the debtor pay him or go to the authorities. If the debtor manages to escape by quickly slipping out of his top robe, which is not secured with a belt, the robe will remain in the hands of the creditor; thus, part of the debt will be paid, and the full settlement will be postponed until some similar, future meeting.

A woman from another kishlak visited us and asked for 4 rubles; she got the money and left promising to pay us back in six months, either in money or oil; then she does not show up for a whole year. Finally, one fine day she returns, empty-handed. "As-salam alaykum!" "Alaykum as-salam!" "How are you living? Are you healthy? Are your children healthy? Have they grown up?" "Yes, thank God." The guest is offered flat bread and tea. There is a long conversation about the harvest, weather, other news, the neighbors' upcoming wedding, and other things. The guest is planning to leave. "Well, I haven't brought you the money; I couldn't get it. But give me two more rubles; I will pay them back next year."

Above, when discussing dwellings, we noted that Sarts keep both the courtyards and the rooms, especially the outer ones, in perfect order. However, as is the case anywhere, the degree of neatness is higher in rich families than poor and in cities than in kishlaks. Almost the same can be said about the upkeep of dishes, kitchen utensils, and bedding. The dishes are washed (but almost never fully dried) and placed in niches; the cauldron is covered with a lid; the bedding, even when full of lice, is neatly folded and put on the top of the chest. Room floors and the courtyard are swept daily, and the latter is sprinkled with water in summer. Food, especially in cities, is also prepared very tidily. Touching food during cooking or eating it with dirty hands is a sin. All the dishes necessary for cooking are washed before food is cooked. Rice and other grains are washed very carefully.

In kishlaks we sometimes saw that when flat bread was rolled out but not yet baked, in the absence of a spare dasturxon, dough was allowed to rise in a robe, which we have never seen in cities. Thus, the outward tidiness of a Sart woman, at least the urban one, can be considered somewhat satisfactory. The opposite, however, can be said about her personal hygiene.

Bathhouses are visited only by men and only in cities. It is considered indecent for women to visit them, so only women of easy virtue or local Jewish women, who follow the custom of going there on Friday nights, can be seen in bathhouses.

However, far from all men visit the bathhouse; but most visitors can be found there at dawn on Friday—i.e., after the customary spousal Thursdays.

The religion forbids the Muslim man to see not only other men's but, if possible, even his own *avrat*, those parts of the body between his waist and knees.[9]

That is why men wash themselves in bathhouses wearing pants or with towels wrapped around their buttocks and thighs. This explains one of the main reasons why the native men and women bathe rarely, even in the summer.

At the same time, while avrat is carefully guarded from other people's gaze by all men and women, men are not embarrassed to work dressed only in pants, and women do not regard it immoral to breast-feed in the presence of men who are not allowed to enter the ichkari [nonfamily men].

The attitude toward religion among the masses of the native people is not different than among other peoples. Religion is foremost treated as a custom that must be followed to avoid negative public opinion, which is the source of genuine fear among the Sarts; at least it is stronger than the fear of heaven's punishment.

Deeds and acts are divided into bad, sins (*gunoh*) that will be punished by burning in hellfire, and good (*savob*), which will be rewarded. Both of these are written by angels in the book of life. It is remarkable that despite being convinced about the existence of angels and the book, Sart men and women think about hellfire comparatively rarely. What they think much more often is how to organize some kind of a savob that would be not very difficult and, more important, not very expensive. It is sinful to spill grain on the ground, but to gather it is savob and a big one. Therefore, no one will miss the chance to perform such a holy act and, after it is finished, to say a short prayer to ensure the deed. There are many savobs like that, so many that you cannot enumerate them: washing one's hair on Friday is savob; picking up bread crumbs is savob; reconciling quarreling people is savob; giving alms to a beggar is savob, and on and on, endlessly. It is possible that the quantity of savobs and the easiness of performing them serve as a source of comfort for hearts with regard to hellfire. Sometimes, a group can cooperate to organize an especially big savob.

Thus, once an elderly Sart who may have needed to fill in some gaps in his book of life offered us the following: "Let us," he says, "build a mosque together. You donate money, and I will manage the construction; *savobga teng sherik bo'lamiz*" (we will be equal partners in the savab). Exactly as if it were a commercial enterprise!

This attitude toward religion is closely connected to superstition since the latter is always a companion of religion.

The superstitions are very similar to those of a Russian peasant. In addition to the devil (shaitan), anti-Christ (*dajjal*), good and evil spirits (*pari* and *dev*), they also believe in the existence of a *domovoi*,[10] the *albasti*, who takes the form of a disheveled old woman with long hair; they also believe in *ajina*, something between a poltergeist and a witch, who in Sart imagination appears as an enormously tall woman with long yellow hair, who can bewitch people and cast epilepsy on them; they believe that an ajina can change her appearance. Thus, one Sart told us that he had seen an ajina who looked like a small flame running down the street. They also believe in the existence of *yolmog'iz kampir*, something like the Russian Baba-Yaga, and there are folktales about her similar to the Russian tales (*kampir* means an old woman). The same term is used for grumbling women (yolmog'iz kampir); women who have not combed their hair properly may be called ajina or albasti. They believe that if they rock an empty beshik (cradle), then the child to whom the cradle belongs will die. Galoshes must always be placed near the door, or enemies of the home's owner will multiply and overpower him.

They believe in the evil eye and never show a newborn child to anyone because of this. They believe that a man will go blind if in certain situations he uses not a clump of clay recommended by the religion but paper, which is a sacred object that should never lie on the ground because the Koran and other sacred books are written on paper.[11] There are so many such prejudices that we could continue recounting them until this day.

Along with believing in ghosts and premonitions, they also believe in magic, sorcery, and fortune-telling. If a wife is afraid of losing her husband's love, she goes to a specialist, a mullah, and for a fee (that may reach 4 rubles) receives from him a tumar, a piece of paper on which is written a special prayer or a poem from the Koran. The paper is folded and sewn into a triangle of silk fabric; this amulet is attached to the shoulder of a shirt or robe. One of our Sart acquaintances had two wives. The enmity between them was terrifying. Once the younger wife told us the following story: "My *kundosh* [co-wife], that base person, almost killed me!" "How?" "Like this. I started getting sick and withering away. I dug a hole in the ground near the hearth in my room and discovered a bowl upside down with a frog in it and a piece of rewarmed fat. She did it. As soon as the fat melted, I would have died. I would have perished in grief."

Or a woman feels that her husband has lost interest in her. She goes to a mullah and asks him to read a magic spell over a piece of bread, dry apricots, water, or something else consumable so that she can give it to her husband to eat or drink without him knowing. Such a magic spell is called *issitma* (heating, bewitching); an opposite spell is *sovutma* (cooling, undoing bewitching).

Magic spells are usually practiced by literate men; in addition to the local Sart mullahs, Jews and Gypsies are also very popular. (By the way, male insanity is said to be caused by wives who feed them donkey's brain, out of spite. This is one of the most widespread beliefs.) Fortune-telling, on the contrary, is mainly done by women. There are two kinds of fortune-tellers: (1) *palvun* or *palbin*,[12] ordinary ones, and (2) *parixon*, a fortune-teller who communicates with spirits (pari). The title parixon is granted to a fortune-teller only if she has seen an ajina with her own eyes.

A certain Sart once worked for us; he was very tightfisted, and because of that he had endless quarrels with his wife about supporting her. Once he came back from home in an unusually good mood. "What made you so happy?" "Oh, *taqsir* (master), this is what happened to me, this thing. . . ." "What?" "My wife has become parixon! I must say that I have been noticing something strange about her for quite a while; I have been asking her but she would not say a word. Finally, she confessed. Parixon, that is what I have become, she said: I have seen an ajina and had visions in my dreams. I will be telling fortunes now, she said. That is fine, I tell her, tell fortunes; you will be earning your own bread, and we won't have quarrels. I am so happy about it, so happy. . . ."

However, the newly minted parixon turned out to be inexpert in fortune-telling and soon returned to the life of common mortals, which restored the family quarrels about supporting her.

Sometimes a fortune-teller also practices healing. But that is something done by almost everyone who has the slightest inclination toward healing the ailments of their close relatives. And they doctor! Once, a young woman from Nanay, the daughter of a rich merchant, was so doctored that the next day she gave up her soul to God.

Some woman or other, we do not remember who, started doctoring her. She gave her something very strong because the poor creature's mouth turned into a huge canker sore, and it is possible that her alimentary canal was also affected. These people take in unimaginable things! A woman gets pregnant in the absence of her husband. She wants to do an artificial abortion. She is told to drink a solution of copper or iron sulfate. She rushes to the bazaar, buys the sulfate, and drinks it. A few days later, another friend convinces her that alum is more effective; she starts drinking that. Then she is told to drink basic *acid fuchsine*, and she tries it, too. One woman was told that the best solution is to drink a bottle of Russian vodka per day. The poor thing almost drank herself to death. This shows such unquestioning trust! But don't you think that it is only women. Oh, no! Men are not much different. It would not be hard, if you wanted to do so, to poison every last Sart, if you just set your mind to it.

We could prove this with a whole range of interesting facts, but, unfortunately, most of them, especially the sins that are most vivid, are inappropriate for print. We will give you one example. One Sart comes to the doctor and in a broken Russian asks for a medicine called, according to him, "shampanskai-mokh." For quite a while, the doctor cannot understand what he wants. Finally, it turns out that the Sart is asking for the Spanish fly (*Lytta vesicatoria*) to ingest, because his wife is still very young and he is no longer potent enough.[13] When some investigation was done on this prescription, it turned out that a while ago in that town there was a Russian medical assistant industriously selling this medicine to increase male potency, and with great success.

We have mentioned before that most of the native population treats religion as a custom that, unless followed, will result in negative public opinion about the person and that Sarts fear this enormously. An even stronger fear used to be caused by the stick of the qozi-rais, who was both the guardian of holiness and the regulator of public opinion.

Once the magic stick was made obsolete, the magic also disappeared; in public opinion divisions appeared, divisions that were few and about which no one spoke, but nonetheless they fully existed. For though the people discussed it little, many of them started to do those things that they had not even thought of earlier. Godliness was disturbed; in the beginning, the range of disturbances was extreme, then they gradually settled down, and currently this movement seems to have reached equilibrium.

On Thursday, so to say, the stick was made obsolete, and the next day, Friday, of a Sart man's three wives, two left his home to move to a brothel, assuming that their life there would be more diverting. He got drunk but in such a way that nobody would see.

The following Friday, he was busy and did not go to the mosque for the *juma* namoz.[14] The next day, he was ashamed. For two Fridays he went to mosque because of either the pricks of conscience or the fear of public opinion. On the third Friday, he did not go again. When he was rebuked for ungodliness, he lost his temper and, summoning his courage, cursed the parents of everyone who nagged him; in addition, he promised to give a good beating to anyone who tried to coerce him in the future. Naturally, nobody dared approach him after that, and he stopped going to the mosque at all. His example turned out to be contagious, and some of those who nagged him in the past also decided that it was inconvenient to stop their work upon hearing the call of the azanchi. For the first time, during the Ramadan holiday, he got openly drunk and beat someone up. They locked him up in jail. When he was released, he got drunk again and began drinking heavily, but since he is a Sart and is frugal, like many of his countrymen, and extremely calculating, he soon stopped. Horrified at what he had done, and most of all at the amount of money he had spent (10 rubles 34 k.), he took a dish of plov and 40 k. in cash and went to eshon, gave his offering, repented, and became a murid, which was the reason why for the next two or three months, until he got tired of it, he would turn his head to the left and say in half voice, "Allah! Allah! Allah!" Sometimes, he would sigh deeply, and "Ya, Xudo!" (Oh, God!) or "Ya, Karim!" (Oh, gracious One!) would slip out of his mouth.[15] In the meantime, one of the wives returned, saying, "Tauba qildim" (I repent), wailed a bit, complained loudly about the harassment she encountered in that dingy place, and began properly spinning thread again, repeating like her husband, "Ya, Xudo! Ya, Falak!" (Oh, God! Oh, Heaven!).[16]

After a while, godliness became boring again. First, the sighs and exclamations disappeared. Then the husband became too lazy to go to mosque, and the runaway wife found a lover with the help of the other wife, her kundosh, who was living in peace with her husband and was, obviously, interested in getting rid of a rival. And these are the people we call fanatics! If there is a need to blame them for something, they should be blamed for what they do, which is not the result of following the dogmas of religion too closely but a result of ignorance and a habit of living the same way as their grandfathers lived, the inability to count even using fingers, and as a result, a habit of being afraid of everything new, good, or bad, since it could destroy what they have currently and not bring anything useful.

We have, however, diverged from the topic. We have diverged starting from the place where we mentioned that after the abolition of the qozi-rais's stick beatings, which ensured strict adherence to religious norms, religious indifference has spread among the masses.

A Muslim woman does not go to the mosque; she prays at home and always finds many reasons to dodge this rite. For instance, it is a sin to pray in a dress or underwear wet by a child or during her period. That is why her attitude toward religion is very unstable. Keeping watch on her has always been harder than watching a man, so it has become customary to turn a blind eye to the fact that, except for the few literate ones, namoz is usually performed only by old women and not even all of them. For the same reason, ablutions, which according to religion, should be completed before prayer, just like prayer itself, are more often performed by men than by women; and due to haste or from unwillingness to take off shoes and wash the feet to the ankle, we often saw [ablutions] replaced with a symbolic sprinkling of soft or hard-soled boots. One poor Sart woman was musing aloud in our presence: "If I were rich," she said, "I would do nothing, would pray to God, sit and praise God's name. But I have no time to pray: I have a lot of work, and what's the point of praying since God has not given me anything!"

When a woman decides to perform namoz, she first washes her face, hands to elbows, and feet to ankles. (More than others, they perform the morning namoz and the next-to-last, namoz-oqshom.) Then she pulls the scarf over her forehead in such a way as to hide her hair and places the ends of the scarf in front. (A man prays in a turban, the end of which, about ½ arshin long, is placed over his left shoulder. Turbans here are mostly white.) Adjusting her dress so that she looks proper before Allah, the praying woman kneels on a felt (or a rug); or a small, clean carpet; or a rug made especially for this purpose of a thick, cotton, light yellow fabric, *joy-namoz*;[17] or a large scarf; or finally, her robe and, turning her face toward the qibla (holy mosque), recites prayers in half voice, accompanying them by bending her body, bowing to the earth, turning her head, and making other symbolic movements.

In respectable and pious families, if someone present in the room is performing namoz, the others either keep silent or speak in half voice. But in most cases, performing namoz alone does not prevent others from talking loudly or even laughing. The noise recedes only at the last moment of namoz, when the one praying, wiping the face with his or her hands, turns to the others with the greeting "salam-alaykum."

We have mentioned fasting before. Women are most willing to perform the following religious rites: pilgrimages, visiting graves of her relatives, lamenting for the deceased, celebrating Kurban and Ramadan, etc. In other words, everything that could be considered both religious rites and entertainment, which is not very varied here and which, as we have seen already, Sart women love a lot, even the elderly.

Most local pilgrimages are to mazars, graves of people who are considered saints for some reason. Sometimes, the name mazar is given to a place consecrated by a special event. In this case, the trees growing there are also considered sacred, and they are not cut, and their branches are used by all of the visitors to the mazar to hang rags, bits of fabric, threads, etc.[18] In Aravan, a village in Marg'ilon district, there is another kind of mazar. At the top of a small cliff face located not far from the kishlak is a carving that reminds one of a mounted horseman in miniature. A spring comes from below the cliff; and in the same cliff face, about half or a quarter arshin above the spring, there is a small, perfectly polished hollow that is big enough for part of a human head to fit in. Sarts believe that the horseman is Caliph Ali's shadow that happened to fall on the cliff wall and that visiting this mazar can help with headaches. Sick people put their heads into the hollow in the rock above the place where the spring comes forth.[19]

There are many mazars; the majority of the most-respected ones are located in the mountains or foothills near Fergana, and they are usually visited in May, June, or July, when the best weather of the year reaches the mountains and before the time when the pastures have been thoroughly grazed.

Each mazar has its own specialties. Thus, for instance, visiting Aravan mazar helps with headaches, and visiting the mazar in Kanibadam called *ko'k-yutal-mazar* is considered the proven treatment for consumption and whooping cough (ko'k-yutal is whooping cough and consumption). The two most notable mazars in Namangan district are *Padsha-ata* and *Bava-ata*; both are situated in the mountains at rather high altitudes; most of the pilgrims, whether on foot or on horseback, coming here in whole caravans, arrive in June.[20] This is what Sarts say about both of these mazars: "If you want to pray about wealth, go to mazar Padsha-ata; and if you want to pray for the birth of a child, go to mazar Bava-ata."

Among those shrines that are famous not only in Fergana but beyond its borders, we must mention *Taxt-i-Sulayman* (the throne of Solomon) situated at the top of a mountain with the same name near the town of Osh.[21]

When setting out on pilgrimage, the somewhat well-off people take a sacrificial ram or a goat. If the road permits, women and children ride in carts. The pious people walk part of the way, driving the ram or goat in front of them. After they arrive at the mazar and perform their prayer, they butcher the sacrificial animal that they brought; the skin and some of the meat are given to the sheikhs of this mazar, who by heritage have a right to receive all the offerings from the pilgrims, and the other part is consumed on the spot, at the mazar, by the pilgrims themselves. (Such an offering is called *xudoyi*, belonging to God.) Sometimes, when visiting a nearby mazar, instead of butchering a ram or a goat, they limit themselves to preparing and eating some food that is considered soul saving (savob).

Often, women visit such nearby mazars unaccompanied by their husbands. Five or six women team up, gather food, hire a cart, and set off.

Discussing the Muslim religion and its everyday meaning, we have already mentioned the level of development of the natives or, to be precise, the amount of knowledge that the native society possesses. That is why here, talking about what women know, we will only mention that their range of knowledge is narrower than the men's. Literate women, who are able to understand with difficulty a few books written in the Turkic language and who can write, with difficulty, some sort of simple letter, are few. Women familiar with theology and law are extremely rare; they are usually asked for advice (by other women) in the same way as men turn to the ulomo, and these women are treated with great respect. Nothing raises a person in the eyes of others and in the society as a whole as much as knowledge, erudition, and wealth.

Due to the illiteracy of the majority of women, writing is often replaced with various symbolic objects. For instance, a woman who misses her husband sends him bedding with a piece of hay and a piece of coal in it. Thus, she tells him that in his absence, longing has turned her yellow, like hay, and black, like coal. To inform someone about a death, they send a dark blue thread. (Dark blue is the color of mourning.)

A rural or kishlak woman is distinguished by her especially insignificant knowledge. Often, she can count to a hundred but not always correctly, for instance, instead of forty (*qirq*), saying twice twenty (*ikki yigirma*), and so on. Most kishlak women cannot count money, do not know how many tanga there are in a tilla, how many *chek* in a tanga, or kopeks in a ruble, and in most cases they have no idea about the units of weight or the number of months in a year. One woman from Nanay said in our presence that her child is less than a year old; it is only seventeen months old.

Both urban and kishlak women, as well as the majority of men, have little idea about the calculation of time. Muslims have a lunar calendar, and the majority of them do not connect the name of the month with a number of days but with the fact of the emergence of the moon. We will illustrate this with an example. A child is born at the end of the moon. The second emerges and recedes; then, the third one emerges; let us say that forty-five days pass after the birth of the child. At the end of this period, the father and the mother say that the baby is three months old, since they have seen three moons since it was born. One can frequently hear that so-and-so has been pregnant for eleven months. Years are counted in the same way, and bearing in mind the above-mentioned confusion, when a child reaches the age of five, they do not say that he has started his sixth year but rather that he is six years old.

We have already mentioned that the moral side of kin relationships among the native people is very weak. We have noticed that in most social strata of the native population, parents tend to love their children much more than children love their parents, and within a group of children, the younger ones are loved more. The attitude toward children is extremely kind among the poor people, and we have seen cases of poor people spoiling their children so badly that the latter grew up to be completely uncontrollable. It is remarkable that the worst cases of such spoiling and all sorts of indulgence toward children can always be found in the poorest kishlak families. We have often seen mothers begging their son or daughter to bring wood, water, or something else from the yard; and the child not only disobeys but even pretends not to hear the mother's words. Then, when she raises her fists at them, they rush out into the street, adroitly avoiding her and still not fulfilling her request or demand. A young girl who lived with us was on very friendly terms with her mother, who was about thirty-five; then, when the girl started growing up, her mother came completely under her influence: she never contradicted her, treated her daughter as a person of a higher position, and received from her a bawling out or admonition. All of this is the reason why children from poor families, especially girls, start helping their parents in the house, in the field, or in other tasks at a comparatively late age. We knew a very poor family in Nanay, where the daughter, age twelve, did literally nothing, and her brother, a strong rosy-cheeked lad, was completely spoiled by his mother and started helping his old father only when he reached seventeen or eighteen years of age, although he used every possible pretext to avoid it. We have often heard stories about spoiling children from the poor people themselves. Rich people, they said, have land, gardens, horses, and sheep; they cherish and love all this not less than their own families, but poor people have only their children, and they focus their love on them.

We can claim without much hesitation that children in cities are taught to work earlier than children in kishlaks, and wealthy families do that earlier than poor families; at the same time, children's relations with their mother are better than with their father regardless of the place or wealth of the family. Respect toward parents, mostly superficial and typical only for relatively well-off families or families where everything is managed by the husband and not the wife, is expressed only while children live with their parents. (Children always address their father with "vy";[22] they sometimes say "ty" to their mother, but this happens comparatively rarely and mostly in kishlaks.)

When a woman marries, she continues seeing only her mother; she either sees her father very rarely or completely ends any relationship with him.

Parents of a married woman are treated with some exterior respect only if they are wealthy. Under opposite conditions, a widowed mother often becomes a house servant at her married daughter's place, performing the dirtiest jobs in the house and receiving her wealthy daughter's old and worn-out dress and shoes in return for her labor. We saw the following scene once: A mother who lived at her married daughter's place out of so-called mercy failed to please the latter by not cooking some dish well enough. The daughter summoned and scolded the old woman in our presence and made her cook the dish again. Despite such situations, mothers often stay with their daughters till their death. Where else would she go if she lost her home after the death of her husband? Wherever she went, she would be treated in the same way. Had she been rich, it would have been a different story. She would have either lived on her own, hiring a poor family to perform agricultural work, or if she moved in with her daughter, she would have separate premises and respect.

For families that observe etiquette and codes of decent behavior, when an elderly man, the owner of the house, enters the room, everyone stands up and does not sit down until he is seated; this includes not only his children, wife, and other female relatives but even his mother.

In the presence of outsiders, a husband and a wife do not express any intimate relationship. The husband usually speaks in a very serious way, and the wife listens to him with an expression of utmost humility. In the presence of outsiders, a husband and a wife address each other only in the formal "you" and never call each other by name, which is considered extremely impolite. In each other's sight, they refer to each other by the name of their eldest child, and if there is no child, the name of the husband's or wife's brother, or they talk about each other in the third person. When out of sight, the husband talks about the wife as "my family," and the wife talks about her husband in his absence without using his name but saying "my husband, my owner, the father of my daughter, etc."[23]

Cases of very strong, loving relationships between spouses are very rare, due to the fact that very few marriages are concluded based on mutual attraction. However, it often happens that the husband and wife whose marriage has been arranged in their absence develop a good relationship, and with time, they form a relationship of habit, strong enough for the marital union to last until one of them dies. But even in these kinds of relationships between husband and wife, because the wife always depends materially to some degree on the husband, total openness is almost never observed between spouses. The opposite is more widespread: half of the wife's actions remain a secret from the husband, and the doors of her real moral world are more often opened to her friends or even female acquaintances than to him.

Although religion and law declare the husband to be the head of the family, it often happens headship falls completely under the wife's influence. We have known families where wives not only kept husbands in strict control but even beat them. One such husband was the district head. A very dexterous and smart man in his official environment and very strict, even harsh with his subordinates, he became absolutely lost when he entered the internal courtyard. Once, when he wanted to get a second wife, his wife slapped him on the face so many times that the sound of that mixed with her shouts could be heard even in the street.

Another curious incident took place in the erstwhile Namangan province. About twenty-five years ago a woman died, a certain Xol-bibi, known among the populace under the name of Xol-mirob-boshi. Her husband, Ho'ja-bek Mirob, was the head of all Namangan provincial *mirobs*, directing the distribution of irrigation water. Even during the life of her husband, Xol-bibi, who was well informed not only about customary law but also all the details of the local irrigation system and who was an energetic, smart woman who never gave in to anyone, always took an active role in her husband's affairs. After her husband died and she was approaching forty, she dressed herself in male clothes, put on boots, a turban, and a sash, and forcing the Namangan population to acknowledge her as their mirob-boshi, she replaced her husband in this position and carried out those duties until the end of her life. Her son Sarimsoq-dodxoh, whom she promoted to the Khan's palace, later became a hokim (governor) of Namangan.

Not only wives of khans but even wives of comparatively low-status officials took direct or indirect part in administrative, political, and other affairs.

If the moral aspect of the local kin relations between children and parents is weak, other kin relations are literally nonexistent, although there is a lot of talk about feelings and relations. Relationships among relatives, even those such as brothers and sisters, do not differ from relations among acquaintances unless there are some additional, material obligations. Cases when relatives help each other out using their own means are very rare. Such an expression of kin feelings and relations can be seen more often among the state employees, who could keep their own fat purse safe by using the opportunities open to them to promote their kin to this or that cushy position.

Thus, we can safely claim that local adult men and women have no feelings toward relatives at all in most cases, except for feelings toward small children, which exist only because of their helplessness. A Russian has an escape here: though he is familiar with the Fifth Commandment, he is also familiar with the saying "Everyone for himself and God is for all." But a Sart has no similar saying or commandment. So he has no way out. Scholars and religious zealots know well that a particular Sart with a huge family literally has nothing to eat. Despite that, they shame him and convince him that he must take care of his parent. "I have to recognize this [obligation], I really have to, but it is so difficult for me, so difficult. We are all sinners in front of God; that is what I think," he says and sighs. But if you listen attentively to the tone of his voice and look carefully at the expression of his face, you see that what he is saying is far from what he is thinking. What he is really thinking is the following: "I must acknowledge [them]; I can't leave a person to die of hunger; I must take care of him, but I cannot do it with all the people I already have to take care of and with my minuscule income. That strength is needed, but I cannot." He will never tell you what this strength is because he does not know. And there are two reasons for him not to know. First, he has never in his whole life given this question any consideration: he has never seen or known in his public life any shelters, poor houses, or other similar institutions for helping the poor and helpless part of the humanity; he, the Sart, never thought about this issue very long and never made an attempt to resolve it. Second, he knows the history of his religion poorly. If he knew the latter well, he would have answered the scholars in the following way: "The Prophet has ordered each Muslim to pay zakat equal to the fortieth part of his capital, livestock, and other property, in addition to the land tax. The Prophet has ordered that zakat should be used in equal proportions for conducting *a faith-based war* and for *supporting the poor and the disabled*. Why have our khans and emirs kept zakat for themselves? Why did they start using it for their own needs? Why did they violate the Prophet's order? Why did they rob the poor and the disabled? Had they not done it, there would have been money for my father."

Turning to the rules of politeness and good behavior prescribed for the native woman, we have to say that these rules are more or less familiar to all the strata of the native society, but they are mainly observed in cities and among the wealthier population, to whom we will refer here.

As we have mentioned before, when a husband, father, or another elderly male relative enters the room, the woman gets up, especially if strangers are present; at the same time she drops her eyes and pulls the scarf slightly over her forehead to cover her hair and acquire as modest and chaste a look as possible. Speaking in the informal "you" only to those younger than her, the native woman addresses adult men as *aka* (elder brother) and a woman who is older than herself as *aya* (aunt) or *bibi* (abbreviated as *biyo*, which means madam).[24]

Guests of lower social status or wealth than the hostess rise every time the hostess stands up. A woman who has arrived from somewhere must visit her acquaintances first. If she wants to make an acquaintance, she brings a gift on her first visit: a piece of fabric (for a shirt or a robe), a plov dish, a dish of flat bread, pistachios and raisins, or something of that sort. If the hosts want to continue the acquaintance, when she leaves, the woman receives a gift of no less value than the one she brought. In the opposite circumstance, if this condition has not been observed, no sooner does the guest reach the door than she starts grumbling and then cursing them for the insignificant respect they showed her.

The hostess stops her work in the presence of guests.

If the expected guests are of the same or higher social status compared to the hostess (such visits are usually paid with a preliminary warning), then the hostess who has no household helpers calls one of her not-so-wealthy neighbors to help her do the cooking. Before guests arrive, the room is swept and tidied, the most festive shirts and robes are displayed in one of the corners, flat breads are quickly baked, rice for plov is prepared in advance, etc. Having tidied up, the hostess dresses up. Guests appear, usually with children and household members. The hostess meets them outside the room; one of the household members or even she herself helps the most respected visitors take off their paranjis and collects the trays with presents brought by the guests. A paranji is always removed in the yard, and wearing it indoors is considered very ill mannered, just as for us it would be rude to sit indoors in a coat, galoshes, and so on. Having removed their paranjis, the guests hug the hostess, ask each other about their health, and express good wishes. Kissing as a greeting is not customary either among men or women, even if they are very joyful.[25] The guests place themselves on quilts spread for them in the front corner of the room; and a dasturxon appears: flat breads, pistachios, raisins, low-quality confections brought from Russia, fruit drops, halvah, fruit in summer, and the ubiquitous tea. One of the women breaks the flat breads into pieces and puts them on the tray or dasturxon. The most important guest takes a piece first, others follow her, and finally the hostess, who should be invited by the guests to partake. To please their hostess, the guests give treats to the children and kiss them, ask them whether they go to school, etc. A conversation starts; the guests examine each other's festive clothing; ask about their cost; gossip; tease each other; exchange news; nursing babies, who are used to being in their cradles, scream; their mothers try to get them to sleep; and, finally, tiring of their cries, send them off somewhere with the teenage children.

When the hostess leaves the room to observe the preparation of plov or some other dish, such as dumplings,[26] the hostess asks the guests not to get bored but to entertain themselves with food and conversation. If it is summertime, the guests, having chatted to their heart's content, go into the yard, visit different rooms, walk to the garden if it is beside the house, make a swing, which is a favorite not only of the young women but even those who are advanced in age, or climb on the roof of one of the buildings and look over into the neighboring yards to see what is happening there. When they see women there, they start a conversation, and when they see men, their faces show fear and confusion, and they rush back with screams and exclamations such as "Voi, o'layin" (Oh, it would be better to die) or "Voi jonim chiqip ketdi" (Oh, my soul has fled!), almost rolling from the roof to the ground. Elderly women are especially amusing in such situations.

Having eaten plov and drunk tea again, the guests go their ways, convincingly begging the hostess not to forget them and to return the visit, and the leftover sweets are carefully collected and locked in a safe place, usually a small wrought-iron chest.

Visits are usually done during the daytime, especially for women; religion advises a Muslim man or woman either to return home before the last evening *namoz xufton* or, if that is impossible, to spend the night where they are. This rule is observed, if not always, at least whenever possible. You do not see anyone in the streets of a Sart town after namoz xufton. The only exception is the month of fasting, when day and night switch places.

Native women's major modes of transportation: for short distances, walking, and for long distances, riding in an araba cart. She rides a horse much less frequently. (It is not customary for women to ride donkeys.) In the latter situation, she never rides on her own. Her husband, teenage son, or some other relative sits in the saddle, and she places herself behind him on the horseback on a folded blanket or other cover. Only Kyrgyz and Gypsy women are used to riding horseback alone (using a men's saddle).

We mentioned earlier the conditions under which a woman appears in the bazaar; and we noted that rules of appropriate behavior and religion require not only that a woman cover her face when she goes into the street but that she makes sure her usually bright adornments are hidden under the chimbet and paranji. This rule is far from always observed. Seeing no men in close vicinity, the woman pulls the chimbet back on her head, uncovers her face, and often does not manage to cover it when she encounters a man around the corner. When two women who know each other meet in a crowded street and recognize each other by their clothes or voice, they come face-to-face, lightly lift the chimbet, and have a chat, after which they part. It is not customary to hug in the street as they do at home. (Men who have not seen each other for a long time do hug each other in the street, sometimes without even dismounting their horses.)

It is not inappropriate for women to talk to female strangers in the street. For instance, one of the authors of this book, the wife, who would wear the same chimbet and paranji in the street as Sart women, was often approached by complete strangers and asked how much she had paid for the bunting for the shirt or adras for a *beshmet* [a type of robe]; both of these items were scrutinized, and then the women went their own ways.

But along with this, custom demands that women should not converse in the street with a man, even if her face is covered. For instance, if a man sees his wife in the street and needs to tell her something personal, he does it in such a way that it is not seen by the passersby; he talks to her in a low voice and looks in a different direction.

Lower-class native women, especially in kishlaks, more or less ignore all the above-mentioned rules, at least with those of their own tribe.[27] Seeing a Russian, a Sart woman turns aside and covers her face with care, often leaning on the wall and pressing her face against it, or she rushes to one side, hiding herself behind the first gate; often the children that accompany her cannot follow her as fast as they should and start crying and wailing in the middle of the street. Less often, when the Sart woman sees no one in the street who might notice and reprimand her for her behavior, she not only does not run away from a Russian but, on the contrary, pulls her chimbet back and looks over the passing traveler with a remarkable good-heartedness and curiosity.

A Sart woman, like a Sart man, is a lover of all possible entertainment and fun, which she calls by the general name *tomosha* (entertainment); she loves holidays and festive assemblies even more.

On the eve of a holiday, the so-called arafa, laundry is done, sweet-dough flat breads are baked in every house, and other holiday preparations are made. In the evening of the same day, women cook plov and take dishes of it to relatives, acquaintances, and neighbors. Usually, everyone gets up very early on the first day of the holiday to be able to sweep the room, wash hair, style hair, and dress up on time. The morning namoz on that day is not at dawn, as it is on ordinary days, but around eight or nine. Men dressed in clean turbans and new robes go toward their mosques; they are followed by the majority of women, who watch the holiday namoz from the street or the roofs of the houses close to the mosque. At the end of prayer, in cities, part of the crowd moves toward the bazaar, where most of the stalls stay open during the day, and another part disperses around the city. If you stop by the gate of a large wealthy household, you will see many men and women coming and leaving throughout the day; until late at night this goes on, a holiday rush. The following day around noon you will hear the peculiar sounds of Sart trumpets, *karnai*, announcing to townsfolk that a performance is starting at the bazaar or some other town square, with a *darvaza* walking the tightrope, an illusionist, a clown, or the bachcha dancing publicly. Crowds of people fill the square and gather in dense groups around the place of the performance; men, women with nursing babies, teenage children, young women. They mix in a multicolored and noisy crowd; crowds of women can be seen on the nearest roofs and araba carts; loud talk, noise; peddlers with raisins, pistachios, halvah, and fruit drops whisk around; trumpets blare loudly, attracting more and more crowds; little by little the crowd throngs, and the few riders who were trapped can no longer move their horses. In the middle of the crowd, part of which, the closest to the arena, is sitting or kneeling in a kind of amphitheater, a good-looking and colorfully dressed bachcha is dancing on a large gray felt rug to the rhythmic sound of the drum and sharp shriek sound of the local clarinet; he lustfully moves his shoulders and body, occasionally shivering his whole body or rapidly whirling in one spot. Catching its breath, the crowd, colorful as an Asian carpet, focuses thousands of eyes on him; here, he is swirling faster and faster, now he is kneeling and is slowly swinging his agile body, dressed in bright atlas, to the left and right, while shimmying his shoulders slightly. A howl comes out of the frantic, frenzied crowd, which is used to expressing approval in these circumstances not with applause but with wild cries. . . .

The holiday usually continues for six or seven days in cities and for only three days in kishlaks, where the absence of acrobats, bachcha dances, and so on makes holiday celebrations much less exciting. The only entertainment available there is limited to visiting each other. In some kishlaks, young girls gather in groups and go from one home to another, dancing in the ichkari and being rewarded with some treats.

In spring, the so-called *Sayil*, which are days for gathering outside the town, are organized in different parts of Fergana at various times in March or April; they resemble our May First. (There are similar Sayil in large kishlaks.)

In Namangan, they are organized three or four Fridays in a row during March and early April depending on the spring. Tents are pitched somewhere outside town, and they sell tea, bread, raisins, and pistachios; peddlers with various candies appear, and dumpling sellers erect their stoves in haste. On the appointed day, starting in the early morning, columns of araba carts, riders, and crowds of walking people start pouring in. Hundreds of groups form; women are usually separate from men. A bachcha dances; sometimes an acrobat appears; less often there is a horse race. By the end of the day all this colorful, bright crowd returns to town, singing songs and beating tambourines.

7 Pregnancy and Childbirth

A Girl

T HERE ARE MANY REASONS for a Sart woman to rejoice over pregnancy, especially her first. First of all, according to tradition, a husband almost never allows a young bride to leave the courtyard until she gives birth to the first child. Second, both religion and the folk mind agree that progeny is one of the best rewards for human virtue.[1] For the same reason, an infertile woman who bears no children hears reprimands and complaints at every step from her husband for the lack of progeny. Being called unfruitful is almost as bad as being called unclean. There are many cases of women trying to hide their infertility by persuading everyone that they are pregnant, but the fetus became stuck inside and they cannot get pregnant again. Such stories about the imaginary fetus stuck inside are rather frequent. We have been addressed many times for advice on what to do with this stuck fetus and what should be done to get rid of it. At the same time, it was only rarely that we would hear complaints about too many children or the difficulty of raising them. Sarts say that a home with children is a bazaar (lively); without children, a mazar (depressing). We have encountered only one case of infanticide, and it was surrounded by exceptional circumstances. A disabled mother, who was born without feet, gave birth to a girl. Lacking the ability to move herself or to ask someone to take care of the newborn, she strangled the child out of despair. Cases of extreme fertility are not rare. More than once we met old women who had fifteen to seventeen children throughout their marriage.

The length of the fertile period, during which native women and, even more so, men maintain their capability for sexual reproduction, is remarkable. We knew families where husbands were fifty-five to sixty and their wives forty to forty-five, and they kept having more children. On average, however, women stop menstruating around forty-five.

A pregnant woman's hygienic situation, including food, does not differ from the nonpregnant one; a pregnant woman performs all the usual work and does not stop sexual activity until the final days of pregnancy. There is a rather indecent saying about it where a pregnant woman is compared to a pregnant mare.[2]

An artificial interruption of pregnancy, or provoking a miscarriage, is done (not always successfully though) only when a woman acquires a lover during her husband's extended absence. First they turn to a cotton swab that is placed into the vagina. Sometimes a pinch of ashes from burning an old sieve is rolled into that cotton; all hopes are invested in those ashes as a medication that the natives believe holds irresistible power.

So a Sart woman is happy to be pregnant. The only case when she may be upset is if the conception occurred during the difficult month of Safar; a child conceived during this month says while still in the womb, "Either I will die, or my father will die, or my mother will die." The pregnant woman expects all sorts of troubles for herself then. But this is an exception. Let's assume that the child was conceived at a favorable time. First of all, various observations start that aim to find out whether the pregnant woman is carrying a boy or a girl. If large hairs appear near the woman's right nipple, it will definitely be a boy, for this observation is made even in some medical books. More often, however, observations are based on the kind of food the pregnant woman prefers, hot or cold. If she prefers hot food, it will be a boy; if cold, a girl.[3]

As in Russia, preference here is given to boys rather than girls. If the first child is a boy, it is considered a special blessing. In this case, wealthy families organize big celebrations; they slaughter a ram, prepare several puds of rice for plov and wheat for flat breads, and the most venerable guests are presented with robes.[4]

A local woman always gives birth either in her own home or at her mother's house, where she usually moves in advance. People present during the delivery are her mother, elder married sisters, or similar relatives from the husband's side; the husband may be present if he wants to, but children, especially teenagers, are always sent away from the house during the delivery. Only in cities are there midwives who specialize in assisting during delivery. Sart women give birth either on their knees or squatting; such positions are preferred above all other possible ones because the local women believe that it facilitates fast delivery. (There is a superstition that a woman with a bad or difficult character usually has difficult deliveries.)

During labor the woman holds on to one of the women present with her hands and at the same time props her back against the chest of another one; the latter embraces the laboring woman with both hands above her stomach and squeezes her every time she sees her having a contraction. If the delivery lasts long, midwives can be changed and other somewhat cabalistic means are tried. For instance, a piece of horse hoof is burned in the room where the delivery is taking place, or the laboring woman is given a drink from a cup that has a prayer written with ink on its inside surface. (We have heard many times that a husband who is present during an especially difficult delivery cries, as he cannot stand seeing his wife suffer so much. At the same time, one cannot stop wondering at the stoicism with which Sarts endure the most unendurable physical pain and very difficult operations.) The newborn is taken by the midwife or one of the relatives who is present, washed, and wrapped in soft old rags, not always clean. The umbilical cord is cut either by scissors or a razor; the end that stays with the newborn is tied up with a thread; the other end is not tied up but is attached to the leg of the woman for fear that it may move back inside. In case of retention of afterbirth for too long, there is a custom in some areas to shoot near the room where the woman is lying.

After the child is born, religion prescribes reciting some prayers over it, but this rule is not followed everywhere or by everyone. After the end of the delivery and the expulsion of afterbirth, the woman must wash, which she always performs herself since the religion does not allow seeing the avrat of others, and only after the ablution she lies down in bed; the newborn is placed next to her on the right. Usually, she stays in bed for six to seven days; in rare cases she is limited to three days in bed. During this time, her food consists of various meatless dishes, if possible, made with qatiq (which is a cold food), and she is cared for by one of her closest relatives. The mother is usually not left alone, not only during the first days after delivery but even during the first six weeks, for fear that the aforementioned yellow-haired ajina may smother the mother and child.

It often happens that, not wishing to embitter a father with the news of a daughter's birth, they first tell him that a son was born, and then, after two or three days he is gradually prepared and advised to accept a daughter. Once, a curious thing happened in Namangan. A child was born in a wealthy man's family. The women present at the delivery, not wanting to upset him, told the father that it was a son. That imaginary son was to be the first boy in the family, since the eldest child was a girl. All the family's acquaintances got invitations through messengers to come and celebrate the event the following day. Rumors spread that on top of plov and other treats, guests would receive robes. The men who gathered in the external yard the following day found a very modest meal and an upset father, who announced to everyone that there was a mistake and instead of the son he was informed about, it was a daughter, so there would not be any special festivities. The same day it was decided that the man should take another wife, who could give him a son.

Upon a successful birth, one of the new mother's male or female relatives goes among the relatives and the close acquaintances with *suyunchi* (joyous news) about the fortunate result of pregnancy and for this receives a reward of a few kopeks from everyone who is told. The following day, relatives and friends come and congratulate the mother and father on the new birth. Sometimes, these visits last for several days. Every female visitor brings plov, flat breads, or pastries and a shirt for the newborn. Most of the time, these guests come in large groups and almost always have children with them; they are noisy and chatty, and nobody thinks that it may be tiring or harmful to the new mother.

As we noted, if a son is born, especially a firstborn, wealthy families may organize a big celebration. When a girl is born, the celebration is much smaller. The most one can expect is that a ram may be slaughtered and plov prepared and several female and male relatives and friends invited. Sometimes, a meal is presented not at home but at the nearest mazar, where the costs of the celebration are covered not by the father but one of his younger brothers, with whom he is especially close.

After six or seven days, about the same time when the mother starts getting up from bed, her mother places the newborn into a beshik, a cradle, where the child, tied down by two large bands, is kept lying without moving, with an arrangement that urine and excrement will fall through a hole in the beshik into a pot fixed under the cradle.[5]

A beshik is always standing on the floor, not hanging; its base is slightly curved so that it can rock. The first tying of the child into this beshik, which is also the first time that a shirt is put on the newborn, is accompanied by a family celebration. On that day, the mother calls her relatives and friends and feeds them flat bread, tea, and plov, and the grandfather or father gives the child a name. They are careful not to give the newborn the name of any of the older relatives, male or female; this is done because when the child grows and starts misbehaving and it is reprimanded or scolded, that older relative, whose name the child bears, might be offended. Parents whose children died, upon the birth of a new baby, wishing that this one would remain among the living and not die like their previous children, usually choose one the following names: Tursun (let it stay), Toxta (wait, stop), Mahkam (robust), etc. Another typical Muslim name is added to this symbolic one: Tursun-Muhammad, Toxta-jon, Mahkam-boi, etc. Often, wishing to do everything to protect the newborn from the fate of deceased brothers and sisters, in addition to naming the baby this way, the baby is given to a nonfamily woman who has milk to breast-feed it for five or six days. After this period, the parents of the child go to the temporary mother with buy-back money. After buying the child back, it is named Sotib-aldi (bought), if it is a boy, or Sotqin (sold), if it is a girl. Then the parents can relax completely and be sure that the child will not die. If twin boys are born, they are called Husayn and Hasan, and twin girls are named Zohra and Fatima; if the twins are a boy and a girl, their names are selected randomly.

Under rule of the khans, there was a law or custom that if triplets were born, one of the children was raised at state expense and the father and mother received some personal reward.

When a child is named, the name of its birth year is also remembered.

In this respect, time is divided into cycles lasting twelve years, and each year of the cycle has its own unique name: for instance, the mouse, the bull, the tiger, the rabbit, the dragon, the snake, the horse, the ram, the monkey, the hen, the dog, the pig.

Thus, for instance, the current year of 1886 is the year of the dog. That is why when the locals ask the question "Which year is this for you?" they often say, "What is your year?"—i.e., what was the name of your birth year?[6]

The new mother starts doing housework as soon as she gets up from bed, but she almost never leaves the house or, to be precise, the courtyard for six weeks. We already mentioned that the child is bathed immediately after it is born; then it stays unwashed until the twentieth day, when it is bathed for the second time and dressed in the second shirt, and if the weather is cold, a padded robe made from silk, if possible.

The first shirt that the newborn wore from the sixth or seventh day is kept for the next child.

In some areas, for instance, in Tajik villages of Namangan district, a boy is bathed on the eighteenth day after birth (i.e., two days earlier than the usual time), believing that in this case, his future bride will require a smaller qalin (dowry), and the girl on the twenty-second day (i.e., two days later), so that in the future a large qalin will be given for her.

After that, the child is bathed more and more rarely, since the natives believe that bathing prevents his growing and getting fat. Before washing, his face and head are rubbed with qatiq (sour milk); the latter is hard to wash off; the dandruff and dirt on the child's head forms some kind of a scab, and because of insufficiently clean conditions, we saw many Sart children with eye diseases, various rashes, ringworm, and other skin diseases.[7]

When the mother has no milk, a wet-nurse is only rarely called; usually, such a child is given cow's milk and after four or five months it is fed a flour and fat mixture. (If a child has a strong belch or other ailments that are considered "cold," the nursing child gets bits of ram fat, which belongs, as we already know, to hot food.)

Abandoning newborns is very rare, at least much less frequent than giving adolescent children to someone else to raise. When a newborn is abandoned, it is taken early in the morning, before the morning namoz, to the mosque; the azanchi, who arrives first to make the azan, the call to prayer, finds the child and immediately announces the news to the parish. One of its members may take the abandoned baby to raise, if he wishes. (There are no orphanages.)

Instead of abandoning a baby, poor native families usually give them away to wealthy families for adoption; in this case, the local qozi creates a document (*vasiqa*) that states that so-and-so has given his or her son or daughter for adoption to so-and-so and renounces forever his or her parental rights for that child.[8]

After six weeks, an urban woman and her new baby visit her mother, who by custom must make her a meal and give her gifts: to her daughter, a headscarf, and to the grandson or granddaughter, a skullcap, a robe, and a shirt. This concludes the celebrations for a baby's birth.

Circumcision of boys usually takes place between ages four and twelve. This ritual, especially in wealthy families, is accompanied by a celebration that can last up to three days.

Preparations, gathering presents and other things, can sometimes take a very long time; but among the sedentary population, the celebration, the to'y, is held in autumn or in winter. If the to'y takes place in a kishlak, then the guests, sometimes several hundred men, settle in all the external yards of all the host's relatives and friends.

Each newly arrived guest goes to the mehmon-xona to give the host a present and greet him, and then he proceeds to the place designated for his stay, where several guests are housed. The home owner bears the expenses for the guest and his horse. On the first day when all the guests are arriving and settling in, they get together in groups and entertain themselves with conversation, singing, bachcha dancing, etc.

One of the important guests is given the title *to'y-boshi*; he manages the festive events and distributes the awards for the races.

Upon hearing about the to'y, friends and strangers from all around send their racehorses to the host, hoping to win the prize.

The next morning on the outskirts of the kishlak, they organize the *uloq*, a race with a goat, which one horseman tries to grab from the hands of another. After the uloq, there are bachcha dances and other festivities in various houses. On the third day, there is a long-distance race (20 to 30 versts) with prizes according to the host's wealth.

Often the prize is a bony cow, hungered during the winter, which the winner does not even manage to bring home, because it dies of exhaustion on the way, having been in no condition to walk even 10 to 15 versts.

After the race, the guests are treated to plov, receive gifts (robes and horses), and go on their ways, after which the villagers or at least household heads of the same parish receive plov and nine flat breads per house.

The circumcision itself is conducted by men after the guests have left, while a meal for women is organized in the ichkari.

In the first years of a child's life, which for girls is up to three, four, or five, when she is first dressed in pants, she is usually dressed in a shirt with a horizontal collar (*mullacha*) and a robe. The head is either covered with a skullcap or a scarf for both boys and girls; but the skullcap is more widespread. The bottom of the shirt or the robe is never hemmed because of the superstitious belief that the child will not live if this is done.

For the first four or five months of its life the child is almost constantly lying in the beshik. Then he gets bored in the beshik; he starts squalling, and this is sufficient to be the beginning of a long period of being carried in arms, which often lasts three, four, or even five years and harms the child's health because a spoiled child who is used to being carried around learns to walk very slowly.

Apart from the fact that all Sart men and women love children, causing a child to cry is regarded as a sin; that is why once he makes a noise, the baby immediately gets attention and his beshik is rocked, or he is picked up and humored in every possible way. The child is dandled by every single member of the family who can pick him up and who is not occupied with work. The ones who do not like dandling the baby are teenage boys, who are often punished for this with curses and kicks. In the families where the mother has to work and there are no teenage baby-sitters wanting to care for the nursing baby, who prevents its mother from working in the day and sleeping at night, Sarts use some not harmless sleep-inducing products.

Sart children get their first teeth at about the age of ten months. If emerging teeth cause pain, there are several ways to deal with the situation: reading prayers, sprinkling with flour, or bathing with the blood of a recently slaughtered, clean animal (used for food).

When the child reaches one year, his hair is cut for the first time.

The hair is cut by the grandfather, father, or some of the elder men in the family; this may be done at home, or the child may be taken to a nearby mazar, where the ritual is combined with preparing plov.

Usually the hair is not cut off completely, but two bunches are left over the temples above the ears; when these bunches grow enough, the hair is braided into small braids, and for girls, their ends are decorated with corals, beads, or amulets. The girl's hair is cut in this way until she reaches age seven or eight, and then it is allowed to grow freely.

The native child usually starts walking at about age one, but there are frequent cases when this ability is delayed. We have seen basically healthy children aged two and three who could barely walk a few steps; this is because the child is spoiled and carried everywhere by adults at an age when it is completely unnecessary. If a one-and-a-half- or two-year-old child gets into an especially bad mood and there is no way to please him, his mother starts scaring him with different bogeys. The most effective ones are *bo'ji* (bogeyman), *bo'ri* (the wolf), and *urus* (the Russian).

Breast-feeding lasts for a very long period, usually until the child is two or three; the child is weaned earlier only if the mother loses her milk or gets pregnant again. The child usually sleeps in the beshik until he can be taught to relieve himself outside, between one and a half and three years old.

The first words that the native child learns to say are "mother," "father," and "mother's breast." Words for mother and father differ in different parts of the Fergana Valley: using Persian words, father is *dada*, and mother, *acha* or *byobyo* (or abbreviated to byo from the Persian *bibi*);[9] or using Turkic, father is *ata* or *aka*, and for mother, *ina* or *opa* (ata is father; aka, elder brother; ina, mother; opa, elder sister). When Turkic names for father and mother are used, there is a rule applied in many areas that dates back to their former nomadic and communal life. Father and mother are called ata and ina only when there are no grandparents in the same house. If these relatives are cohabiting, grandfather is called ata (father), grandmother is called ina (mother), father is called aka (elder brother), and mother, apa (elder sister).

When talking to a small child and teaching him to talk, the mother and father do not use the correct words but words that often do not even resemble the correct ones, simple sounds that can be easily learned and pronounced by the child. For instance, instead of issiq (hot), the child is taught to say *pa-pa*; instead of *emchak* (breast), *mama*; instead of *chiroyliq* (beautiful), *ayai*, etc. Similar to us, locals have the habit of mispronouncing the words with "r" on purpose when they talk to children, which is especially popular among women; however, children who mispronounce "r" are very rarely seen. Much more often girls aged eight to twelve mispronounce words with "r," which is nothing but an attempt to be coquettish and fashionable.

We met healthy, beautiful children with round, wholesome faces and rosy cheeks everywhere, but round, muscular arms and legs or proportionately developed stomachs are found mainly among children before ages two or three. Later, by the age of five or six, their legs and arms become thin and narrow, and stomachs, disproportionately large. In their sixth or seventh year, most children retain some roundness in their faces only, which may be due to high cheekbones. All of this is evidence that the nutrition of native children is insufficient, which coupled with the terrible hygienic situation, cannot help adversely impacting the number of deaths and diseases. In winter, the city is plagued by smallpox, while crowds of children run in the dirt or snow wearing unbelted short robe, or barefoot, or else in galoshes worn on bare feet, and often without pants; why they do not die by the thousands boggles the mind.

As soon as the child starts walking, his mother significantly reduces attention to him and almost never bathes him. He bathes on his own initiative, mainly in summer, in some muddy ariq, where he and his companions, boys and girls, wallow for days on end.

Apart from the extremely widespread skin diseases, which are a direct consequence of the dirt in which a child lives, other frequent childhood diseases are indigestion, smallpox, measles, scarlet fever, whooping cough, flu, and edema. We have already discussed medical treatments earlier.

A child who dies, similar to an adult, is buried immediately or as soon as possible—i.e., on the same day or the morning of the next day. After a child's funeral, its mother avoids leaving the yard and goes into mourning; the deceased child is considered an angel who prays for the sins of its parents.

If both parents die, orphaned children are raised by their relatives, and the property they receive is entrusted to a guardian. There are three types of guardians: (1) natural, such as grandparents, uncles, and other male relatives, or the mother if she is familiar with inheritance laws; (2) those appointed in the will; and (3) those appointed by the authorities in the absence of the first two.

Religion regards guardianship and bringing up orphans as ways of enacting godliness, but in the majority of real-life cases the situation of orphans, especially small children, is extremely unenviable. Children who were left something from their father's inheritance, if their mother remarries a different husband, often receive nothing except food from their stepfather, and they have to buy clothes with their own money.

We should also point out that in middle-class families, the situation of all children, especially boys, differs little from the situation of hired workers and other servants. They are always dressed worse than their father and scarcely better than the workers, they rise when the house owner enters the room, they hold the reins when the latter mounts a horse or dismounts it, they sweep the floor, drive the plow, etc. That is why the relationship between the workers and the home owner's sons is often better than between the sons and the father. (This is not so obvious in wealthy houses where the conditions for children are different.)

When a child reaches the age of three or four, he gets out of hand, so to speak; another one usually takes his place. The mother, concentrating her care on a newborn, leaves the comparatively grown-up one to the older children, who are always lazy about this duty, or to his own devices.

This is also is when the child receives footwear for the first time, not only in poor but even in middle-class families; these are usually boots or galoshes that are worn over bare feet in winter only, because in summer he goes barefoot.

Girls in wealthy or well-off families start dressing up when guests come or when they go visiting; they are dressed up in silk shirts and robes, decorated with corals, etc.

If there are several children in the family, one of them, usually the youngest, becomes the favorite, *erka* [spoiled], indulged by everyone, dressed up and spoiled in the most unconscionable way.

As soon as the child starts understanding speech, he becomes if not an active then at least a passive participant in conversations among elders. In the child's presence, they discuss everything and everyone, calling everything by its name. The child is sent away only in those cases when the adults are afraid that he will carelessly repeat what he heard and harm the speakers. Thus, six- or seven-year-old Sart children know all about things that are often kept as a mystery from many of our fifteen- to seventeen-year-old young ladies,[10] yet in spite of this, we have not noticed that it does them any harm to have such a relationship with their parents.

The only thing that we can attest in this regard is that most Sart children talk with extreme sensibility and credibility; we should also add that the children of the poor and middle classes are more sensible than children of the wealthy, and urban children are sharper than children from kishlaks. Finally, the children of the urban poor classes are even a bit too experienced and sober minded: having reached age nine or eleven, they know perfectly not only where, what, and how to buy or how to sell things with profit but even where, what, and how to pilfer.

As soon as a child begins talking freely, his parents gradually teach him the basic dogmas of religion and some of the most popular prayers, as well as the rules of politeness, to the extent they know them. In any decent and well-off family, the six- or seven-year-old child starts greeting guests with salam, addressing them with the formal "you," and not touching food served to guests. At the same time, children in poor families learn from their mothers to beg, cajole, and scrounge. However, they cajole things only from strangers. In poor homes, where there is not always an extra piece of flat bread or a bowl of some porridge, but also in wealthier homes, especially in cities, children are disciplined so much that they rarely ask for food.

A Sart girl whom we took into our home never asked for anything in the beginning, until she relaxed and grew familiar with new rules and ways; she only looked into our eyes intensely, signaling that if we gave her something to eat, she would not be averse to that. This habit was instilled in her at home so intensely that it took us a lot of effort to break it. Not daring to ask, she was caught stealing more than once. Later, when she learned not only to ask but also to eat enough to satisfy her hunger, her stealing disappeared completely.

No matter how sensible a Sart child is or how capable of understanding the conversation of adults, it interests him very little; that is why if he has eaten enough and the weather is not too cold outside, he always looks for an opportunity to disappear from the house and go to the street. Heat does not deter him. A boy or girl, four or five years old, bronze colored, often with a bare head or completely naked, sits in the middle of the street with his or her playmates and builds a qo'rg'on, a fortress constructed from a thick layer of the street mud.

At age five or six, he or she starts participating in various children's games in the street, whose actors include both boys and girls up to the age of eight or nine.

They play ball, knucklebones,[11] throw stones, and play hide-and-seek. Another popular and noisier game is called *oq-terak*. Children are divided into two equal teams. Each team holds hands and forms a line; both lines stand facing each other. One of the lines sings the words:

"Oq terak mi? Ko'k terak?
Bizdan sizga kim kerak?"

(A white or a gray poplar?
Which one of us do you want?)

The name of this or that child is called. The child who was called runs toward the opposite line and tries to break it; if he succeeds, he takes one person from the opposite line into his line; if he fails, he stays in the opposite line, and the game continues.

In the early spring, before it becomes really hot, most boys abandon all the other games and engage exclusively in flying kites, which are made in a great variety of forms, from rectangular to bird or dragon shaped. The girls, who are not allowed to participate in that activity, run around with balls.

Almost all the children's games are accompanied with various refrains, songs, or adages.

Several boys and girls, ages five to nine, are playing ball in the street. A caravan of camels passes by. The children stop playing, gather together, jump, and sing:

"Lo'q-lo'q, tuyalar!
Achchiq, achchiq tuyalar!"
(Camels, camels!
Bitter camels!)[12]

A group of Kyrgyz men passes by, and a jumping crowd of children sings:

"Kyrgyz, Kyrgyz, qirildi;
Bir burchakka tiqildi;
O'layi, o'layi, deganda,
Ketmon olin yugurdi!"
(Kyrgyz, Kyrgyz all died;
All crowded in one corner,
And when the hungry death came,
They all grabbed spades and ran in all directions.)[13]

(This is mocking the Kyrgyz, who have been left only with land in the mountains and who take up farming only in situations of direst necessity.)

A group of children playing in the middle of the street sees a Sart approaching with an appearance that pranksters find funny. Jokes and hushed laughter are heard. The Sart comes closer. The children let him pass, stepping aside, and one of the sharpest bows with an air of extreme importance, pressing his palms to his stomach and saying, "As-salam alaykum"; the Sart responds in a similar manner—"Alaykum-as-salam"—and passes by. The children wink to each other and shout as he recedes: "Baka!" [*qurbaqa*] (frog). The Sart slowly turns his head, producing the greeting corresponding to the situation; and the naughty boys and girls disperse in all directions with shouts and shrieks of laughter, hiding behind gates and doors from the anticipated chase.

Similar pranks are played on Russians, too. When Qo'qon was conquered, and children there, like most children from large cities, were especially daring and mischievous, some not-too-clever Russians immediately sensed a political undertone to the children's pranks and appealed to the authorities to introduce corporal punishment for challenging the national pride of the Russians; they even suggested punishing the parents of the mischievous little Sarts in order to instill the idea of respect to everything Russian.

Children enjoy not only songs and chants but also rhymes and riddles.

In the early spring, one of the most popular songs that one can hear is

"Lailak keldi, yoz bo'ldi;
Eski chopan buzvardi."
(The storks have come, the summer has started.
The old robe is torn up.)

Here are some of the riddles:

(1) "Tap-tap etadi
Tagidan karvon o'tadi."
(It produces the sound: tap-tap
And a caravan passes below it.) Answer: A sieve to sift flour.
(2) Snow is falling on one side and hail on the other.
(Cleaning seeds from cotton. Cotton fiber goes to one side of the chig'iriq and seeds; chigit, to the other.)
(3) It walks and walks and does not look back. (Water.)
(4) "Havuzning ustida bulak
Bulakning ustida chiroq;
Chiroqning ustida qalam;
Qalamning ustida changal;
Changalning ichida to'ngiz."
(Above the pond a spring, above the spring a lamp, above the lamp a reed pen, above the pen a thicket, and above the thicket a pig.) Answer: Mouth, nose, eyes, brows, hair, and an insect.

Fairy tales are the favorite pastime for children on long winter nights, and their tales are very similar to ours (golden fish, Baba-Yaga, flying carpet). Here are some examples.

The first fairy tale: There once was a Sart. His wife died; he was left with a son and a daughter. Then he married another wife. After a while, the new wife got pregnant and became ill tempered. Once she told her husband, "Slay your son; I will eat him." The Sart was sorry for the boy, but he also wanted to please his wife. He called his son to go into the garden to collect stalks for kindling. After a while he returned without the boy and told his wife, "Go under the tent roof; you will find what you asked for under a sheaf of brushwood." The wife went out, found, and boiled the stepchild under the sunshade and threw the bones out into the yard. The next day the stepdaughter saw the bones, recognized them as her brother's bones, and burst into tears. She cried and cried, then collected the bones, put them into a small satchel, and hung it on a mulberry tree. The bones turned into a turtledove. A peddler passed by. "Sing a song to me, turtledove!" "Give me a needle, and I will sing." The peddler gave it a needle, and it sang him a song. He liked it. "Sing me another song!" "Give me another needle." The peddler gave it another needle, and it sang him another song. The father went to the mosque and saw a turtledove on the mulberry tree, not singing. "Sing me a song, turtledove." "Close your eyes and open your mouth; then I will sing you a song." The moment when the father closed his eyes and opened his mouth, the turtledove threw a needle into it. The needle went right down into his innards. The father died instantaneously. The stepmother went out into the yard to bake bread and saw the turtledove on the mulberry tree. "Sing me a song, turtledove!" "Close your eyes and open your mouth; then I will sing to you." As soon as she closed her eyes and opened her mouth, the turtledove threw the needle into her mouth; and the stepmother died instantaneously. Then the turtledove flew down to the ground, did a somersault, and turned into a good-looking boy.

The second tale: Once, in a certain kingdom, there lived a sultan who had forty vizirs. One of them was his favorite, and the rest of the vizirs envied him and decided to do him in. Once they came to the sultan and said, "Taqsir [my lord], you need to decorate your palace like this: make two ponds from the shell of a walnut so that water would flow from one into the other. Order your favorite vizir to do that." The sultan called his favorite vizir and told him to accomplish this in forty days. The vizir became sad and went for a walk in the steppe to think how he could avoid the sultan's anger. There, Saint Khizr[14] appeared to him, gave him two walnut shells, and told him to dig them into the ground in the yard of the sultan's fortress. The vizir went there, dug, and placed the shells in the sultan's yard: suddenly water appeared and began flowing from one shell into the other. The envious men saw what he had done, and they went to the sultan again. "Taqsir, you should build a house that would touch neither the ground nor the sky. Tell your favorite one to make it for you." The sultan called his favorite vizir and told him, "Build me a house within forty days that will touch neither the ground nor the sky. You need only find the masons, and I will provide the materials and the other workers." The vizir grew even sadder and went wandering around the world out of grief. An old man joined him while he was walking. They walked together and reached the city where the vizir's companion lived. The old man invited the vizir to be his guest. It turned out that the old man had a beautiful daughter: she fell in love with the vizir and married him. On the first day after the wedding, the vizir was sitting and sighing. His young wife asked him what was wrong. He told her that the sultan had ordered him to build such and such a house. The young wife said, "Go to the field, and catch a young lark." The vizir went to the field, caught a young lark, and brought it to his wife. Within a few days, she taught him to cry, "Loy! G'isht!" (These were the words that native masons use to make the workers bring them cement, loy, and bricks, *g'isht*.)

Then they went to the sultan. The vizir said, "My workers are ready; tell them to start working." Bricks and cement were piled up and day laborers gathered. The vizir surreptitiously threw the lark up, and it flew into the sky and started crying, "Loy! G'isht!" The workers kept throwing bricks up, but they kept falling down, never having reached the invisible masons. Only then the sultan understood that this task was impossible, and later he realized that the very idea was an intrigue of the envious vizirs.

The third tale: Once upon a time, on the bank of a wide, deep river with clear water, there was a large *tugai* (a thicket of bushes, reeds, etc.). It was inhabited by wild boars, goats, hares, foxes, and other wild beasts. They all lived in peace and harmony because there was enough food and space for all. It would have been a wonderful life, but a tiger moved into their tugai. It started catching and eating the wild boars and goats, hares, and foxes. The animals gathered for a meeting. They argued and discussed the matter but could not come to any decision. Then the fox suggested the following: "Rather than all of us living in constant fear, let us decide the following: we will form a line and voluntarily go and offer ourselves as a snack to the tiger; I will go and negotiate with him about it, and for this you will excuse all my progeny from being in that line." The animals agreed. The fox went to the tiger and said, "Taqsir, why should you chase us all over the place and worry; better that you should lie here peacefully, and I will bring you different animals every day to eat." The tiger agreed. The fox started bringing some of his friends, but soon the tiger was not satisfied with this: he started chasing and eating animals in addition to those that came to be eaten voluntarily. The animals were alarmed and called another meeting. A jerboa took the floor and said, "Hide in your holes and dens for a few days, and don't leave them; and don't go to the tiger voluntarily to be eaten by it; I will fix the rest." All the animals went into hiding. The tiger waited for a day, then for another day, but nobody came. It got hungry and became angry. Then the jerboa came to him and said, "Taqsir! There is a new tiger in our tugai; it looks like you, but it is even fiercer. It has strangled many animals, and the others ran away, so our kingdom is deserted now. Of course, you are stronger than your adversary, and you should fight him to restore order. Kill him, and then all the animals will return to our tugai and will start coming to be eaten by you again."

The tiger agreed. The jerboa took him to the place where his adversary was hiding. It brought the tiger to a steep bank of the river and said, "Look down; it must be there."

The tiger looked down and saw its own reflection in the water; he thought that it was his enemy, jumped down, and drowned. Ever since then, peace and calm have reigned in the tugai.

* * *

Stories are usually told in winter, in the evening, when adults are unoccupied. Then spring comes, and it gets warm. Everyone starts working. Children who got used to winter and to hearing tales pester their parents: please, tell us a tale, tell us a tale. The parents are busy, and they send them away; children start crying. The children are then scared with a story that anyone who listens to tales not in winter but in spring or summer will grow teeth in the wrong places. Although listening to tales is fun, children are afraid of teeth growing out of place, and they run into the street, where they spend most of their time till the next winter comes.

From age eight or nine, girls play mostly with other girls and not with boys. From this time until she is given in marriage, her main toys are dolls (*qo'g'irchoq*), which are mostly ugly and which she makes herself. Girls sew shirts, robes, bedding, and pillows for their dolls. The dolls get married, bear children, and die. Usually, several girls play dolls together. They sing songs at doll weddings and wail at doll funerals. Sometimes, when girls get bored with playing dolls, they play *mehmon-mehmon* (guests): some girls play guests, and others, hostesses; or they play wedding, where one of the girls is the bride and one of the younger brothers is convinced to play the groom. Girls of this age have fistfights very rarely, but they yell at each other without any restraint. Since cursing is extremely widespread among the Sarts, especially in the lower classes, nobody pays attention to cursing children and nobody tries to stop them, which is why children attain a degree of perfection in that art. Children curse with passion and authority; they have an enormous vocabulary of stereotypical phrases. The only limitation the society and parents impose on them is that they use only the curse words and phrases that are appropriate for their gender.

We have seen cases when a mother would slap her daughter not because she heard her cursing but because she was using curses that were used only by men— i.e., she was promising actions that she would not be physically capable of doing.

At about this age, eight or nine, girls are taught to saw, clean cotton, and spin. It is usually the mother who teaches the girl and, more rarely, a female relative. If there is opportunity and interest, it is also the age when the girl is taught literacy. As a result of the latter, girls can often read the Koran or parts of it without understanding what they are reading; they sometimes can read books in the Turkic language, with difficulty; less often they can write a short letter with many spelling mistakes. Truly literate women are very rare. However, during the rule of Omar-khan (1816–1821), there were two female poets in Qo'qon: one of them wrote under the pen name Zinnat and the other under the pen name Maxzuna. It is said that one of them would come to the khan's court wearing male dress with her face uncovered, and she possessed a general's title, *dodxoh*. Both of their works were included in the *Majmu-i-Shuara*, a collection of poems written by Omar-khan himself and his court poets.[15]

Girls are taught to read and write by a female teacher, otin, and classes usually take place at the teacher's home, applying almost the same method that we mentioned previously when we described the elementary school for boys (maktab).

When the girl's hair grows long by the age of nine or ten, it is braided into several small braids with one or two braids put over her ears.

She stops wearing skullcaps and starts tying a scarf over her head like adult women do.

At about the same time a girl in a wealthy family receives a complete set of jewelry, such as necklaces, rings, earrings, and bracelets; she starts paying more attention to her appearance and studies the details of the native science of flirting. It often happens that though she used to speak correctly, she now starts mispronouncing her "r"s or "sh" sounds, which, as we noted, is one of the weapons of flirtation among native girls. At the same time, she starts putting makeup on her eyelashes and dyeing her eyebrows, and before holidays she colors her nails and palms with saffron.

If parents want to marry her off in a hurry, they start adding years to her real age; instead of ten or eleven, she is now turning twelve.

If the girl is the eldest child in the family, other siblings call her apa or byovyo; they are somewhat afraid of her and obey her, sometimes more than their mother.

But it is her misfortune if she has an elder brother; her importance in the family is close to zero; she is just a baby-sitter or mother's helper; she has no voice even in the least important family affairs. The younger children notice this readily, and it is very hard for her to keep them disciplined or to have any influence over them. All importance rests on the elder brother.

In towns, when a girl reaches twelve or thirteen (and in kishlaks sometimes later than that), she starts wearing the paranji and chimbet. She is now called *balog'atga yetdi* (having come of age) or *ko'zga qo'rinib qoldi* (becoming attractive, making an impression). The girl turns into a young maiden, a bride.

8 The Maiden
Marriage Proposal and Marriage

A MAIDEN'S FIRST PARANJI is usually sewn not of the gray fabric that women typically wear but from white ticking with narrow red stripes.[1] Otherwise, her clothes and hairstyle remain the same as for younger girls. In cities, even in the poorest families, maidens are provided with soft boots; no longer are they allowed to walk barefoot, and galoshes on bare feet are worn only in summer at home.

All her street games with friends and peers are ended. The maiden starts participating more and more in household activities such as cooking, cleaning cotton, and spinning.

Now she can play and frolic at home as much as she wants, but when she is out in the street, she should behave, and she actually does behave, in a very reserved and proper way.

She rarely leaves the house alone, especially if she needs to go far. Often she is accompanied by one of her younger brothers or sisters. However, it is not considered shameful if several girlfriends get together and go somewhere without being accompanied. Such groups of maidens who are all of one age go together to Sayil, acrobatic performances, or bachcha dancing during holidays, etc.

The main forms of fun and entertainment for this age are dolls, which girls often are not done with even in the first years of marriage (fourteen or fifteen), and gatherings. Like women's gatherings, girls' gatherings can be divided into types: festive and work related. The latter are gatherings of maidens (and women) at someone's home, where they often bring their own work, or gatherings for help, when acquaintances are invited to assist with cleaning cotton or beating fiber, sewing bedding, or picking cotton. Most of these gatherings are accompanied with dancing, beating a tambourine, and singing. The dances are very similar to bachcha dancing. Singing is usually performed poorly, though some tunes are very melodious. They try to sing as loudly as possible and with the highest notes, which results in shrieking and yelling the song; in addition, many women (as well as men) sing in a nasal way, considering this especially delicate.

At the same time that the twelve- or thirteen-year-old girl starts wearing paranji and chimbet, adults start treating her differently. Women address her as if she were their peer and often, in her presence, mention the possibility of her getting married soon. If she continues playing dolls, she does that only with girls younger than herself. With friends her own age, her entertainment is not dolls but singing songs, dancing, and talking. Dreams are frequent topic of conversation, some of which can be fantasies, but almost all of them deal with what is going to happen to her in the future when she is married. It often happens that at the age of twelve or thirteen, the girl is overtaken by a strong desire to get married, and all her thoughts are directed exclusively to this. One of our Sart female friends open-heartedly confessed to us that when she was given away in marriage (around twelve or thirteen), she was very happy about it and was jumping and running around the house on the wedding day as if crazy, settling down only after she got spanked for completely forgetting the necessary wailing that a Sart bride must perform.

In her childhood, a girl makes girlfriends among her peers by playing together. Maidens make friends mainly by exchanging their thoughts; similarly to women, they grow close quickly, but we have not seen any long-term, close friendship among them. Their friendship starts quickly but also ends equally quickly, if not quicker, and the reason can be some very insignificant cause.

By the age of thirteen or fourteen the maiden's character is formed almost completely: it is generally identical with the character of a young woman. Very rarely does her character change under the influence of the early years of married life. But for the majority of young women who know fairly well what to expect after that milestone, marriage makes almost no impact on character. A much more important event, which happens later, is the birth of the first child. We have often seen examples when until nineteen or twenty, the young Sart woman remains exactly the same in habits and character as she was when she was given in marriage at age thirteen or fourteen. Restless, hot tempered, and sometimes even mean, she changes completely after giving birth to the first child; she becomes extremely calm and relaxed, starts working little by little, and does not show the hot temper that until recently was one of her main characteristics. We should note, however, that this kind of development in native women cannot be considered universal. It should rather be considered one of the best possible developments, because the main features of a young woman's character will remain with her to the grave.

While the maiden's character is formed, certain changes take place in her. By the age of fourteen or fifteen, sometimes earlier, her facial features coarsen. This is probably the result of climate and the sun's rays, as well as unsatisfactory nutrition and hygiene conditions in which most natives grow up and live. Frequently a maiden who was unbelievably good-looking and delicate in childhood grows much coarser and ugly before she gets married.

Menstruation begins on average at age fifteen. Sart women note that the age depends on the wealth of the family where the girl is raised. For instance, Sart women told us that daughters of butchers begin to menstruate at age twelve,[2] while daughters of arabakeshes, who are always busy with transporting goods to faraway places, start around eighteen or nineteen. The father who travels for extended periods of time often leaves the family without means of subsistence; this results in long periods when the family has to be satisfied with the most meager food, which explains delayed menstruation. (A bride's average age at birth of her first child is between sixteen and twenty, but the actual cohabitation between the husband and the wife starts right after the marriage—i.e., usually between thirteen and fifteen—and for most, menstruation begins after the girl is married.)

Old spinsters are comparatively rare and found mainly among the daughters of xo'jas, who, as we have mentioned earlier, themselves marry both maidens and women of the qoracha (commoners) indiscriminately but give their daughters in marriage only to men of their own rank, other xo'jas.

Several reasons explain the lack of spinsters here. First of all, Sarts are not very fastidious or demanding regarding beauty; second, if qalin is not expensive, a Sart always considers marriage to be an advantage because he acquires a partner in work; third, because of the comparative freedom of divorce, the risks of marrying are low for both parties; fourth, religion approves of marriage as something that is beneficial for every person, and especially beneficial for wives, who in a husband acquire a protector and defender of their rights; fifth, the utmost dream and wish of every Sart is leaving offspring to succeed him and the possibility of seeing descendants in his old age, so every Sart tries to marry young. Thus, for every maiden who is not extremely ugly, getting married is really almost guaranteed; all the more so because she does not even participate in the selection of the groom, because the proposal is made and accepted by the matchmakers and her parents, while she is not involved.

However, there are cases when a maiden remains unmarried until she is twenty to twenty-three. Usually, the reasons for that are these rather unusual conditions: either there are persistent rumors that she is an extremely bad worker, or the groom is too poor and it takes him several years to collect qalin, so the wedding has to be postponed, or, finally, the rich and haughty parents reject proposals for a long time, hoping to marry their daughter to someone more appropriate. (About three years ago one wealthy Sart family in Namangan delayed the search so much that their twenty-three-year-old daughter ran away with a Tatar.)

On average, native maidens marry between ages thirteen and fifteen, as we mentioned. Sometimes, there are cases of much earlier marriage, at ten or eleven. Such a young girl may move in with her husband, but she does not enter into a physical relationship with him; when the physical relationship starts with such an underage girl, she has been forcibly intoxicated with opium, and it is often followed by serious pathological consequences for her.

Native [men], like the majority of other ethnic groups, strongly prefer a virgin bride rather than a *juvon*, a woman who has lost her virginity, like a widow or a divorcée. Apart from the general human motivations, this is also explained by the following: first, religious belief pronounces that in the afterlife a woman will be the wife of her first husband (i.e., the one she married as a virgin); second, religion encourages marrying young women who are virgins (Koran, chapter 5, verse 7; chapter 4, verse 29; chapter 2, verse 235). But if a Sart decides to marry not a virgin but a juvon for some reason, he does not differentiate between a widow and a divorcée, as long as all the other conditions for this marriage, such as the age of the bride, the expenses for the wedding ceremony, etc., are appropriate. Most pay no attention to the number of previous husbands the divorced women had or her previous behavior.

In real-life situations, especially among the poor strata of the population, we have frequently encountered examples of women who engaged not only in clandestine but in open prostitution, who by promising to quit this way of life, easily managed to find a husband who completely ignored her past, because marriage is regarded as a way of redeeming one's past.

However, there are adverse conditions that force a man to prefer marrying a woman to a maiden. It is the case that qalin is paid only for a virgin. A Sart who marries a widow or a divorcée takes on only the expenses related to the wedding (feeding guests), which never exceeds 30 or 40 rubles among the poor classes and in some cases could be as low as 4 silver rubles.

Qalin is paid for a bride who is a juvon only in the following cases:

1. If she is not yet divorced from her husband, because she seeks a divorce, the law demands (under some circumstances) that she repays to her first husband the qalin that he gave when he married her.[3]
2. If the divorced woman owes money to her relatives who repaid her qalin to her first husband when she divorced him.

Under those conditions of divorce and subsequent remarriage, the [new] groom pays the required amount of money either to his bride's first husband or to her relatives. However, as we will see below, the divorcing woman is not always subject to these conditions because, first of all, divorced women and widows are able to act as free people, since after they entered their first marriage, their parents' power over them collapses, so they are now able to decide their own fate; and second, men can marry them without paying qalin, which significantly reduces their expenses for the wedding.

When giving a daughter in marriage (or a son marries), parents always prefer a marriage [to someone] closer both in physical distance and in kinship than to those far away; at the same time, when relatives intermarry, it is necessary to observe only the limits established by religion (Koran, chapter 4).

A bride and her relatives prefer marriage to someone nearby, because if she goes too far away from the parents and other relatives, the young woman will find herself in a distant land, will miss her family in the beginning, and will not have reliable defenders of her interests and rights. The parents of the groom prefer a marriage to a close relative, since there are hopes to settle affairs as between relatives, paying a lower qalin.

In cities, it is not uncommon that the groom does not know and has never seen his bride; he sees her for the first time after the wedding, when she is brought to his house. This manner of arranging a marriage and undertaking a wedding is considered normal and necessary; therefore, the Sart often does not admit to actually having seen his bride before the wedding or before the engagement. Rules of decency require concealing the fact that the bride was looked over (and perhaps much more than that) long before the wedding. In most cases when a Sart marries a girl from his own kishlak or urban quarter, he knows very well whom he is marrying and what his future wife is like. First, he saw his bride when she was a girl, when she ran around in the streets with her face open; second, if that did not happen, his female relatives arranged for him to be able to look at the girl before the proposal was made or before the wedding—for instance, during sumalak, a ritual that was described earlier—third, when a marriage is arranged in a kishlak, the groom can see the bride during the cotton harvest, etc. As far as the maiden is concerned, it is much easier for her to see the groom since men do not hide or cover their faces.

Thus, most of those getting married, if they live in the same village or the same urban quarter, always have the opportunity to look each other over. (Not to mention close neighbors, which presents an even easier case.) At the same time, marriages based on love or, at least, some kind of mutual attraction, do not happen very often. This is because, first, consent to a proposal is usually given not by the girl but by her parents, who are mainly concerned with purely material questions; and second, because there are very few situations where it would be possible to have a fully free, moral coming-together between a man and a maiden. That is why marriages based on love are seen not among maidens but young widows and divorcées, who due to social position as more or less self-sustaining women, have much broader opportunities than maidens do to interact with men under very diverse conditions. For instance, we knew a young, unmarried arabakesh who happened to be driving a woman whom he did not know from another city to his hometown. They spent about three days on the road. The conversation was lively. It turned out that his passenger was a young widow who was not opposed to remarriage. During the journey, when they were crossing unpopulated regions, she would lift her chimbet, revealing her face. The arabakesh looked her over and decided to marry her. After some debate, the young man's father agreed to his son's marriage to a widow, and they married.

No matter how rare love-based marriages are for maidens, they still happen. We knew a wealthy merchant family, whose daughter, age fourteen or fifteen, fell for the neighbor. Once they were caught together; naturally, the matter did not pass without a beating and scandal. Despite that, a couple of months after the incident, it became clear that the daughter was already in the second half of her pregnancy, and the parents had to hurry to marry the pregnant girl and her lover willy-nilly. The elder sister ran away with a Tatar man, and the local poet could not forgo this opportunity to write a long and rather caustic *hajv* (satire).

In the old times there used to be a custom of arranging marriages when the children were still in the cradle (*beshikkerti*). The reasons for such matchmaking are usually the following: first, a friendly relationship between the parents of the boy and the girl; second, because this way of proposing marriage allows for plenty of time between the agreement and the wedding, so paying qalin is much easier. This custom continues among the nomadic population, where costlier qalin is demanded than what Sarts usually pay.

Similarly, the custom of arranging a marriage when the children are age nine to twelve is also gradually disappearing. Recently, this is rare and practiced only in wealthy families, where the fathers were either wealthy merchants or from the elite class of the khan's servitors.

As we said, the native maiden gets married around the age of thirteen to fifteen. Young men, who themselves or whose parents can pay qalin immediately, marry starting at sixteen to eighteen. Parents decide that it is time to marry their son or at least arrange a bride for him. After discussion, they decide on a particular girl. They send matchmakers, relatives, or close acquaintances to the girl's family. When arranging a marriage to a bride from a stranger's family, the matchmaker not only examines the girl but also pays attention to the cleanliness and tidiness of the house, since it is believed that the mother of the bride passes on both good and bad qualities.

If the proposal is accepted, the bride's mother presents the matchmaker with a scarf, towel, or some other present.

(Sometimes the family asks for some time to think; the relatives of the bride visit the home of the groom and carry out their own examination, after which the groom's matchmaker goes, a few days later, a second time, to get the answer.)

On the day after the matchmakers bring the consent, men set out to the house of the bride and arrange the amount of qalin, *mahr*, and other details.[4]

If a mutual agreement is achieved, the male or female relatives of the groom visit the house of the bride for a third time, taking plov, flat bread, and various presents (depending on their wealth), such as galoshes, looking glasses, cotton or silk fabrics, etc. In wealthy houses, the value of the first present (*sar-silla*) can sometimes be very high, and similar presents will be given in return. On those trays that carried the groom's gifts to the bride's home are placed items of similar value, and they are taken to the groom's house. Such exchange of presents is called *idish-qaitar* (return of dishes).

People who delivered presents from the groom are treated to a meal in the bride's house, after which one of the men present announces, "Allah akbar" (God is great), and this concludes the engagement ritual on behalf of the main parties.

In poor families, the first present to the bride is usually not very valuable. In cities it is customary to send, along with those gifts, a cartload of fuel and supplies for the meal, in exchange for which the groom receives scarves, sashes, robes, or something like that.

Qalin is usually paid by the parents of the groom; the latter personally pays if he owns property after separating from his father and elder brothers. The amount of qalin varies widely. We knew marriages where it was only 12 or 15 rubles; maidens given under such conditions were either full orphans or came from extremely poor parents. In wealthy merchant families, the size of qalin paid by the groom or his parents rises to several hundred rubles; in addition, the bride's parents add an approximately equal amount of money to the sum received from the groom; all this goes toward providing a dowry and organizing the wedding. Qalin is paid in money (cash) only in cities. In kishlaks, it is paid mostly in livestock and wheat.

Depending on the age of the groom and the bride as well as the wealth of the groom, either qalin is paid immediately or the payment is spread over a significant amount of time and done in installments. In the second case, the installments are usually paid annually on the eve of Ramadan, and the bride receives not only the planned installment but also presents, such as shoes, clothing, and fabrics. The groom's parents try to keep the best possible relationship with their quda [future in-laws]; however, this is not always easy. Often the bride's parents start getting hard to please when they are receiving partial qalin and dismiss the matchmakers, who showed up with a bony little cow or mare, hoping to get away with poor payment this time, without much fuss, like relatives.

The amount of qalin paid for a maiden by a family of average means, both in cities and in kishlaks (in addition to the money paid by the groom for the wedding feast), rarely exceeds 70 to 80 silver rubles. One of the indispensable parts of qalin in most areas is 5 to 15 puds of uncleaned cotton bolls. The bride's family cleans and processes it partly into thread and partly into stuffing for bedding, pillows, etc. Upon receiving the qalin, the bride's parents are obliged to use that amount to provide their daughter with bedding and pillows when they send her to her husband and to produce a full set of clothing for both of the newlyweds, as well as provide a wedding feast.

Customarily, qalin can be regarded as the groom's payment for all the expenses related to concluding the marital union. It does not have the character of the groom buying the bride, since the bride's parents, after receiving qalin from the groom, must spend it for all of the customary expenses.

Even when the amount of qalin exceeds the anticipated wedding expenses, most of the natives regard the extra money that the parents receive not as a payment for their daughter but as a reward for expenses and care they provided when they were raising her. The importance and the role of qalin change only later, if the wife initiates a divorce without sufficient legal cause. Then the husband can demand a return of all of the money that he spent to get married. In the latter case, qalin is a sort of guarantee against his wife leaving him arbitrarily and groundlessly. A similar guarantee for the woman, though of a much smaller size, is mahr, which, according to custom established through local practice, is the wedding gift from the groom to his future wife and at the same time a means providing her financial safety in case of a divorce initiated by the husband.[5]

Mahr is received by the woman in two ways: either when she is getting married or after that, as well as at the time of divorce.

The first case is more rarely practiced among the natives than the second one, usually only between well-off or rich people or if the parents of the bride doubt the ability of the would-be husband to fulfill his obligations conscientiously toward their daughter.

Conditions on the amount of mahr are always included with the other conditions of the marriage.

Payment of mahr is usually expressed by transferring into the wife's name a house, a small garden, a land lot, etc. This property becomes part of the wife's heritable property and, as we have already mentioned, provides her with the practical means of living in case of a divorce.

If mahr is given to the wife in the form of land or other real estate property, in most cases the husband manages the revenue it brings, and the wife keeps only the document confirming that she has the right to alienate it from the rest of her husband's or family property into her own exclusive use and possession.

The cost of such mahr in middle classes rarely exceeds 100 or 150 rubles. More often when marriage is contracted, mahr is not immediately requested from the husband; only its amount is set.

In most cases the amount of mahr is equal to the qalin, but in case of marriage to a widow or a divorcée, it (mahr) is much smaller than the mahr given for a maiden, as low as 2 silver rubles.

As we have already said, the period of time between the match and the wedding varies, lasting from several days to several years. In wealthy families the age of the bride and the groom is the main consideration when determining the timing, since there are cases of matching underage children and even small children, but most parents do not allow marriages too early for either sons or daughters.[6]

In poor families, the major factor lengthening the time between the match and the wedding is payment of qalin. Because of the groom and his parents' poverty, the payment of qalin often drags out for two or three years, in spite of the fact that the bride has already come of age.

Under such conditions, especially if the family of the bride is as poor as the family of the groom, the matter rarely proceeds without scandals and squabbles, and the results often adversely affect the well-being of both sides.

This is how it usually happens. If the matchmaking is conducted between families that are related or well acquainted, it often happens that during the matchmaking the size of the qalin or the amount of expenses for the wedding that the groom and his parents must provide according to custom are not exactly settled. The reason negotiations remain unsettled is that both sides hope to trick each other. The bride's parents feed on the hope of getting more, because of the lack of exact arrangement, and the groom's parents console themselves that they might give less. When it comes to paying the real money, the conflict often escalates so quickly that it takes all the elderly people from the village to calm the sides down.

But this is often not the end of it. We noted that in poor families the payment of qalin is often spread over several years.

Installments are paid on a yearly basis. The bride's parents urge faster payment. The groom's side spends beyond their means to meet the demands, harms their own economic well-being, and still cannot accumulate sufficient funds to fully pay qalin.

At the same time, the parents of the bride, who are receiving qalin in installments, start spending it for their daily needs and try not to think about the future wedding and the need to provide clothing for the newlyweds.

The day of the wedding comes. Most of the qalin was spent long ago. Then the old Sart saying often comes true, that after the wedding of the daughter, there is nothing left in the parents' house, not even a broom.

Needless to say, in such cases, instead of bedding, pillows, and dresses, the parents provide their daughter some sort of useless trash, and when she comes to the house of her husband, she often encounters dire poverty brought about by efforts the groom's family made trying to pay qalin.

Despite the obvious inconvenience and often even adverse consequences of this custom, paying and receiving qalin and the subsequent obligation of providing the dowry, the custom is so established in practice that nonobservance would be considered indecent, while women often pride themselves on the amount that was paid.

However, recently, changes to this custom have been seen among the poor population, especially in cities and large towns.

There are cases when qalin is replaced with expenses for the wedding only and the groom makes his own dowry for the wife according to his own means. This leads to two extremely important consequences: first, it eliminates the extremely disadvantageous financial transfer of qalin from one party to another. Second, the abolition of qalin frees the woman from some of the obligations, oppression, and disadvantages that she encounters in case of divorce when the qalin was paid to her parents, because if the groom does not pay qalin but covers only the wedding expenses, the amount of money he can demand back in case of a divorce (initiated by the wife) is reduced considerably and in most cases can be covered with mahr.

Probably like everywhere, the position of the bride is enviable. Everyone is trying to please her, including her own parents. If the groom is well off, she receives presents from him, buys sweets for herself, and dresses in fashionable clothes, which she never before or again could afford.

According to custom, after the marriage arrangement, the bride carefully hides from all the relatives of the groom, and the groom equally hides and avoids meeting the relatives of the bride. Sometimes this leads to comic scenes. In small kishlaks, it is natural that everyone knows who is engaged to whom. The groom goes to a small kishlak market, approaches an araba with melons surrounded by a crowd of people, and does not notice that the father of the bride is standing almost next to him. If he has not noticed it, the people in the crowd have and start giggling. The groom and the father of the bride look around, notice each other, seem petrified for a few seconds, and run in different directions, surrounded by laughter.

In some kishlaks, there is a semiofficial custom that the groom meets with the bride long before the wedding or even sleeps with her. (This custom is not practiced in cities.) This is how it is done. After the engagement has been concluded and part of the qalin has been paid, one of the female relatives of the groom goes to the bride's mother and arranges with her which evening the groom can see his bride. On the appointed night, when it is quite dark, the groom, carrying some presents and some sweets, starts toward the bride's house. He is taken to some faraway room so that he does not encounter his future mother- or father-in-law. At this meeting, the purpose of which is to give the engaged pair the opportunity to get to know each other and get used to each other before the wedding, at least one of the bride's female relatives is present. In her presence, the engaged couple lies down to sleep, and her main obligation is not to leave the room but observe them so that they do not go too far. Before dawn the groom must leave so that nobody sees him.

These visits continue for a while without any hindrance, and later no relatives are present so that the engaged couple enters into a physical relationship.

We knew a case when the payment of qalin took a long time, and the parents had to hurry with the wedding because the bride was in her last month of pregnancy.

An engagement's cancellation after payment of at least partial qalin is very rare since it is not beneficial for the side that announces the cancellation. The groom (if the refusal comes from him) loses the portion of qalin that has been paid, and the parents of the bride (if they initiate the refusal) must immediately repay everything that the groom has given them.[7]

The same calculations are made in case of the death of either the groom or the bride. If the groom dies, the bride's parents retain qalin; if the bride dies, qalin paid for her has to be returned.

Weddings are usually conducted in the fall or in winter, since, first, this is the time when everyone is free, and, second, all the necessary food, grain, cotton, etc., for the wedding can be prepared in spring or summer.

If the groom does not delay qalin, the wedding date is set in advance. On the eve of or a few days before the wedding, a bride's party (majlis) is conducted, which is mainly attended by her girlfriends, as well as women acquainted with her family. They sing songs, dance, and eat together.[8]

The marriage ritual itself usually takes place in the evening, in the house of the bride, and does not feature any special festivities. A local imom is invited from the mosque; and the bride is placed in the corner of the room behind a curtain. The groom comes with two or more witnesses from his relatives. The imom asks the groom and the bride if they agree to marry each other. A maiden, whose shyness is taken into account, is allowed to respond with silence; a woman must give an appropriately open answer.[9]

When this mutual agreement is obtained, the imom says a prayer and the marriage, *nikoh*, is considered concluded.

The groom and his accompanying witnesses then are treated to a meal and leave.

According to the groom and the bride's wishes, the marriage contract is written and signed at the same time as the marriage is concluded. It states the amount of qalin and mahr that have been paid or the obligation to pay the latter upon request.

The document is concluded by the seal of the local qozi.[10]

Delivering the bride to the groom is conducted in various ways in different regions. In cities, it usually takes place when the nikoh is finished and, in most kishlaks, only several days later. In Namangan, it is done at night; in Qo'qon, at dawn; and in many kishlaks, during the day.

A few hours before the young bride is taken away, female relatives and acquaintances get together in her home. The bride is dressed in a clean shirt, always white and usually lacy, and her head is covered with several scarves tied in the form of a turban. She sits down in the middle of the room dressed in this way, and her female relatives and friends surround her and start wailing.

Having wailed to their hearts' content, they raise the bride up and cover her with a chimbet and paranji. Her father guides her out of the room. As soon as they step into the courtyard, all the wailing stops. In the street, one or two arabas are waiting and a crowd of small children, some of them with tambourines. The bride seats herself on one araba along with as many women as can possibly fit; her dowry is piled onto the other. The column sets off. The horse barely manages to pull the araba with all the women sitting on it; boys grab its wheels and pull them to slow it down, beat the tambourines, and shout a wedding song at the top of their voices:

"Hoi keladur ko'zi bilan
Yar, yar, yar—do'st, do'st, do'st!
Bir birisin izi bilan
Yar ma padar!"[11]

The column creeps to a halt as it reaches the groom's gates. By that time everyone who could not fit on the araba has gathered there. They guide the bride into the courtyard, and the crowd stops at the gate. One of the matchmakers takes the bride by the waist and, walking slowly forward, shouts out the names of the groom and all his relatives, male and female, according to their seniority, and greets each person separately with a salam.

Thus the procession enters the yard. Then the matchmaker announces for the last time, "To the great and the small, to everyone as-salam!" The women enter the house, and the men go into the mehmon-xona, and then the feast starts; its extent, character, and length depend on the host's wealth.

The bride is placed behind a curtain, where she stays for three days, without showing herself to the new kin. This is how the celebration ends. In some areas, the mother and the father of the bride come the following day to visit her, bringing plov with them, as well a robe for the father and the mother of their son-in-law. In other areas, mainly in kishlaks, on the morning of the third day after the wedding, the bride goes and spends a whole day with her parents. In the evening they send for the groom and his parents, who are treated to a meal and given presents, after which the bride returns to her home and no longer hides from the new kin.

The newlyweds are usually placed in a separate room.

The cases when they move in not with the husband's parents but with the wife's are comparatively rare and take place only when the bride comes from a wealthier family than the groom or if the latter has neither parents nor a place of his own.

Living with the husband's parents, the young couple do not divide their resources, since they mostly have none. They eat from the same pot as their parents do; their clothes are either provided by the husband's father or bought with their own earnings.

In the first couple of months the old parents avoid burdening the young bride with housework, giving her some time to look around and get used to the new family and its way of living. Later, the mother-in-law gradually makes her do almost all the housework.

At the same time, these two women often start quarreling, and within a year the young couple starts seriously considering moving to a separate place. There are many reasons that make them want to do so. The young wife thinks that she has been tasked with too much work and that the mother-in-law rebukes her too often for being lazy and a sponger. The young husband is unhappy that his father gives them too little money from the common share for his bride's clothing, etc.

Since these stories occur repeatedly in almost every family, in many areas, among the wealthier families, it has become popular to let the young couple move out and live separately one year after the wedding. Often this separation is initiated by the old parents themselves, and the year is given to the new couple to get used to each other and let the young wife learn to do housework on her own.

In most such cases, the parents facilitate this voluntary separation by providing the young couple with a separate house, working livestock, and all the necessary utensils.

Either the house for the young couple is built on the same lot where the parents' garden is, or another lot is purchased nearby; at the same time, a son from an agricultural family continues working on his father's land as a qo'shchi [plowman] (see the conditions for that above) or receives a temporary right to use some of his father's land, which he exploits for his own profit until the final division, usually at his father's death.

However, despite what was said above, there are frequent cases even in wealthy families when the old parents provide the young couple with such miserable things and conditions that the separation no longer looks like a division but more like a simple eviction of the young people out from under their parents' roof.

In poor families where the parents cannot provide the young with what was described above, the young couple divides from the elders using their own means and often to their own material loss.

The young wife can no longer bear the nagging of the mother-in-law and pressures the husband to separate before they have the means to acquire their own house. Under these circumstances, what frequently happens is that the young stay in the same courtyard as the parents (but in different rooms) but use their own cookpot and utensils, eating and working separately from the parents.

Naturally, this does not guarantee the absence of quarrels, and at the same time, the means and living conditions of both families become much worse.

One daughter-in-law once told us that she would have separated from the parents if she had 2 or 3 rubles to buy a cookpot and utensils. We wondered what she planned to cook in that pot, if these were the material realities of her life.

At the same time, there are examples, mainly from wealthy merchant families, of parents and several married sons living together without any division. Everyone lives together in one or several adjacent yards, and they do not divide until the death of the elder man, the father. After that, this shared household, which had been sustained only by will of the patriarch, falls apart.

Thus, we can say that Sarts, both parents and their married children, strive to live separately, and as far as parents are concerned, the opposite is mostly found among the wealthiest merchant families, where petty calculations happen rarely and the material benefits of cohabitation and common economy are especially obvious.

The young wife gets used to her husband rather quickly, even if she has not known or seen him before the wedding. At the same time, the majority of couples start having quarrels and disputes, since there always is an abundance of reasons.

The main reason, the first to appear, is the young wife's absence from her courtyard. The natives are accustomed either not to allow the young wife to leave the yard at all or to permit that very rarely until she gives birth to the first child.[12]

The custom is observed everywhere, and everyone knows about it, but in practice the young wife, as well as her mother or other relatives, regards every new instance as something not only unexpected but unbelievable.

Suppose a family marries their son and daughter at nearly the same time. They observe [the seclusion rules] carefully with regard to the daughter-in-law; but at the same time, when the old mother goes to visit her own daughter, she starts wailing over her, "You have been put into a cage, my dear; you have been put into a prison, into hell; you see only the sky and walls"; and so on. All this adds to the young woman's discontent, who even without this is forced into a new position, unfamiliar for her, of being a stay-at-home woman, a position that has nothing to do with her girlish habits or inclinations. She endures it for a while and then starts quarreling with her husband.

A story like that developed right in front of our eyes in one of the Sart families that we knew. Their daughter was given as a wife at the age of fifteen. Things went well for the first two or three weeks. The young wife stayed at home, even started to do housework, and did not seem to mind her situation. In the meantime, her mother and stepfather managed to fall out with their son-in-law over the qalin that remained to be paid within several days of the wedding, according to a separate clause. They complained to the young wife. Little by little, she imagined herself as an unhappy, secluded woman and began crying; quarrels with her husband followed; the young thing[13] turned out to be very provoking, and matters often reached a point of a fight. Finally, she announced to her husband that if he did not give her full freedom, she would run away from him and enter the brothel. Such cases are not that rare. One often hears how interference from the wife's relatives upsets the life of this or that family.

We knew another case. One not very wealthy family consisted of only a husband and wife; they had no children. The latter caused certain tension in the relationship between the spouses; moreover, the wife had a large goiter[14] and was generally ugly. She began noticing that her husband started having affairs. Instead of talking to him and coming to some decision (like a divorce), she called all her relatives in his absence. They had a council and decided on the following punishment for the unfaithful husband: for a start, his best silk robe will be torn apart and turned into a sleeveless robe for the insulted wife. The verdict was immediately executed by all of them. The husband came home and discovered that the robe was missing. When he learned what exactly happened, he was angry that for at least five years he could not forgive his wife this misdeed, and their relationship forever remained hostile.

When the husband really likes his young wife, cases of uncontrolled jealousy are frequent. We knew a family where the husband not only never allowed his wife to leave the courtyard but even strictly forbade her to talk loudly in the internal yard so that the people who enter the external yard would not hear her voice.

So there are more than enough reasons for quarrels and disputes between the spouses, especially if the husband does not live at home and the wife depends directly on him for her subsistence.

Their quarrels sometimes last for several weeks and are accompanied with loud cursing, promises to run away, enter the brothel, break all the dishes, etc. As for the husband, he also warns the wife that he will beat her half to death, throw her out of the house, and destroy some parts of her body so that her promise to enter the brothel would become impossible.

However, these promises are only words: cookpots, dishes, and parts of the body remain undestroyed; the wife does not run away, since she has nowhere to go, no means, and no one to go with; and she does not evict herself because her husband has no money to pay her mahr.

Nevertheless, the talk about the divorce reappears on every useful and unsettling occasion and starts only three or four months after the marriage is concluded.

In general, we would not be mistaken if we say that a peaceful and quiet life is the lot of very few families. Things very rarely develop toward a real divorce, but talk about it goes on very frequently in all the quarrels and family disputes, especially in lower classes. Now we should also mention that all Sart women, smart and rather hot tempered, are big fans of love affairs. These are the reasons why it is a rare married woman with some degree of freedom who does not have a lover or even several lovers.

They meet under various conditions. We do not need to mention that neighbors, men and women, always have an opportunity to observe each other; let us ignore the cases when some merchant's wife starts an affair with one of the clerks or employees of her husband when he is away, as well as examples when a love affair is started not for the love of that art but for material benefit—i.e., when the woman, simply put, engages in prostitution.

Let us turn out attention to those young and middle-aged women who do not have male friends or acquaintances but want to flirt with someone.

First of all, we should say that there is nothing in the depths of the native life that can be kept in secret and that would not, sooner or later, become known at least to some people. A woman gets wind of the fact that in some quarter or street there is a widow, usually not too wealthy but not too poor either, who receives guests in the evenings, both men and women. The young lady asks her husband's permission to go for a couple of days to visit a relative who lives 5 or 10 versts away; she takes with her a tray with flat breads or plov and rushes with these gifts to the land of opportunity. There she immediately joins the group of the numerous female friends of the widow and, having enjoyed herself, returns to her house as if nothing happened. She brings her relatives' best regards to her husband and tells him how they live; she lies shamelessly and gets confused in her lies but already starts planning her next runaway either to the same widow or other places mentioned by her new friends.

There are some cases like the following. Let's assume that you, dear reader, are here, in some place like Namangan, you know the Sart language, and do not despise Sart women. As the evening approaches, you put on a robe and a skullcap to look less Russian, get on a horse, and go riding around the Sart city. It is summer. The evening is hot and dusty. The sun has just set. All around, in various tones, the droning voices of the azanchi call you to the evening prayer. Merchants riding their sturdy pacers are leaving their stalls and caravanserais and are going home. Women in gray and blue paranjis with and without children are moving along the streets in all directions, hurrying to get home before dark. You start moving toward the outskirts of town.

The further the streets are from the center, the more deserted they are and the darker it gets. Ahead of you walks a Sart woman, wearing a new festive paranji. You catch up with her and start talking to her in a low voice. Only if you are really unlucky, she will turn into a side street or turn herself away or will lean against the wall and wait in that position till you pass by. More often, she will start talking with you, first cautiously and then more boldly. You know fairly well that at least half of what she is saying is a lie when she tells you things about herself and her husband, but, of course, you could not care less.

Continuing this flirtatious conversation, you keep riding and she keeps walking for quite a while; occasionally, when you meet other riders or walkers, you go to opposite sides of the street to keep up appearances.

In the meantime, it has become completely dark. You found yourself in the gardens, at the outskirts of the city; there is not a single soul around. Your companion sighs and declares that she is lost and has no idea what to do. Naturally, you offer to let her sit behind you on the horse, so you take your foot off the stirrup and lean to the left. The young woman looks around, sets her foot into the stirrup, grabs you with both hands, and rather deftly jumps on the back of your horse. . . .

9   Polygyny, Divorce, Widowhood, and Death of a Woman

Religion allows a Muslim man to have no more than four wives at the same time. The number of wives he can have over time, according to Sharia, is unlimited. For instance, if he already has four wives but for some reason wants to marry a fifth one, he must first divorce one of his current wives, and then religion does not prevent him from replacing her with a new one. A woman who becomes a widow or divorces her husband can also remarry an unlimited number of times.

The eldest, senior wife is considered the mistress of the house; she is responsible for the overall supervision and management of the household economy and the performance of the work she decides to do; the rest of the work must be performed by the younger wives on her order. The latter call her byovyo (bibi, elder sister, aunt, mistress) and must treat her with the respect they would show an older close relative. (We will see below that in most cases these rules are not followed.) If the first wife dies or is divorced, her position is usually taken not by the next one in line but by the one that the husband loves most.

Outside each other's presence, the co-wives of one husband call each other kundosh. The word can be translated "she with whom one divides the days." The origin of the term is the requirement, based on religion and law, that a husband who has several wives must sleep with each of them (without the obligation to do anything else) no less than once in four days.[1]

In the majority of cases, all the wives live in the same yard where their husband lives, but each has a different room. Rich people who have property in several kishlaks or cities often have wives who live separately in their own houses on land that is close to their places of birth. That was very frequently practiced by the khan's servants in former times. A young man from a good family, let us say in Namangan, gets married and starts a family.

After a while he begins service and is requested to move to Qo'qon, to the khan's court. His wife's relatives do not agree to her moving to Qo'qon. So he goes there alone. He cannot visit Namangan often; then he buys a house in Qo'qon or a garden, starts a household, and takes a second wife. A year or two later, he is sent to Osh. Neither his Qo'qon nor his Namangan wife agrees to go there. This makes him marry a third wife.

Something similar happens sometimes nowadays. A married urban man buys land in a kishlak 30 to 40 versts from the city and starts using that property.

There is nobody who can keep an eye on the latter because he is busy in the city with his trade or business. Then he marries in that kishlak. The wife either lives on her husband's newly acquired land if there is house on it or stays with her parents, who take responsibility for overseeing his property.

If the husband cannot take one of his consecutive wives into his house, she stays with her parents, but he must pay for her expenses and must visit her at home.

A husband with several wives is advised by the religion to treat them all equally so that there is no jealousy or unfriendliness among them; religion recommends that he give the same clothes to one as he gives to the others. These rules, naturally, are almost never observed, and that is why in addition to the inclination of Sart women to quarrel and squabble, examples of peaceful coexistence of several wives under one roof are extremely rare.

A Sart takes a second wife. In a very short period of time, the elder wife starts feeling that her new kundosh, first of all, does nothing and, second, treats her without respect. She stops giving bread to the second wife as a punishment. The latter complains to her husband. The husband, who is more compassionate toward the new, younger wife, scolds the older one. The older one attacks the younger one. The latter, who feels that she has some protection, regains confidence and returns the attack. The squabbles happen daily. The husband first starts to calm and pacify the feuding sides. But nothing of the sort. The more time passes, the fiercer the quarrels become. One day the husband loses control, gives both wives a good beating, and orders them to prepare their food separately. (We have seen such a situation in a wealthy Sart family, whose head held an important public position.)

Need we say that if any one of the wives lacks control, there would be enough reasons for quarrels and squabbles like the ones that we described. One very beautiful Sart woman, whose husband took a second wife, told us that she would have lived in peace with her kundosh if she were at least a tiny bit better. "She is so ugly and stupid that I am ashamed to call her my kundosh. That is the reason why I hate her," said the offended beauty.

Thus, in the majority of cases, the pleasure of having several wives comes at a very high price, and there are abundant examples of Sarts who grow tired of family quarrels and divorce the extra wives, leaving only one of them, the most appropriate, and swear off taking multiple wives.

At the same time, most Sarts think that the possibility of living peacefully with several wives depends directly on the tact and agreeableness of the husband himself and his oldest wife.

We cannot help agreeing with this opinion, since we have seen several examples showing that this opinion is well reasoned. Thus, for example, we knew a family that consisted of a husband and three wives, the first of which had four small children, and the two younger ones had no children yet and fulfilled all the housework, allowing the eldest to simply take care of her children. The first wife was the one who insisted on taking both younger wives because prior to them she had to take of the children, milk the cows, and do all the other housework. Asking her husband to take one or two more wives, she pointed out to him the need for one or two women domestic workers; but these could not be substituted for wives, since in kishlaks it is very difficult to find a housemaid, oqsoch, and there were no suitable women relatives. We both heard about the life of that family and have visited them on many occasions, sometimes completely unplanned.

We have never encountered any family quarrels; on the contrary, it was hard not to be surprised by the friendly relations among the three wives and how they managed to arrange their lives without quarrels and squabbling, despite the fact that the oldest wife had extreme advantages.

In another wealthy merchant family, the wife sought and selected a second wife herself for the same reasons that the previous wife did, and she was mainly interested in ensuring that her future kundosh was a hard worker as well as good-natured.

Unfortunately, we do not know how the life of that family went after the second wife was introduced.

And though it is rare, there are still examples of cohabitation of several wives without quarrels and squabbles and when the oldest wife does not resist the subsequent marriages of her husband but even encourages them. (There is, however, one more condition when two wives of the same husband not only live in peace but even become friends; it is when one of them has a lover and the other covers up that relationship, getting personal benefits from doing so. We knew two examples of this. In one family, the conspirator was the senior wife, and in the other, the junior one.)

Still, cases of peaceful coexistence of several wives should be seen as exceptions rather than the rule, since most of the examples of polygyny that we saw or knew about showed absolutely the opposite character.

The oldest wife is almost always against the subsequent marriages of her husband and tries by any and all means to prevent him from concluding such marriages.

A vast number of the latter are concluded against the will of the oldest wife and thus against religious requirements; although religion allows a Muslim man to have four wives simultaneously, it requires him to take a second wife only if the first wife has agreed.[2]

It is now clear that under these conditions the chances of peaceful existence of several wives under the same roof are scarce, and the more so because the Sart woman is very hot tempered.

For this reason, most native men who do have several wives try to house them each separately, if possible; if all the wives live in one courtyard, then not only does he give them separate rooms, but they also cook their food separately so that they have little occasion to interact. It is clear that such conditions, which first and foremost require a lot of financial and other expenses, can be met by only a few husbands, so of necessity, few avail themselves of the right of polygyny.

Observing native life, we saw that polygyny in cities, where there is a concentration of proletarians who are willing to give their daughters away for a tiny amount of qalin, is practiced much more frequently than in kishlaks, and by wealthy [men] much more frequently than by those of few means or the poor. As far as low-income and poor kishlak and rural families are concerned, cases of possessing two or more wives are extremely rare. With all the conditions that we enumerated above, polygyny among this part of the native population should and usually does lead to financial ruin.

Among the wealthy village population, the possession of two wives is mostly practiced among those Karakalpaks, Kipchaks, and recently sedentarized Kyrgyz who have considerable amounts of arable land at the bottom of the valley, as well as livestock that go up to mountain grasslands every summer. In such families, one wife stays permanently on the land, and the other spends spring, summer, and part of the fall in the hills and mountains with the livestock.

Among the urban rich, possessing several wives is considered some kind of ostentation, a necessity that every respectable and affluent man should have, similarly to the way we consider having a beautiful and expensive actress or singer as an ostentation; but the huge difference between the two phenomena lies in the consequences for the women. When our kept mistress is thrown out, she becomes almost a pariah; but one of the four wives of the Muslim man, divorcing him, does not lose any of her human rights but finds another husband for herself always and without difficulty. On the contrary, she gains by becoming a free person, since she does not need to obey her parents anymore; nor does she depend on any of her subsequent husbands economically, because in most cases they married her without paying qalin.

Later the attitude of the natives toward polygyny will probably change; it is quite possible that instances of polygyny will decrease considerably unless conditions of divorce become more complicated, but this is something that the future will show, and we will only say, *qui vivra, vera.*[3]

What is much more interesting and instructive is the past of this phenomenon.

Previously, during the khan's rule, every person lived under heavy clerical and governmental oppression.[4] The clergy (like scribes and Pharisees of the Old Testament way of life) reminded the government about the need to strictly preserve religion as the basis of the theocratic state and also offered to monitor the members of society, to convince, to persuade, and, when necessary, to appeal to the authorities. Naturally, anyone who held a slightly important social position did not dare to compromise himself with some forbidden act, so when necessary, he looked for a way or outcome that was allowed by Sharia and was, thus, lawful. Having been bored with his wife and feeling the need or an inclination to get new and fresh experiences, he took a second wife. Why would he risk his life and reputation by taking a mistress, when Sharia gave him a different, more convenient, and absolutely legal way, especially if he had the financial means?

All this concerned only the wealthy people, and naturally it did not eradicate love affairs or prostitution, since there were conditions for their existence alongside polygyny; nevertheless, this mentorship and punitive policy of the khan's government led directly to extending the boundaries for polygyny in the society, as well as introducing customs such as bachcha, and the main enthusiasts of introducing these fashionable things were the khans themselves, who had innumerable wives, bachchas, and concubines.

Thus, gradually, polygyny came to be seen as an institution that allows a man to satisfy his sexual whims and appetites in a lawful way and that can at the same time make him look good in the eyes of others.

That is why, even now, the inertia of those old habits makes every Sart who has not yet experienced the ordinary pleasures of polygyny strive to try it, if he possesses a sufficient amount of money.

Only the most reasonable, or those who learned from bitter experience, or those who witnessed or heard about the charms of living with several wives at once, or the most calculating ones say to themselves, "Let the others get ten wives; I would rather survive with just one. If I have difficulty coping with one, what would happen with two! No, my dear, get married if you want to; do it, but don't drag me into it, not on your life!"

For some, this wisdom is achieved at such cost that they forbid their children to take more than one wife at the same time.

So among the wealthy strata, polygyny is practiced mainly as a lawful means to satisfy a man's comfort and sexual needs. It allows those who are well-off to bring several workers into the household or to have wives tend to several homes that belong to one man but are located in different places. Among the poor strata, where the household is usually not that complicated and thoughts about additional comforts are low priority, polygyny is rare, especially in kishlaks. Still, there are cases when lust overpowers a poor man, and he obtains two or three wives despite the fact that he can barely feed one. Thus, we knew two Kyrgyz families near the kishlak of Nanay, each of whom has two wives, and the second wives were taken under the pretext that the first wives were barren.

The property of the first childless family consisted of a yurt, a four-year-old colt, and a cow. They had no land; the husband was engaged in very unprofitable hunting (in the mountains) and making wooden utensils.

The other family also had no land; what they had was a bad yurt with holes in the roof, two milking goats, and three children; the husband was engaged in making charcoal.

Apart from the reasons for polygyny such as desire for comfort or the wish for an extra worker in the house, there are several other reasons mentioned by men: (1) childlessness of the first wife, (2) the lack of a son, (3) the fact that the first wife was not a virgin but a widow or a divorcée when she was taken.[5]

We have already mentioned that the oldest wife always regards her husband's subsequent marriages with animosity, while religion advises and even obliges a Muslim man to obtain the permission of the first wife before he takes the second wife; moreover, he must give the first wife the same presents that he gives the second wife as a bride; in other words, he must give to the first wife the same amount of money or presents that he plans to spend on the second wedding.

We knew several examples of this kind, when the first wife, who did not agree to her husband's second marriage, initiated divorce on the pretext of his second marriage. In one of these cases, the upset wife not only divorced her unfaithful husband but gave him a good beating on the second day of the wedding. The divorce took place a few days later and with ease since the woman had sufficient means, had her own house, garden, and land.

Without going into details of the theoretical side of Islam's complicated and entangled divorce law, we will limit ourselves to listing, generally, briefly, the main instances in local native practice of solving this question.

The divorce, *taloq*, is given freely if both spouses agree to it.

The wife has the right to demand a divorce in the following cases:

1. If her husband has given her a beating, without reason, that left visible marks on her body;
2. If her husband takes a new wife without her permission;
3. If he does not give her money for food for six months;
4. If he takes her away (without her agreement) from her permanent home to another place that is more than three days' journey away;
5. If he goes insane;
6. If he turns out to have leprosy (*moxov*).

The preliminary dissolution of the marriage is effected by (both spouses or one of the spouses) pronouncing the word "taloq," after which religion recommends waiting three days.[6] This time is given to both of them to think over the step they are taking. If there is no reconciliation made during this period, the spouses go to the qozi with the required number of witnesses to declare their decision to divorce and to obtain a document of divorce.

If the husband initiated the divorce without valid cause, he must give the wife whom he is dismissing the promised mahr, and he loses the right to demand return of qalin or his wedding expenses.

If such a divorce is initiated by the wife, she loses her right to mahr and must also return the qalin her husband paid for her.

As far as the possibility of restoring the marriage, there are two main kinds of divorces:

1. If before the divorce is completed, the word "taloq" was pronounced once or twice, Sharia allows simple reconciliation between the divorced spouses and without requiring a new marriage ceremony;
2. If the word "taloq" was pronounced three times, the marriage is considered annulled, and the divorced wife can remarry her husband only if she marries someone else first and then divorces him.

In this case, her husband marries her as a stranger and not like a wife whom he divorced, and the new marriage should be concluded with a new ceremony.

After the divorce, the woman settles down either with some relatives or in her own house, if she has one.

A woman who is divorced from her husband has the right to enter a new marriage if she is not pregnant, only after three menses have passed (Koran, chapter 2, verse 228). This period is called *idda*, and its purpose is that there is no doubt about the fatherhood of the first child born after the divorce.

In a case when the woman is divorced while she is pregnant, she must wait until the pregnancy ends before she can remarry (Koran, chapter 65, verse 4).

In case of divorce, the wife has the right to keep little children until they reach the age of seven, and the father should provide support for them. The father can take children under the age of seven away from their mother if she enters a new marriage after the divorce.

If the mother is missing, the above-mentioned rights to her little children go to either to the mother's mother or their adult sister (capable of exercising rights) or to a maternal aunt; only if these relatives are absent does the right go to the paternal aunt.

When a child reaches age seven, the father can take the child to live with him; when the child comes of age, a son can live where he wants, but a daughter must live with her father or father's father.

However, by mutual agreement children can be split up between divorced parents: usually the boys stay with the father and the girls with the mother.

If her husband dies, all the woman's obligations with regard to qalin disappear. The woman becomes free, but social customs can prevent her from quickly remarrying, so she usually waits for a year to a year and a half, sometimes two years.[7]

A Sart widow either stays with the children in the house that her late husband left or moves out somewhere.

If the children are of age, the property left by the husband is immediately divided and the widowed mother either settles down with one of her children or with her relatives. (We have discussed her situation earlier.)

If the children are small, she usually stays in the house left by her husband, and, if she is not too old, she usually remarries in a year or two. Cases of women remarrying at age forty or forty-five, if they are well preserved, are not that rare, especially if she has a house, a garden, and some other property that brings her permanent and sufficient income.

A Sart woman wears mourning clothes (dark blue shirt, dark robe, and a blue sash worn during wailing) from four months to a year after her husband's death. Most of them take off the mourning clothes after the one-year commemoration of death.

We noted that most elderly Sart women are very agile, active, and hardworking. The Sart woman fades most noticeably between the ages of eighteen and twenty-five; later, especially after thirty, her visible aging slows down and happens in stages, while the changes of her moral world become almost nonexistent. She is energetic, always ready to chat and laugh, a lover of all possible female gatherings, brisk and hardworking at the age of forty and forty-five, and remains unchanged till her death, which happens around the age of fifty-five or sixty unless she is weakened by some occasional hard illness.

Cases of men living till the age of seventy or eighty are not rare but are almost exceptional among women. (We knew an old woman who was ninety and whose husband was one hundred. She continued spinning thread, and he continued weaving crude cotton fabric. Of course, they both regarded this work as a diversion.)

Fatalists as they reach old age, both men and women similarly greet death with remarkable calm, believing that *ajjal*, the hour of death, has been determined for every person in the book of fate and that nothing can postpone this timing even for a moment. We were once present at the death of a mullah, who was not very old. Thieves had wounded him the previous night, and he was dying; he retained consciousness almost until the end. With extreme calmness and without paying attention to the people that surrounded him, he recited his own dying prayer in a noticeably weakening voice.

As soon as the person dies, his or her relatives immediately start lamentation.

Neighbors start coming as they hear the wailing and chanting; relatives and friends are informed that so-and-so *qazo keldi*, met his or her fate. (Upon hearing this piece of news, people usually say, "Xudo rahmat bo'lsin," May God be merciful to him or her.)

Then the dead man's or woman's jaw is tied with a scarf so that the mouth does not gape, eyelids are closed, the hands are stretched along the sides, and the body is covered with a piece of fabric.

In the meantime, relatives and friends come together, and *yuguchi* [*yuvgich*], male or female bathers of corpses, arrive. Women go into the ichkari, and men go into the mehmon-xona. Lamenting goes on in both places. A man is lamented by women; a woman is also lamented by women and only her closest male relatives: a husband, sons, and brothers.

A wife and a husband lament each other with the words "gulim-oi!" (oh, my flower) or "oshiqim-oi" (oh, my love). These exclamations (and similar ones) are called out in a singing manner resembling crying, and between these phrases there are wailing and moaning without words.

In wealthy families, everyone who came to the funeral receives a piece of calico or other cloth in which small coins are wrapped.

Usually, the corpse is washed only by the yuguchi, always in a separate room. Since touching a corpse is considered polluting, yuguchi put small sacks over their hands, like gloves. Having washed the naked corpse, they dress the body in a shroud made of white cotton cloth that looks like a sack with openings at both ends. When the corpse is shrouded, the open ends are tied over the head and the feet. Then the corpse is put on a long funeral bier covered with a sheet (or any fabric or robe or the paranji of the dead woman), and it is carried to the outer courtyard. Here, in the presence of all the men who have gathered, an imom recites *janoza* (something similar to our funeral service), at the end of which all those present say their last salam over the deceased.[8]

The bier with the corpse is either carried by people or placed on an araba. The accompanying people, men only, carry a staff and a blue scarf in their right hand. There is comparatively little wailing done on the way to the cemetery, only if the dead person is a rich man, so usually the funeral procession moves in silence.

The grave looks like a large hole, deep as a man's height, with a niche made along its western side from north to south. When the funeral procession arrives at the cemetery, the corpse covered with the sheet is lowered into the grave, and the corners of the sheet must be held over the open grave all the time until the grave-diggers place the corpse into the niche. The corpse is placed on its back, with head to the north. The opening of the niche is covered with bricks or stones and the grave is covered with earth. Then the imom recites a prayer, and everyone goes home.

The women come to the grave the following day and wail as they did at the house.

Yuguchi receive either money or clothes belonging to the deceased woman for their services. If the deceased had no daughters, her husband sells her clothes and pays for the funeral repast.

Those women relatives who wail for the dead woman receive her paranji or some of her old clothes.

On the third day, called *uchi*, relatives and the closest friends get together for a funeral repast. Apart from the meal, there is a special lamentation by women for the deceased man or woman. They dress in dark blue shirts, wrapped with blue sashes, holding a staff and a blue scarf with the right hand.

One by one or all together, they go to the center of the room, swaying, wailing, and chanting in the same way as they did on the day of the funeral.[9] Often, women get so entranced while performing this ritual that they start scratching their faces, tearing their hair, etc.

In the first three days, no food is prepared in the house of the deceased, even if a child lives there, but it is provided by neighbors and relatives.

On the sixth or seventh day, and in some areas on the fortieth day, relatives get together again. One of the women washes the bedding for the deceased's family. All the people present receive a meal and a piece of soap to wash the linens that they wore at the funeral. This custom is called *kir* (dirty, dirty laundry).

In wealthy families, a lamp is kept burning for forty days in the place where the dead person was lying or was washed.

The next remembrance is organized on the fortieth day of the death and one year after it.

10 Prostitution

THE READER KNOWS ALREADY that during the khan's rule the Muslim government and its agents, one of which was society itself, punished not only prostitution but even ordinary adultery with death. Nonetheless, both of these were practiced, and not infrequently, because catching a man or a woman in the act was difficult, even impossible,[1] and there was no shortage of motivations pushing a woman toward prostitution or an adulterous relationship with a man, then as now. Men have always been inclined to diversify their experiences in the sexual sphere. Women, great seekers of love affairs and all sorts of pleasures of that kind, also love to receive even small gifts, since most of them have always been financially dependent on their husbands and have never been in a good position to satisfy their needs and desires for flirtation. The young wives of those who have several spouses, then and now, are often left unsatisfied; and poverty, which was as widespread then as it is now, made women try all possible means to struggle against need. Thus, the only difference between the past and the present lies in the fact that previously, the fear of punishment forced men and women to be extremely cautious, which is why prostitution was clandestine, while nowadays it is practiced both secretly and openly. There were, however, historical moments in the past when the clandestine prostitution encouraged by the epicurean khans spread to an enormous degree, at least in Qo'qon, for instance, during the reign of Madali-khan. (See the *Short History of Kokand Khanate*, V. Nalivkin, 1886.)

These days, remembering their recent past, Sarts assiduously assure us that before the arrival of Russians, because of the strictness and vigilance of the khan's rule, not only was there no prostitution, but even unlawful relations were unbelievably rare exceptions. It is impossible to believe these tales both because of the histories of the Qo'qon Khanate written by natives and because the early days of our own existence here tell us the opposite. Here are some facts. In autumn 1875, as soon as the right bank of the Syr Darya (now Chust and Namangan districts) was occupied [by Russian forces], prostitutes, mainly married women, were brought in very large numbers and without difficulty, by their own husbands, to our squad, which stationed in Namangan. Starting from the next year, 1876, we already knew Russians who obtained Sart women, and the latter in most cases liked their position since their new life was materially incomparably better, and their freedom was much greater than before. At the same time, many native women began asking our Russian administration to divorce them from their husbands since they wanted to enter the ranks of open prostitutes. All this reveals that the contingent of future open prostitutes was prepared long ago and only waited for the moment to openly and legally announce their own existence.

In 1875, when the Russian administration was established in Namangan, one of its members turned to an elderly local man who belonged to the previous khan's administration with questions about the extent to which local prostitution existed during the khan's rule and whether there were many secret prostitutes in Namangan. The Sart answered that, if the truth is told, all women of Namangan between the ages of twelve and sixty must be called prostitutes. Naturally, he exaggerated a bit, but he may have been close to the truth. Later, we became convinced that only a rare woman is not inclined toward temporary love for a certain reward, that a rare woman would refuse a honorarium of 3 to 5 rubles, and that in native life such rewards may decrease to negligible amounts, bearing in mind that Russians are usually charged 5 to 10 times more than Sarts.

The latter, however, is valid not only in the sphere of prostitution. If a Sart sells a horse for 20 rubles, he will sell it to a Russian for no less than 30; Russians always pay more for everything, and they themselves are to blame for that. Occupying a new province and receiving increased pay for wartime, we give free rein to the broad Russian nature. We throw money right and left and brag by competing to spend more money in a certain period of time.

At the beginning of the [18]70s in Tashkent, we paid street boys 15 or 20 kopeks for holding the horse at the porch for fifteen to twenty minutes. Such wasting of money, especially here, where money is scarce and capital is dear, cannot go without consequences. Such extravagance in the Russian's nature first shocked Sarts and then made them come to the conclusion that every Russian is Croesus.[2] And if he is Croesus, taking a few spare rubles from him is not a sin for the Sart, who is poor compared to Croesus. This attitude has become customary and is unlikely to change soon, despite the fact that with time Sarts are gradually becoming convinced, as they become broadly acquainted with the imagined Croesus, that many [Russians] are acquainted, not just theoretically but in practice as well, with complicated debt obligations and other no less complex financial operations.

So currently there are two types of prostitution here: open and clandestine.

The first brothels appeared in towns of the newly occupied Fergana province right after occupation. One of the first acts of the first local prostitute was that she immediately started walking along the streets with an open face. This was something between spitting in the face of the old society that oppressed her and a sort of a "Marseillaise" she sang on the ruins of the regime that recently threatened to stone her. It was a sort of glee of freedom, a greeting to those who forgave her in advance, gave her the right of citizenship,[3] and removed her eternal fear for her life.

Nevertheless, according to tradition a Sart woman wearing her national costume but with uncovered face was not in harmony with her native surroundings, not only in the eyes of Sarts but even in the eyes of those Russians who lived in Turkestan for a long time and were used to seeing Sart women in the streets with their faces covered. Understandably, all of this must have shocked the Sarts. In this area, a Sart woman walking with an uncovered face would be like a woman walking in her nightshirt along the streets of a European city. To add insult to injury, one of the district towns had temporarily organized a reception ward for a clinic on the premises of the district administration, where among others, prostitutes were treated. Sarts started a rumor that, according to Russian law, every public building needs to have a brothel whose inhabitants will be supported by government funds. At the same time, both the number of prostitutes and of women who started walking with uncovered faces grew steadily. The pious Muslims were not only angered but proclaimed the end of the world was upon them. In the beginning, local public opinion was so opposed to open prostitution that the administration received several requests to provide a place for a brothel somewhere outside the city limits, as far away as possible and in an unpopulated area.[4]

However, this did not last too long. Antagonism receded little by little; open faces became less shocking; there turned out to be many visitors even from the local men, and finally, it turned out that keeping a brothel is a troublesome enterprise but not without profit. Recently, a new brothel was opened in one of the local cities by a cleric, a qori who previously occupied himself with learning and reciting the Koran by heart.

In the first years of the existence of brothels, prostitutes were recruited in various ways. Many were women who either were divorced from their husbands or ran away from them.

Entering the ranks of prostitutes, they entered the pay of the brothel's founders, Sart men, and much less often lived in groups of two of three supporting themselves. Often there were cases like the following one. A wife who could not legally divorce her husband or a maiden who was still dependent on her parents ran away and came to the owner of the brothel to take her as a prostitute. Naturally, she is readily accepted with enthusiasm, pampered, and provided with festive dress, on credit, which she is obligated to repay from her future earnings. In the beginning, she enjoys her unprecedented freedom and the merry pastime so much that she becomes afraid that her husband or parents might track her down and take her home. Then she is told that she can easily avoid this by giving the owner of the brothel a document declaring that she owes him so much money that neither her husband not her parents would be able to pay. She signs such a document and finds herself in debt bondage.

Here it should be noted that any similarity to Russian debt bondage is imagined, since a document of the kind mentioned above has no effect; it is not recognized, and every such prostitute could easily obtain liberation through facilitation of the Russian administration.

That is why the way of recruiting women and maidens into brothels has changed from previously into a new, fixed form. The owners of brothels are almost exclusively Sart men, and the women in brothels are their legal wives, which is the reason why there are not more than four prostitutes in each brothel (corresponding to the number of legal wives). Wishing to open such an establishment, a Sart takes three or four wives and starts a trade in them.

Usually it is divorced women and rarely maidens who enter such a marriage. The latter is explained by the fact that most parents do not dare give their daughters to such institutions with their own permission, fearing public opinion; as far as divorcées and widows are concerned, we have already seen that they can make their own decisions, and their behavior after the first marriage is not used by the public to shame them.[5]

In the first years of the existence of brothels here, the main visitors were soldiers, Cossacks, and the dregs of the local Russian society. After a while, many Sart enthusiasts also appeared; in the last few years crowds of them surround brothels during all the days of Ramadan and Kurban, when local brothels turn into crowded clubs for the Sart rabble; and in the last few years at Sayil[6] there are always dozens of prostitutes, who have become an indispensable part of public festivities these days.

Currently, when the practice of open prostitution in Fergana has established itself in a comparatively short period of time, it is difficult to predict the fate of prostitutes who leave the profession for various reasons. Actually, we know a few cases when young women, tiring of this kind of life and leaving the brothel forever, found husbands within a short period of time; but these examples can be considered as serendipity that cannot predict the further fate of the majority. We can expect that the fate of open prostitutes here may be similar to that in Europe. However, one of the main reasons for this is the belief that a woman who has been a prostitute for too long loses the ability to bear children, and the reader already knows how the native men regard barren women.

Secret prostitutes are in a completely different position. First of all, we must say that their name is legion, and the specifics of their positions depend on their observance of a universal human rule: everything is possible as long as it is done on a legal basis or, more important, follows the rules of the specific society. (We think that we are not mistaken about this being a universal rule.)

Open prostitutes are called *jallob* (prostitute); secret ones, *kupia* (secret) without the word jallob; thus, a secret prostitute is not recognized as a prostitute.[7]

The number of maidens [never married] who are either open or secret prostitutes is comparatively small. As far as secret prostitutes are concerned, this is also explained by the fact that a maiden marries very early and so in most cases would fall into prostitution only after her marriage.

The number of secret prostitutes among young girls has started growing only recently when cases of selling virginity are appearing repeatedly.

We knew several examples of selling virginity under the following conditions. The girl is married to an old man; in two or three months she divorces him because he is impotent, and her parents or the relatives that raised her sell her virginity, while she enters the category of secret prostitute.

The level of payment to a prostitute among Sarts is rather low; it starts from 10 to 15 kopeks and never exceeds 5 silver rubles. Only the most ostentatious secret prostitutes manage to get valuable presents from their admirers. The tight-fistedness of Sarts can be demonstrated by the following fact. In autumn 1883, a group of gymnasts and dancers came to Namangan. The performances for Sarts were organized in a caravanserai; the price of each ticket was 15 kopeks. There were often such scenes: a rich merchant stands at the gates of the caravanserai and bargains to buy the ticket for 8½, 9, or 9½ kopeks.[8]

In the last three or four years the secret prostitute has literally made a bloodless revolution among the majority of the local Muslim population. She has almost completely replaced the bachcha. Only a rare friendly male gathering happens without her; she appears here as a dancer and there as a woman of easy virtue. At such parties, you can meet representatives of the local administration, big local merchants, and sometimes even local clergy. She dictates fashions, forces the pious Sart to watch her dancing, listen to her songs, and even drink wine with her; fooling her admirer, an old man from the local bourgeoisie, she marries him, enters high society, recruits new associates, divorces her husband, obtains her own house, and organizes a small but very merry place of entertainment. Thus, she carouses until her common sense tells her at some point to find a quiet shelter, get married again, and contribute to the cause of free love only as a broker.

There are many secret prostitutes who deal not only with prostitution but with pimping. "If I do not please you, I can introduce you to my daughter or my younger sister or my niece." If there are many secret prostitutes, there are even more pimps, since in addition to women, men also engage in this craft; sometimes these are fathers, brothers, and even husbands.

In the beginning, the Russian administration tried to combat the development of secret prostitution by demanding that the women who were caught bear witness, but these efforts were almost completely in vain, since it was impossible to keep an eye on the legion of secret prostitutes due to the peculiarities of local life.[9]

You are invited to someone's party, *bazm*. You arrive. In the mehmon-xona you find five or six women and several men. One of those women, dressed in silk, bracelets, and corals and other decorations, dances; the others sing and play tambourine. You ask who they are. This one is the daughter of such and such merchant, this is the wife of an elder, this is the former wife of some provincial governor, etc.

A few more questions make it clear that most of them are more or less available.

* * *

For a farewell, we want to tell our reader a Sart saying: *Hamma odam bir odam.* All people are the same.

Glossary

The modern Uzbek spelling of a word is given first, frequently followed by a transliteration from Cyrillic of the Nalivkins' presentation of the term. In some cases, several variants of the Uzbek term appear, and occasionally the Arabic version of a word is also presented.

In modern Uzbek:

A' is a lengthened *a*.
G' is a guttural *g*, sometimes represented as *gh*.
J is pronounced as in the word "jump."
O' is a rounded, forward long *o*.
Q is a hard *k* sound produced at the back of the throat.
X is a hard *h* sound, *kh*.

adno/adna: lowest level of study
adras: cotton and silk fabric, usually with brightly colored stripes
ajina/adzhina: yellow-haired poltergeist or witch
a'lam/aglam: assistant to a judge (qozi)
albasti: poltergeist in the form of an old woman with long hair
a'lo/ala: superior; the highest level of study; excellent
apa or opa: elder sister
araba: two-wheeled cart
arabakesh: cart driver
arafa/rapa: eve of a holiday
archa: creeping evergreen
ariq/aryk: small irrigation canal
arshin: Russian measure equal to 28 inches or 71 centimeters
asamusa: cane plant; the "Staff of Moses" plant
atala: gruel made with flour
atlas: silk fabric, warp-died to produce brightly colored patterns; ikat
attor/attar: seller of perfumes
aul: nomadic encampment; cluster of multiple yurts (felt houses)
avrat/aurat (Arabic): parts of the body that should not be shown to others, such as genitals, according to Islamic concepts of decency
avsat/ausat: middle level of study in a madrasa
Azami: another name for the Hanafi school of Islamic jurisprudence
azan: call to prayer
azanchi/muezzin (Arabic): one who recites the call to prayer
bachcha: dancing boy
badraf/badrap: latrine, outhouse
baqqol/bakal: small grocer
bek: owner of a military land grant; a district governor during the Khanate period

beshik/bishik: cradle

beshkokil/beshkakil': five braids, a hairstyle

bibi: honorific added to a woman or girl's name, meaning elder sister, aunt, or mistress

bit: lice

bit-ko'z/bit kuz: slanted or narrow eyes

bo'lish: cylindrical pillow

boshoq/bashak: ears or stalks of grain

boybachcha/baibacha: son of a rich man (boi)

bo'za/buza: fermented grain drink similar to beer

buqoq/bukak: goiter

caravanserai (English)/karvon-saroi (Uzbek): a sort of hotel for merchants traveling by caravan

chaksa/chaksy: obsolete Uzbek measure of weight: 1 chaksa equals about 13 pounds, according to the Nalivkins, or 0.33 Russian pud, between 5 and 6 kilograms

chala-mullah: half or incomplete mullah; only partially learned

chaqa/chaka: small copper coin

chaq-chaq/chak-chak: chatter; idle conversation

charx/charkh: spinning wheel

chechak: smallpox

chek (Russian): check; chit; receipt; pin

chig'iriq/chagrik: hand-turned cotton-cleaning apparatus used to separate cotton fiber from cotton seed

chigit: cotton seed

chilim: water pipe; hookah

chimbet/chashmband/chachvon: Uzbek terms for a large, thick net woven of horsehair, used as a veil draped over the top of the head and down the front of the body, obscuring everything beneath it from the eyes of others; the wearer can see through it but not clearly

chiroq/chirak: lamp

chiroq poy/chirak pai: lamp holder

chit: cotton fabric; chintz

chivin/chimyn (dialect variant): flies

chordana/chardana: cross-legged

chorikor/chairikar: sharecropper

Chor-kitob/Char-kitab: "Four Books," a Persian book that formed part of the curriculum for the maktab

choy/chai: tea

choydush/chaidush: teapot

choyrak or chorak/chairik: obsolete measure of weight equal to 5 puds or 16 kilograms

choyshab/chaishab: bed sheet

choy-xona/chai-khana: teahouse

dajjal/dadzhal: anti-Christ

dallol/dallial: witness; broker

dallolchilik: the act of witnessing

dars-xona/dars-khana: classroom in a madrasa

darvoza-xona: gatehouse

dasturxon/dastarkhan: tablecloth; a cloth laid out with food for guests
dehqon/dekhan: farmer; agriculturalist
dehqonchilik: farming; agriculture
desiatina (Russian): measure of land equal to about 1.09 hectares
dev/div: evil spirit
devol, devor/dival: wall
devona/divana: holy fool; dervish
domla/damulla: teacher in a primary Islamic school, a maktab
do'qon/dukan: a shop, often one that produces and sells handmade items
duo-xon/dua-khan: someone who provides others with healing prayers
duro'ya or duraya/duriya: scarf; in the Nalivkins' time, white muslin scarf edged with lace
durracha: small scarf
dutor/dutar: two-stringed lute
eshon/ishan: sheikh; leader of a Sufi order
falbin, polvun/palbin: fortune-teller
farz: moral obligation
fatvo/fetva: decision made by an Islamic judge
Fergana/Ferghana/Farg'ona (Uzbek): various renderings for the name of a valley, Fergana being the most familiar to an English-language reader
garm-sel: hot summer wind
g'isht: brick
go'ja/kucha: soup or porridge with grain and yogurt
go'za/guza: Central Asian cotton (*Gossypium herbaceum*) with short fibers growing in pods that have to be opened manually
grazhdanstvennost' (Russian): citizenship or subject-citizenship
gumboz/gumbaz: dome
gunoh/gunakh: sin
guvala/guvalia: elliptically shaped dried mud bricks
guzar: small bazaar; crossroads with shops
halol/halal (Arabic)/khalial (Russian): pure; righteous (refers both to foods that Muslims can eat and to deeds that they should do)
halvah/helva: a sweet, usually made of butter, flour, cream, sugar, and some additional flavoring
Hanafiya/Khanafiia: one of the four Islamic schools of legal interpretation, founded by Imam Abu Hanifa
haq-ullah: tax paid to a religious authority; God's share
harom/haram (Arabic)/kharam (Russian): forbidden (refers to foods that Muslims should not eat, such as pork, as well as deeds that are considered sinful)
hashshar/ashar: mutual assistance in labor for tasks such as building houses or cleaning irrigation systems
hayat/khaiat: small plot of land used for farming or gardening
Hayit/Khait: a religious holiday, either Qurbon Hayit (festival of the sacrifice) or Ro'za Hayit (festival at the end of Ramadan)
hazina/khazina: pantry; treasury; storehouse
hokim/khakim: governor

hovuz/khauz: artificial, usually lined pond or pool in a courtyard

hujra/khudzhra: (architectural) cell or small room in a madrasa or caravanserai

ichkari: interior courtyard of a house and the rooms surrounding it that housed the family and was off-limits to nonfamily males; similar to harem, harim, zenana, birun, and other such terms

ijab: marriage proposal

imom/imam: preacher and prayer leader in a mosque

ipak: silk

iparkak: type of light silk fabric similar to atlas

irshod/irshad: document testifying to the bearer's skills or accomplishments; a certification

ishton/ishtan: loose pants or trousers worn by women under a long shirt

isiriq/isyryk: herb, rue (*Peganum harmala*), that is burned for smudging or incense

isiriqchi: someone who burns isiriq, fumigating the bazaar

issiq/issyk: hot

jallob/dzhalliap: woman who has been married and divorced countless times; prostitute

jida/dzhigda: Russian olive

jigit or yigit/dzhigit: young man

jiyak/dzhiak: woven decorative strips used to edge women's pants

jo'ra/dzhura: male friendship circle; also called gap, gashtak, or mashrap

joriya/dzhuria: female slave

joy-namoz/dzhai-namaz: place of prayer; a carpet or fabric on which one performs the prayers

jugara/dzhugara: sorghum

juvon/dzhuvan: previously married woman; widow or divorcée

juvoz/dzhuaz: oil press (for sesame, cotton seed, and other vegetable oils)

juvozkash: person who runs the oil press

Kaaba: the black stone at the center of the Sacred Mosque in Mecca, the focal direction of prayer and center of the Hajj pilgrimage ritual

kampir: old woman

kappon/kapan: bread bazaar

karaul (Russian)/qorovul (Uzbek): guard

ketmon/ketmen: hoe with a wide, deep iron blade that can be used as a digging, cultivating, weeding, or chopping tool

kibitka (Russian)/bo'z ui (Kyrgyz)/ger (Mongolian): felt house; yurt

kiima: pitcher

kishlak/qishloq (Uzbek): unwalled village, from the Turkic word for winter settlement

ko'k/kuk: blue

ko'k yutal/kuk iutal': whooping cough

kopek (Russian): coin equal to 0.1 ruble

koranda/keranda: tenant farmer

kosa: bowl for stew

ko'za: jug for water

kudungar: fabric finisher

kufr (Arabic): lack of faith; unbelief

kul: male slave

kuloh/kulia: conical red felt hat worn by a dervish

kundosh/kundash: co-wife

kunjara/kundzhara: oilseed hulls

kupia: secret prostitute. (This may have been a local variant of some other term, but it is not attested in the major [late Soviet period] dictionaries, maybe because it was nonstandard or because Soviet dictionary makers did not include some crude terms.)

Kurban/Qurban (Uzbek): Eid al-Adha, Islam's annual festival of the sacrifice

kyrchoo, kurchoo (Kyrgyz)/kurchou: rope encircling a yurt midway along its walls

loy/lai: mud

lozim/liazim: pants or trousers; "necessaries"

lutchak or luchchak/liutchak: apricot or peach; a type of wheat with ears that lack bristles

Maddah: dervish or holy man

madrasa/medresa: school of higher Islamic learning

mahr/makhr: Islamic marital gift, a portion of which the groom gives to the bride upon marriage (prompt mahr) and a portion of which he promises her in case he decides to divorce her (delayed mahr)

majlis: council

makruh/makrukh: Sharia determination of "reprehensible," which means that this action is looked down on and discouraged but not haraam or forbidden

maktab: primary school that teaches reading, writing, and basic Islamic knowledge

mastura: veiled, covered woman who stays in the home

mata: woven cotton fabric

mazar: tomb; cemetery

mehmon-xona/mikhman-khana: room in a house for entertaining male guests

mirob/mirab: head of a local irrigation system

mirza: scribe; title for a local official

mol-xona/mal-khana: barn for livestock

mosh/mash: mung beans

mosh-xurda or mosh-guruch/mash-khurda: stew of rice and mung beans

mudarris: lecturer in the madrasa, appointed for his expertise in one of the Islamic sciences

muezzin (Arabic): one who calls others to prayer

mufti: religious scholar and judge appointed to direct the district judges (qozi)

mullah/mullo (Uzbek): person who has Islamic theological education. (Unlike Muslims in many parts of the world who refer to a mosque preacher or a teacher as mullah, Uzbeks called preachers and teachers domla.)

mullocha qo'ynak: shirt or dress with horizontal, rather than vertical, neck opening

mum: oil or wax

mumiyo: tarry, mineral-laden substance sourced from natural seepages in some mountains; also known as shilajit in Ayruvedic medicine

murid/miurid: disciple in a Sufi order; follower of an eshon

musafir: stranger; foreigner

mutawalli (Arabic)/mutevali (Uzbek): caretaker of a waqf property

muttaham/muttakham: parasites; exploiters

namoz/namaz (Arabic): prayer that is formal, public, and required, which is performed five times daily in Arabic. (It can be contrasted with dua, voluntary prayer that can be offered at any time, with any content, and in one's own language.)

namoz oqshom/namaz aksham: evening prayer

namoz xufton/namaz khuptan: nighttime prayer

navruz/nauruz: "New Day," the day marking the start of the New Year on the vernal equinox (March 21), according to Persian traditions that were widespread in Central Asia

nash, nasha: hashish

nikoh/nikakh: religious marriage ceremony

nimker: assistant; apprentice. (The term is not attested in modern Uzbek but is related to Tajik nimkora, meaning incomplete, half-finished.)

non/nan/lepioshka: flat bread

nosvoy/nasvai: snuff; chewing tobacco

objuvoz/abdzhuaz: water mill

oblast' (Russian): province

obrez/abrez: hole in the floor for disposing of water used for ablutions

o'choq/uchak: fireplace inside the house for food preparation and heating

oftaba, obdasta/aftaba: long-necked pitcher for pouring water over the hands and for ablutions

oqshuvoq/shuak: wormwood

oqsoch/ak chach: literally, white-haired; elderly woman servant

oqsoqol/aksakal: literally, white beard: a senior; elder

o'rda/urda: citadel

o'roqchi/urakchi: reapers who use sickles

o'rtoq/urtak: friend

osh-taxta/ash-takhta: small board with legs, for kneading

osh-xona/ash-khana: kitchen

otashdon/ateshdan: small pit in the floor of a dwelling room that holds coals for heating

otin/atun (also buvotin, bibiotin, otuncha, and various other terms): woman teacher who gives Islamic primary instruction for girls

paisa: obsolete measure of weight equal to about 50 grams

paranji/parandzha: woman's veiling robe

pari: good spirit; fairy

parixon: fortune-teller who has seen a spirit

paxsa-devol/pakhsa-dival: rammed-earth wall

paxta/pakhta: upland cotton (*Gossypium hirsutum*), different from Central Asia's indigenous go'za

paxta-dek: white, like cotton

Payshanbalik/Paishambelik: "Thursday" money or goods, given weekly to the maktab teacher by each of the pupils

piyola/piala: tea-drinking bowl

plov/osh (Uzbek)/pilaf (English): festive dish made of rice, carrots, onions, and meat

pud (Russian)/pood (English): measure of weight equal to 36.11 pounds or 16.38 kilograms

qalami/kaliami: woven cotton fabric

qalandar/kalandar: wandering Sufi mystic

qalin/kalym, kalyn: bride wealth, a payment from the groom's family to the bride's parents

qassob/kasab: butcher

qatiq/katyk: soured milk, similar to yogurt

qibla/kibla: the direction toward the Kaaba in Mecca, in mosques marked by a niche; the direction toward which Muslims pray

qobul/kabul: acceptance; agreement

qoracha/karacha: the "black" or ordinary people, deriving from the concept of black bone, as contrasted with white bone or aristocratic

qo'rg'oncha/kurgancha: small, walled fortress

qori/kari: one who knows the Qur'an by heart and recites it on behalf of others

qori xona/kari-khana: building where a qo'ri may live and where he recites

qorovul/karaul: guard

qorovulbegi/karaul-begi: leader of the guard

qo'shchi/koshchi: plowman; hired farm laborer

qovurma/kaurma: fried

qo'ynak, qo'ylak/koinak: shirt or loosely shaped dress

qozi/kazi/qadi (Arabic): judge in an Islamic court

qozi-rais/kazi-rais: leading judge, appointed by the government to oversee and implement Islamic law

quda/kudai: future in-laws; a term referring to the relationship between parents of a groom and parents of a bride

qumg'on/kumgan: copper pitcher

Qurbon Hayit/Kurban: Muslim Festival of the Sacrifice, called Eid al-Adha in Arabic

quroq/kurak: patchwork

rabot/ravat: inn

rais: local authority; administrator who had the authority to enforce moral laws and Sharia norms

ramazanlik: donations that children collect during Ramadan for their teacher

rasmiy: customary

risola/risala: treatise

ro'mol/rumol': large scarf used to cover a woman's head and hair

ro'za/uraza: Muslim month of fasting, or Ramadan

Ro'za Hayit: festival for the final three days of Ramadan; Eid al-Fitr in Arabic

salam/saliam: peace, a term of greeting; extended form, as-salam alaykum

saman: chopped straw

sandal: low, tablelike platform placed over a pit with heating coals where the family sat to stay warm, with feet under the sandal and a blanket over the sandal. (The sandal can still be found in some rural homes in Uzbekistan.)

sandiq/sunduk: trunk for storing clothing and valuables

sarrov: rafter plate or support

Sart: an ethnic name used widely to denote the sedentary population of Central Asia. (The Nalivkins use it to mean both Uzbek/Turkic speakers and Tajik/Persian speakers.)

Sartianka (Russian): Sart woman

saqich: pine tar for chewing; now used as the term for chewing gum

satukchi (dialect)/sotuvchi (Uzbek): seller of goods

savob/savap: good deed; meritorious act

savod: literacy

Sayil: community celebration of springtime

sazhen' (Russian): measure of length equal to 2.13 meters or about 7 feet

shafe: defender; one who provides security for a debt

shaitan: Satan; the devil

sharbat: cold or icy sweetened fruit juice

Shariat (Russian, Uzbek): Islamic law or Sharia

shart-noma/shartnama: legal document, such as an endowment for a waqf

shavla: gruel with rice, fat, carrots, onions, and mutton; watered-down plov

Sherikan or sheriklik: partnership fee

shipang: dual-pitched roof

shogird/shakird: student at a madrasa

sipara: one-thirtieth of the Qur'an, a division that allows the reciter to recite the full Qur'an in one month

sopol: slipware crockery

sotishqin, sotqin/sashkyn: for sale, in particular when a hujra in a madrasa is sold

sovuq/savuk: cold

soy/sai: ravine

sud: interest paid on a loan

Sufi: a Muslim mystic; also used in Uzbek with several other meanings, including muezzin and pure or godly man

sumalak: sweet paste made by boiling down sprouted wheat; associated with the spring festival

supa: platform used for resting, eating, napping, and other activities

sura: chapter of the Qur'an

surpa: goat hide used when raising dough

tahsil: study days; work days

taloq/talak: divorce

tandir/tandur, tanur: clay oven for baking bread

tanga/tenga: unit of money in Turkestan before transition to the Russian ruble

tanob or tanap or shanab: a measure of land that varied widely. (In Namangan district it was approximately 850 square meters, the measure of land one person could plow in a day, using oxen.)

taqsir/taksyr: sir

tashqari/tashkari/anderun (Persian)/selamlik (Turkish): outer rooms and outer courtyard of a house (hovli) complex, a place for men and for male guests

ta'til: days of rest; days off

tilla/tillia: unit of money larger than a tanga

tishqoli/tishkaly: dye for blackening teeth

toboq/tabak or tavak: earthenware dishes

tog'ora/tagara: large serving bowl

tol/tal': willow tree

toloq/talaq (Arabic)/talak (Russian): divorce

tomosha/tamasha: entertainment

to'shak/tushak: narrow, padded mattresses

to'y/tai: feast celebrating a life-cycle occasion, such as marriage, birth, or circumcision

tugai: thicket

tumar: amulet

Turkistani: a native or indigenous person from sedentary Central Asia. (Contrast with Turkestan, the Russian spelling of the territory's name.)

tuurduk (Kyrgyz)/turduk: felt forming the walls of a yurt

uezd (Russian): district

ug'ir keli/ugir kili: mortar and pestle

ulama: false plaits; hair additions

ular: snowcock, a type of pheasant

ulomo (Uzbek)/ulama (Arabic): scholars who are expert in Islamic law and theology

uloq/uliak: a game in which horse riders compete for possession of a goat carcass; also known as buzkashi

un-osh/un-ash: noodles served in boiled water and sour milk, without meat

usma: plant extract used to dye eyebrows and to make them grow

usta: master of a craft

ustakor: shop foreman

val: basket loaded with weights and dragged behind a horse for threshing

vassa: lathwork

vershok: Russian measure of length equal to 1.75 inches or 4.5 centimeters

versta (Russian)/verst (English): Russian measure of distance equal to 0.6629 mile or 1.06 kilometers

viloyat/vilayet: province

voy-dod/vai-dad: a cry for help

waqf (Arabic)/vaqf (Uzbek)/vakif (Russian): charitable foundation that supports an Islamic institution such as a madrasa, mosque, or hospital

xalifa/khalifa: one who has acquired a degree of mastery; in a Sufi tariqat, a spiritual mentor; in a workshop, a foreman

xirmon/khirman: earthen threshing platform

xo'ja/khodzha/khwaja (Persian): lineage groups in Central Asia that claim descent from the Prophet, the first caliphs, or certain Arab saints who brought Islam to Central Asia

xoldor/khal'dar: having a birthmark or a beauty mark (xol)

xona/khana: a room

xonagah/khanaka: a room for prayer and worship

xo'rda: rice gruel

xo'sh kelibsiz: you are welcome, a greeting

xurjun/khurdzhun (also khurdzhum): large saddlebag woven of cotton or wool

xurmacha: bowl for preserving milk

yaktak/iaktak: men's everyday shirt

yangi chikkan/iangi chikkan: newly produced; the latest

yasmiq/iasmyk: lentils

yaxshi/iakhshi: good

yuvgich: one who washes the dead. (The Nalivkins provide the variants goguchi and yuvguchi.)

zaif (Arabic): weak or light, used metaphorically to mean "woman"

zakat: religious obligation, an annual contribution of 2.5 percent of one's income to charity

zolotnik (Russian): measure of weight equal to 0.01 pound or 4.26 grams

Notes

Editor's Introduction

1. The city that was at the center of this Khanate is present-day Qo'qon, Uzbekistan. Alternative spellings for "Qo'qon" include "Kokand," which was the standard Russian form and the form most widely used in English; "Kokan," which was the Nalivkins' spelling; and "Khoqand," a transliteration from the Arabic alphabet used in many scholarly works.

2. Sergei Abashin, "The 'Fierce Fight' at Oshoba: A Microhistory of the Conquest of the Khoqand Khanate," *Central Asian Survey* 33, no. 2 (2014): 215. Alexander Morrison provides a valuable introduction to the Russian conquest of Central Asia. See Alexander Morrison, *Russian Rule in Samarkand, 1868–1910: A Comparison with British India* (Oxford: Oxford University Press, 2008), 11–50.

3. Sergei Abashin, "V. P. Nalivkin: 'Budet to, cho neizbezhno dolzhno byt'; i to chto neizbezhno dolzhno byt', uzhe ne mozhet byt'," *Minaret* 12 (2008), http://www.idmedina.ru /books/history_culture/minaret/12/abashin.htm. Nalivkin's Gur-tiube is present-day Gurtepa in southern Namangan province. All translations in this introduction are by Marianne Kamp.

4. Natalia Lukashova, "V. P. Nalivkin: Eshche odna zamechatel'naia zhizn'," *Vestnik Evrazii*, nos. 1–2 (1999): 39.

5. Vladimir Nalivkin, "Posluzhnoi spisok," May 1906, reproduced in D. I. Arapov, ed., *Musul'manskaia sredniaia aziia: Traditsionalizm i XX vek* (Moscow: Rossiiskaia Akademiia Nauk, 2004), 277; S. B. Mukhamedov, "Vzgliadi V. P. Nalivkina na problem islama v Turkestane," in *Tarihshunoslik o'qishlari 2010: Konferentsiia materiallar to'plami* (Tashkent, Uzbekistan: Yangi Nashr, 2011), 188.

6. Recollections from Nalivkin's daughter, Natalia, in "Materialy k biografii Vladimira Petrovicha Nalivkina," 1957, O'zbekistan Davlat Arxivi [Uzbekistan State Archive] (Uz. Dav. Arx.), Fond 2409, opis 1, delo 7, lists 2–3.

7. Historian Jeff Sahadeo describes the Russian administration's knowledge-building projects in Central Asia and Nalivkin's role in *Russian Colonial Society in Tashkent, 1865–1923* (Bloomington: Indiana University Press, 2007), 58–80. For a discussion on Russian Orientalist training, see David Schimmelpenninck van der Oye, *Russian Orientalism: Asia in the Russian Mind from Peter the Great to the Emigration* (New Haven, CT: Yale University Press, 2010); and Robert Geraci, *Window on the East: National and Imperial Identities in Late Tsarist Russia* (Ithaca, NY: Cornell University Press, 2001).

8. Sources vary on the details of Vladimir Nalivkin's birth. His daughter, Natalia, cited 1855. "Materialy k biografii Vladimira Petrovicha Nalivkina," l. 195b. Academician Boris Lunin dated his birth 1852. Lunin wrote that Nalivkin graduated from gymnasium in St. Petersburg in 1864, which would have made him very precocious. Boris V. Lunin, "Svet i ten' odnoi zamechatel'noi zhizhni (Vladimir Nalivkin)," 1999, Uz. Dav. Arx., F. 2409, op. 1, d. 13, l. 2. Historian Natalia Lukashova pointed out the contradictions in the various sources but views 1852 as the correct year of birth. Lukashova, "V. P. Nalivkin," 38.

9. Lukashova, "V. P. Nalivkin," 39.

10. Alex Marshall, *The Russian General Staff and Asia, 1800–1917* (Abingdon, UK: Routledge, 2006), 9, 20–24.

11. M. M. Kazem-bek, *Obshchaia grammatika turetsko-tatarskago iazyka* (Kazan, Russia: Universitetskaia Tipografiia, 1846). Nalivkin identified a few of his scholarly sources in Vladimir P. Nalivkin, *Kratkaia istoriia kokandskago khanstva* [A short history of Kokand] (Kazan, Russia: Tipografiia Imperatorskago Universiteta, 1886), which he wrote concurrently with *A Sketch*. L. Z. Budagov, *Sravnitel'nyi slovar' turetsko-tatarskikh narechii* (St. Petersburg, Russia: Tipografiia Imperatorskoi Akademii Nauk, 1869–1871).

12. Boris V. Lunin, *Istoriografiia obshchestvennykh nauk v Uzbekistane: Bio-bibliograficheskie ocherki* (Tashkent, Uzbekistan: Fan, 1974), 257. See also Boris V. Lunin, *Sredniaia aziia v dorevoliutsionnom i sovetskom vostokovedenii* (Tashkent, Uzbekistan: Nauka, 1965), 226.

13. Ol'ga Pugovkina, "M. V. Nalivkina: Pervaia zhenshchina-etnograf sredei azii (na osnove vpechatlenii zhizni v ferganskoi doline)," *O'zbekiston Tarixi*, no. 1 (2011): 62–69. D. Iu. Arapov instead identifies her as attending the Saratov Women's Institute. See D. Iu. Arapov, "Vladimir Petrovich Nalivkin," in Arapov, *Musul'manskaia sredniaia aziia*, 14. Lukashova puts Nalivkina at Smolny. See Lukashova, "V. P. Nalivkin," 55. Her daughter, Natalia, wrote that Maria attended Saratov Institute. See "Materialy k biografii Vladimira Petrovicha Nalivkina," l. 1.

14. Ivan Borisovich Nalivkin, "Vospominaniia o V. P. Nalivkin," 1957, Uz. Dav. Arx., F. 2409, op. 1, d. 9, l. 19. This description sounds more like the education that Smolny Institute provided than the education in an 1870s women's gymnasium. Anna Kuxhausen offers a description of Smolny Institute's curriculum and a contrast with a state gymnasium in *From the Womb to the Body Politic: Raising the Nation in Enlightenment Russia* (Madison: University of Wisconsin Press, 2013), 121–143.

15. In 1873, there were fifty-five girls' gymnasia in Russia with 8,713 girls enrolled. Christine Johanson, *Women's Struggle for Higher Education in Russia, 1855–1900* (Montreal: McGill University Press, 1987), 31; Thomas Ewing, "From an Exclusive Privilege to a Right and an Obligation: Modern Russia," in *Girls' Secondary Education in the Western World: From the 18th to the 20th Century*, ed. James C. Albisetti, Joyce Goodman, and Rebecca Rogers (New York: Palgrave Macmillan, 2010), 165–179; Barbara Alpern Engel, *Mothers and Daughters: Women of the Intelligentsia in Nineteenth-Century Russia* (Cambridge: Cambridge University Press, 1983), 23–24.

16. Vladimir Nalivkin, memoir, Uz. Dav. Arx., F. 2409, op. 1, d. 9, l. 20, cited in Pugovkina, "M. V. Nalivkina," 63. Nanay was a mixed village, with Sart and Kyrgyz families. While the book is about Sart women who followed fully sedentary farming lifestyles, the Nalivkins clearly also interacted with Kyrgyz, even going to summer pastures with them.

17. V. Nalivkin and M. Nalivkina, *Russko-sartovskii i sartovsko-russkii slovar' obscheupotrebitel'nykh slov, s prilozheniem kratkoi grammatiki po narechiia Namanganskogo uezda* (Kazan, Russia: Tipografiia Imperatorskago Universiteta, 1884). They also published a brief description of Sart grammar based on Andijon dialect in the same year.

18. Paragraphs of geographic description from the first chapter of *Sketch* also appear in V. P. Nalivkin, *Short History*, 2–4.

19. Lukashova, "V. P. Nalivkin," 40, quoting Nalivkin's archived writings.

20. V. P. Nalivkin, "Posluzhnoi spisok," 280. The thirteen-year gap between the birth of the second (Boris, 1878) and third (Natalia, 1891) raises questions. Nalivkin mentioned the arrival of two babies during the Nanay years (1878–1884), and he may have named only his surviving children in 1906. Family portraits taken when daughter Natalia was a young girl include other unidentified children who perhaps were other Nalivkin offspring who did not survive. See twelve family photographs, Uz. Dav. Arx., F. 2409, op. 1; I. B. Nalivkin, "Vospominaniia," Uz. Dav. Arx., F. 2409, op. 1, d. 9, l. 20.

21. Abashin, "V. P. Nalivkin"; Lukashova, "V. P. Nalivkin." See also Alexander Morrison, "Metropole, Colony, and Imperial Citizenship in the Russian Empire," *Kritika: Explorations*

in Russian and Eurasian History 13, no. 2 (2002): 355–356. For more on Central Asian representatives in the Duma, see Adeeb Khalid, *The Politics of Muslim Cultural Reform: Jadidism in Central Asia* (Berkeley: University of California Press, 1998), 31–35.

22. Abashin, "V. P. Nalivkin."

23. Daniel Brower, *Turkestan and the Fate of the Russian Empire* (Abingdon, UK: Routledge, 2003), 179–180. In 1916 the Russian Empire initiated conscription among Kazakhs, Uzbeks, and other Central Asians for service in wartime labor battalions. Indigenous Turkistanis rose up against the Russian administration in demonstrations and then in violent attacks against Russian settlers. Brower misidentifies Vladimir Nalivkin as "Nikolai" Nalivkin. Sahadeo reviews the complex turn of events in 1917, including Nalivkin's role. See Sahadeo, *Russian Colonial Society*, 187–206. See also Khalid, *Politics of Muslim Cultural Reform*, 272.

24. Abashin, "V. P. Nalivkin."

25. Lukashova, "V. P. Nalivkin," 58. The detail that he shot himself, unmentioned by either Lukashova or Lunin, comes from "Materialy k biografii Vladimira Petrovicha Nalivkina," l. 5.

26. For example, see Charles Steinwedel, "How Bashkiria Became Part of European Russia, 1762–1881," in *Russian Empire: Space, People, Power, 1700–1930*, ed. Jane Burbank, Mark von Hagen, and Anatolyi Remnev (Bloomington: Indiana University Press, 2007), 94–124; and Austin Jersild, "From Savagery to Citizenship: Caucasian Mountaineers and Muslims in the Russian Empire," in *Russia's Orient: Imperial Borderlands and Peoples, 1700–1917*, ed. D. Brower and E. Lazzerini (Bloomington: Indiana University Press, 1997), 101–114.

27. Morrison, "Metropole, Colony, and Imperial Citizenship."

28. Lukashova, "V. P. Nalivkin," 84; Lunin, *Istoriografiia obshchestvennykh nauk*, 252. The medal was indeed awarded. Russkoe Geograficheskoe Obshchestvo, "Perechen' nagrazhdennykh znakami otlichiia russkogo geograficheskogo obshchestva (1845–2012)," 2012, http://www.rgo.ru/sites/default/files/upload/spisok-nagrazhdennyh_8.pdf.

29. Quoted in Lunin, *Istoriografiia obshchestvennykh nauk*, 252.

30. Brower describes this imperial knowledge production in *Turkestan and the Fate of the Russian Empire*, 43–56. Examples of the scholarly, commissioned research are A. P. Fedchenko, *Puteshestvie v Turkestan*, 2 vols. (St. Petersburg, Russia: Knizhnyi sklad M. Stasiulevicha, 1874–1880); N. A. Maev, *Russkii Turkestan: Sbornik izdannyi po povodu politicheskoi vystavki* (Moscow: Universitetskaia Tipografiia, 1872); N. Severtsov, *Obshchye otchety o puteshestviiakh 1857–1868 godov* (St. Petersburg, Russia: Trubnikov, 1873); Aleksandr von Middendorff, *Ocherki Ferganskoi Doliny* (St. Petersburg, Russia: Tipografiia Imperatorskago Akademii Nauk, 1881); and L. F. Kostenko, *Turkestanskii Krai: Materialy voennostatisticheskogo obozreniia Turkestanskogo voennogo okruga* (St. Petersburg, Russia: Tipografiia Transhelia, 1880).

31. A. P. Fedchenko, *Puteshestvie v Turkestan*, vol. 1, bk. 2, *V Kokandskom Khanstve*. (St. Petersburg, Russia: Knizhnyi sklad M. Stasiulevicha, 1875), 99–100.

32. Edward Said makes this clear in *Orientalism* (London: Penguin, 1977), 37–40.

33. Schimmelpenninck van der Oye, *Russian Orientalism*, 5.

34. A. P. Khoroshkhin, *Sbornik statei kasaiiushchikhsia do turkestanskago kraia* (St. Petersburg, Russia: Tipografiia i Khromolitografiia A. Transhelia, 1876), 116–117, 219, 223.

35. Ibid., 227.

36. A. P. Khoroshkhin, *Sbornik statei kasaiiushchikhsia do turkestanskago kraia*.

37. Nathaniel Knight, "Nikolai Kharuzin and the Quest for a Universal Human Science," *Kritika: Explorations in Russian and Eurasian History* 9, no. 1 (2008): 85.

38. Sergei Abashin, "Problema sartov v russkoi istoriografii XIX– pervoi chetverti XX v.," in *Natsionalizmy v srednei azii: V poiskakh identichnosti*, by Sergei Abashin (St. Petersburg, Russia: Atelia, 2007), 95–176. Abashin discusses the continuation of this debate into present-day

Central Asian historiography in "Vozvrashchenie sartov? Metodologiia i ideologiia v post-sovetskikh nauchnykh diskussiiakh," *Antropologicheskii Forum*, no. 10 (2009): 252-278.

39. Middendorff, *Ocherki Ferganskoi Doliny*, 409. For Middendorff's broader discussion of ethnography, see *Ocherki Ferganskoi Doliny*, 389-412. V. Nalivkin made direct, repeated reference to Middendorff's work in *A Short History of Kokand* for the purpose of arguing against Middendorff. In 1883 he published a critical review of Middendorff, focusing arguments on Uzbek ethnogenesis and land use in Fergana. Lunin, *Istoriografiia obshchestvennykh nauk*, 251-252.

40. Lukashova, "V. P. Nalivkin," 40.

41. The scholarly debate over the terms "Sart" and "Uzbek" gained political force in the 1920s, when the Soviet Union delineated the Uzbek Soviet Socialist Republic, and many people who previously had been recorded as Sart, Turk, Kipchak, or Kuruma became identified as Uzbek. Whether this was an erasure of earlier identities or a recognition of self-naming practices remains debated. Anthropologist Peter Finke reviews the scholarship on Turkic sedentarization and identity in *Variations on Uzbek Identity: Strategic Choices, Cognitive Schemas and Political Constraints in Identification Processes* (Oxford: Berghahn, 2014). See also Yuri Bregel, "The Sarts in the Khanate of Khiva," *Journal of Asian History* 12 (1978): 121-151; Alisher Il'khamov, "Arkheologiia Uzbekskoi identichnosti," in *Etnicheskiii atlas Uzbekistana* (Tashkent, Uzbekistan: Institute Otkyrtogo Obshchestva, 2002), 268-302; Abashin, *Natsionalizmy v srednei azii*; Marlene Laruelle, Sergei Abashin, Marianne Kamp, Adeeb Khalid, and Alisher Il'khamov, "Constructing a National History in the Language of Soviet Science after the Collapse of the USSR: The Case of Uzbekistan," *Ab Imperio*, no. 4 (2005): 279-359; and Abashin, "Problema sartov v russkoi istoriografii XIX–pervoi chetverti XX v."

42. Barbara Evans Clements, *A History of Women in Russia* (Bloomington: Indiana University Press, 2012), 114. Vernadskaia's ideas were published in the 1850s.

43. William G. Wagner, *Marriage, Property and Law in Late Imperial Russia* (Oxford: Oxford University Press, 1994), 103, 109.

44. Richard Stites, *The Women's Liberation Movement in Russia: Feminism, Nihilism, and Bolshevism, 1860-1930* (1978; repr., Princeton, NJ: Princeton University Press, 1990), 75-105.

45. Laurie Bernstein, *Sonia's Daughters: Prostitutes and Their Regulation in Imperial Russia* (Berkeley: University of California Press, 1995), 85.

46. The Nalivkins were perhaps unaware that the survival rate for abandoned infants in Russia's orphanage and fosterage system was disastrously low in the late nineteenth century. David Ransel, "Abandonment and Fosterage of Unwanted Children: The Women of the Foundling System," in *The Family in Imperial Russia*, ed. D. Ransel (Urbana: University of Illinois Press, 1978), 189-205. See also Kuxhausen, *From the Womb to the Body Politic*, 71-74.

47. Gordii Semenovich Sablukov, *Koran: Zakonodatel'naia kniga mokhammedanskago veroucheniia; Perevod s arabskago* (Kazan, Russia: Tipografii Imperatorskago Universiteta, 1877).

48. I. B. Nalivkin, "Vospominaniia," ll. 7-8.

49. Lunin, "Svet i ten'," l. 27.

50. Many sources attest that potatoes and tomatoes were introduced and widely adopted in the 1930s, but there is little evidence about when eating cucumbers and fresh herbs became widespread. It is possible that the Nalivkins simply did not mention them or that they came into wide consumption later. For more on cadastral surveys and rural taxation, see Beatrice Penati, "Beyond Technicalities: Land Assessment and Land-Tax in Russian Turkestan (ca. 1880-1917)," *Jahrbücher für Geschichte Osteuropas* 59, no. 1 (2011): 1-27.

51. Tian'-Shanskaia (1863-1906) was the daughter of the famous explorer and geographer Pyotr Petrovich Semyonov (1827-1914), who added Tian'-Shanskii to his name to connect himself to the Central Asian Tian-Shan mountains, the site of his most famous adventures.

52. The 1897 census for Turkestan provides evidence that daughters were about 10 percent less likely to survive infancy than sons. *Pervaia vseobshchaia perepis' naseleniia rossiiskoi imperii, 1897 g.*, vol. 89, *Ferganskaia oblast'* (St. Petersburg, Russia: Izdatel'stvo Tsentral'nago Statisticheskago Komiteta Ministerstva Vnutrennikh Del, 1897), 18.

53. Wagner, *Marriage, Property and Law.*

54. Linda Benson, "A Much-Married Woman: Marriage and Divorce in Xinjiang," *Muslim World* 83, nos. 3–4 (1993): 227–247. For a brief explanation of the many migrations and resettlements of Turkistanis between Fergana and Kashgar in the nineteenth century, see Abashin, *Natsionalizmy v srednei azii*, 53–64.

55. See, for example, the works cited in the bibliography by Soviet period ethnographers N. A. Kisliakov, M. A. Bikzhanova, F. D. Liushkevich, and K. Sh. Shaniiazov; historians and Orientalists Boris V. Lunin, and Dilarom Alimova; and post-Soviet ethnographers Sergei Abashin, G. Sh. Zununova, and Svetlana Peshkova.

56. Lukashova, "V. P. Nalivkin," 51.

57. Since the late 1980s, the varied spring holiday celebrations in Uzbekistan have been pulled together under one name, Navruz, which is now designated as a national holiday with roots dating back to Zoroastrianism. Laura Adams explains Navruz's establishment as a national holiday in *The Spectacular State: Culture and National Identity in Uzbekistan* (Durham, NC: Duke University Press, 2010).

58. Marianne Kamp, *The New Woman in Uzbekistan: Islam, Modernity, and Unveiling under Communism* (Seattle: University of Washington Press, 2006); Peter Finke, *Variations on Uzbek Identity*, 86.

59. *O'zbek tilining izohli lug'ati: Ikki tomli*, ed. Z. M. Ma'rufov (Moscow: Izdatel'stvo Russkii Iazyk, 1980); *Uzbeksko-russkii slovar'*, ed. S. F. Akobirov and G. N. Mikhailov (Tashkent, Uzbekistan: O'zbek Sovet Entsiklopediiasi Bosh Redaktsiiasi, 1988).

1. A Short Sketch of the Fergana Valley

1. A verst is a Russian measure of length equal to 0.6629 miles or 1.0668 kilometers.

2. An arshin is a Russian unit of measure equal to 28 inches or 71 centimeters.

3. The authors use *tol*, which means willow or holly; they probably meant *majnun tol*, or weeping willow. They use *jida/dzhigda*, known in the West as Russian olive.

4. An araba is a cart with two wheels, drawn by draft animals.

5. The authors use the Russian term *glinobitnyi*, which can translate either as wattle and daub, or as *pise*—rammed earth. Neither is exactly accurate as a description of vernacular house construction for Fergana Valley houses, which did not use a reed framework (wattle) or a wooden form to be filled with clay (rammed earth). House construction is discussed in chapter 3.

6. For a discussion on Bukharan Jews in Russian Central Asia, see Audrey Burton, "Bukharan Jews, Ancient and Modern," *Jewish Historical Studies* 34 (1994–1996): 43–68; and Catherine Poujol, "Approaches to the History of Bukharan Jews' Settlement in the Fergana Valley, 1867–1917," *Central Asian Survey* 12, no. 4 (1993): 549–556. For a discussion on Hindu (Indian) merchants in Russian Central Asia, see Scott Levi, *The Indian Diaspora in Central Asia and Its Trade, 1550–1900* (Leiden, Netherlands: Brill, 2002).

7. Rather than use the Central Asian names for these foods, as is their practice throughout this text, the Nalivkins use these Russian terms, *pel'meni* and *pirozhki*, for somewhat similar Central Asian foods. Unlike Russian pel'meni, which are small, boiled, meat-filled dumplings, *manti* are meat or vegetable filled, fist sized, and steamed. Russian pirozhki involve raised

dough filled with meat, while Central Asian *somsa* have flaky pastry dough, often with a meat filling, are palm sized, and are baked in a *tandir*, a wood-fired clay oven.

8. This process makes the surface of the silk fabric shine.

9. Atlas is woven silk fabric, with resist-dyed warp, like ikat. Kanaus is a rough silk, woven fabric. Iparkak is not attested in Uzbek, Tajik, or Russian, but the Nalivkins describe it elsewhere as a lightweight silk fabric. In Uzbek, *ipak* is silk. Adras is half-silk, half-cotton woven fabric.

10. Russian *soldatka* could mean either a soldier's wife or a woman who was a camp follower.

11. The authors seem to mean below-zero temperatures when they mention Celsius values, though they do not specify that. If the authors suggest that average temperatures in December and January are –5 to –15 degrees Celsius, this equals 5 to 15 degrees Fahrenheit. If they mean the numbers to be positive, as indeed appears in the text, the average temperatures would be 41 to 59 degrees Fahrenheit. Neither seems quite accurate for the Fergana Valley. In 2010, average winter temperatures in Namangan were –5 to 5 degrees Celsius.

12. More recent data show Namangan at 476 meters (1,551 feet), Marg'ilon at 487 meters (1,587 feet), and Andijon at 492 meters (1,614 feet).

13. Asamusa (Uz) or *asoi musa* (Tajik) means the staff of Moses, a plant used for making walking sticks or canes.

14. A sazhen' is a Russian measure of length equal to about 7 feet or 2.13 meters.

15. The Nalivkins use the Russian word *kibitka* for yurt. The Kyrgyz term would translate as felt house.

16. Lutchak or luchchak is attested only as the name of an apricot or peach.

17. The author indicates planted fields surrounded by earthen walls. Hayat now means a planted area near a house, with or without a wall.

18. The Nalivkins use the traditional Russian heating stove as their comparison.

19. "Salam alaykum," or "The peace of God be with you," is a standard Muslim greeting.

20. The Nalivkins refer to non/nan (Central Asian bread rounds baked in a tandir, a clay oven), using the Russian word *lepioshka*, which can mean a flat bread or a flat cake.

21. The Nalivkins describe it as *kul'turnyi*, which in this context could mean civilized or planted.

22. Khudoyor Khan was the penultimate ruler of the independent Khanate of Kokand; an internal coup led to Russian conquest in 1875, a military action in which Vladimir Nalivkin took part.

23. The Nalivkins use the Russian term *tuzemtsy*, meaning indigenous or people from this land.

24. Sumsama is not attested.

25. Authors' note: Apart from these two ethnic groups, there are small numbers of Jews, Gypsies, and Hindus.

26. The Nalivkins' term here is *rod* (clan or lineage group).

27. *Sartianka* is Russian for Sart woman. The sentence seems illogical: Why should the fact that Uzbeks and Tajiks are culturally the same mean that Russians call Uzbek women "Sart"? Many Russians used the term "Sart" to refer to both Uzbek and Tajik speakers who were urban or sedentary farmers, and the Nalivkins seem to suggest that what they say about Uzbek women in Fergana Valley would equally pertain to Tajik women.

28. Authors' note: The majority of the books were in Persian. It was also the language of most official documents and papers before the Russians arrived.

29. Modern Uzbek presents this word as *qimirlaidi*. The Nalivkins judge the Persian "ah" pronunciation in words such as "nan" as correct, and the Uzbek "aw" (as in "law" or "raw"), represented in modern Uzbek with "o" rather than "a," as in the case of "non," as wrong.

30. Sharia is Islamic law. The Nalivkins use the word loosely to refer to all the texts that shape Muslim moral thinking. They render the word as *Shariat*, as it appears in Russian and in Uzbek. They use the Russian/Christian term "tithe" to convey the meanings of both *zakat* (charitable donations) and taxes.

31. Plov/palau is rice with meat and carrots, or pilaf.

32. A chorikor is a sharecropper or tenant farmer; a qo'shchi is a plowman. Koranda is one who pays rent for land in the form of a portion of the harvest.

33. Authors' note: These are mainly poor urban dwellers who are currently unemployed and residents of the kishlak who for some reason failed to obtain a land lot as chorikors.

34. A desiatina is a Russian measure of area equal to 1.0925 hectares. The Uzbek term is *tanap/tanob* (shanap may have been a dialect variant or misprint), and its dimensions varied significantly by region. The Nalivkins' measurement makes a tanob equal to about 850 square meters, so the smallest landholdings were about 200 square meters. The largest holdings were 275 hectares.

35. Authors' note: "The good and fat animals we selected for sacrificial offerings to God; you will receive his grace for that. Say the name of God over them, when they are standing there; when they stop breathing, eat their meat and feed it to the poor who ask you for it and the beggar, who does not even dare ask. We have given the animals to you assuming that you will be grateful. It is not their meat or blood that rises to God; it is your piety." Koran, chapter 22, verses 37–38.

Editor's note: Nalivkin's translation is of Qur'an 22:36–37, and the first line of the verse refers specifically to "the sacrificial camels we have made for you as among the symbols from God." Uzbeks refer to the Muslim festival Eid al-Adha, festival of the sacrifice, as Qurban.

36. *Syrat* here is a reference to Qur'an 19:71.

37. The Nalivkins do not explain how they knew this, who established this rule, or how it was enforced locally.

38. Vladimir Nalivkin was himself an avid hunter, going out nearly every day in the appropriate seasons, according to his granddaughter's memoir. Z. Nalivkina, untitled notes about her grandfather, Vladimir Nalivkin, O'zbekiston Davlat Arxivi [Uzbekistan State Archive], Fond 2409, opis 1, delo 12, list 6.

39. The Uzbek term is xo'ja; the Persian, *khwaja*, referring to lineages claiming descent from the early Arab Muslim missionaries to Central Asia. Nalivkin presented the term as *khodzhi*, turning the Persian singular into a Russian plural (replacing "a" with "i"). However, his term would mean one who made the hajj. A more thorough explanation of the xo'ja is found in Bruce Privratsky, *Muslim Turkistan: Kazakh Religion and Collective Memory* (London: Routledge, 2001).

40. Qoracha means from the "black" or common people. This draws on a differentiation between the *oq suyak* (noble, white bone) and the *qora suyak* (common, black bone).

41. Some of these goods were produced in Russia, while others, such as tea, were imported via Russia, usually from China.

42. Makruh is an Arabic term, a Sharia determination of "reprehensible," which means that this action is looked down on and discouraged but not *haraam* or forbidden.

43. The Nalivkins use the Russian term *tsygan'ka*. In Central Asia this ethnic group is usually called Lo'li, which sometimes appears in Russian as Liuli.

44. Qalandar was a particular order (*tariqat*) of Muslim mystics; more generally, wandering Sufi mystics are called dervish.

45. Guzar is a crossroads where there are shops.

46. The supa, or sitting platform, is placed beside a small water channel to make it a cool resting place.

47. Satukchi is a variant of *sotuvchi*, a salesperson, someone with goods to sell.

48. A xurjun is a woven saddlebag for a horse or camel. A xurjun was also hung on inner walls as a storage container.

49. Jiyak are woven, decorative strips used for edging women's pants.

50. Ramadan, the Islamic month of fasting, is known as Ro'za (Uzbek spelling) in Central Asia, from Persian, "a day of fasting."

51. Azan is an Arabic term, a call to prayer, "Allah Akbar" means "God is the greatest."

52. Anthropologist Russell Zanca discusses the enduring appreciation for fat in Uzbek cuisine in "Fat and All That: Good Eating the Uzbek Way," in *Everyday Life in Central Asia*, ed. J. Sahadeo and R. Zanca (Bloomington: Indiana University Press, 2007), 178–197.

53. Uzbek qovurma simply means fried, from the verb *qovurmoq*, to fry.

54. Aulie-ata is now Taraz, Kazakhstan; Tokmak is in Kyrgyzstan; and Vernyi was the Russian fort that became Almaty, Kazakhstan.

55. Semirechie (Seven Rivers, or Jetti-su) was the name of the province that now makes up most of southeastern Kazakhstan.

56. Perovsk is now Kyzyl Orda, Kazakhstan.

57. Authors' note: "If any trade transactions or deals happen among you, you will not be blamed for giving no receipts. Have witnesses present at the time of discussing the conditions of the deal among yourselves. . . ." Koran, chapter 2, verse 282.

58. Qozi (Uzbek)/kazi (Russian) means judge in an Islamic court (Arabic, *qaḍi*). Nalivkin seems to draw on local understandings of Islam in his explanations. The Qur'anic verse he cites is selectively quoted, as it begins with the insistence that a written document is always necessary for trade.

59. Authors' note: "Witnesses cannot decline if they are called to witness." Koran, chapter 2, verse 282.

60. Authors' note: "Those who are greedy in charging interest will be resurrected in the same way as those whose mind was touched and taken away by Satan. . . . God allows profit from trade but interest is forbidden. . . . If the person is burdened by poverty, you should wait till his wealth improves; but it would be best if you turn the debt into alms. . . ." Koran, chapter 2, verses 276–281.

2. Religion and Clergy

1. Hanafi/Khanafiia is one of the four "schools" of law and interpretation in Sunni Islam. Azami is another name for this school of Islamic law, founded by Imam Abu Hanifa (d. 767 CE/148 AH).

2. These translations adhere word for word to the Nalivkins' text, and the difference between them and the Qur'an's authoritative translations is substantial. Multiple translations of the Qur'an were available in Russian, but the Nalivkins used Sablukov's 1877 translation. Sablukov, an Orthodox Christian missionary, used words and names familiar to his Christian readers where possible, such as Maria, who is Maryam in Qur'an, or Mary in the English New Testament. However, instead of their Magomet, I spell the name of the Prophet Muhammad in the more commonly accepted way. At the time, there was no translation of the Qur'an into Uzbek or Persian, and there is no evidence that the Nalivkins read Arabic.

3. Sablukov's translation differs from a more standard understanding. Abdullah Yusuf Ali uses this phrasing: "the Record [of Deeds] will be placed open." *The Meaning of the Holy Qur'an* (Brentwood, MD: Amana, 1991).

4. Authors' note: In various places of our work, we use verses of the Koran from the Russian translation by G. Sablukov, published in 1877.

5. Authors' note: Birth sisters may both become wives of the same individual but at different times.

6. The Nalivkins identified this as verse 123, but in a more standard translation, it is 124 and ends "and not the least injustice will be done to them." Ali, *The Meaning of the Holy Qur'an*.

7. Sablukov uses *postoronyi*, a word that means stranger, outsider, or extraneous. Usually this Qur'an passage is understood as referring to elderly women, not to outsiders.

8. Authors' note: A wife cannot be called "mother" or "sister" even as a joke; and the husband cannot be his own wife's teacher. A violation of this rule is one of the reasons for divorce.

9. The Nalivkins use *dukhovenstvo*, meaning clergy or priesthood. Islam has no similar role; many scholars would say that to call Muslim religious leaders "clergy" is a misnomer.

10. Implied here is a contrast: Russian Orthodox clergy were members of a hereditary estate, appointed to positions based on lineage rather than on knowledge or expertise. See Laurie Manchester, *Holy Fathers, Secular Sons: Clergy, Intelligentsia, and the Modern Self in Revolutionary Russia* (DeKalb: Northern Illinois University Press, 2008).

11. Violent crimes and cases involving Russian citizens went to the Russian colonial administration instead of to the qozi's court.

12. Nalivkin writes *zemlia*, land or soil. This seems to be a miswording: Now Ruz (New Year at the vernal equinox, commonly celebrated across Turkic and Persian cultures) takes place when the new wheat sprouts.

13. Petrushka, a character from Gogol's novel *Dead Souls*, was a servant who read everything he found.

14. This would be a dialect variation of *savod chiqti* or *savodli chiqti*, meaning that he or she became literate or he or she can read.

15. Central Asians regard the space in front of the wall opposite the door as the place of highest honor in the room, the *to'r*; guests, family members, or in this case schoolchildren sat in descending order of their importance and age, with the youngest and least important nearest the door.

16. Authors' note: Those who have especially clear and beautiful handwriting earn 60 kopeks.

17. *Mukhtasar al-Wiqaya*, by 'Ubaydallah b. Mas'ud (d. 747/1346), is a work of Hanafi *fiqh* (legal interpretation) that was commonly taught as part of the madrasa curriculum.

18. This may refer to Sheikh Sirajuddin's *Ilm ul-Faraiz* (*Ilm-i Feraiz*) or *Faraiz al-Sirajiyya*, a thirteenth-century work, which has been translated as *The Muslim Law of Inheritance, Sirajiyya*.

19. Authors' note: Property (mainly land) that generates profits used by that institution; a waqf is a charitable foundation set up to support a particular institution in perpetuity.

20. A shogird (Persian) is a student in higher education.

21. A mutevali/mutawalli (the Arabic word in its accepted English form) is the caretaker of the waqf property who sees to the fulfillment of its conditions. Frequently the donor assigned this role to his lineage in perpetuity.

22. A thorough discussion of the standard madrasa curriculum for this time period can be found in Allen Frank, *Bukhara and the Muslims of Russia: Sufism, Education, and the Paradox of Islamic Prestige* (Leiden, Netherlands: Brill, 2012).

23. The Nalivkins provide the term *tauzi*, which seems closest to *tavsiia*. The Noble Mishkat, probably meaning *Mishkat al-Masabih* by Muhammad Khatib al-Tabrizi, is a work on hadith.

24. The Uzbek term *sotishqin* or *sotqin* means on sale or for sale.

25. An eshon/ishan is the leader of a Sufi lineage or order, also called *pir*; qori (Uz) is a Qur'an reciter. Duo-xon is from the Arabic *dua*, voluntary prayer, and the Persian *khondan*, to read, meaning one who recites prayers, often at pilgrimage sites.

26. The Uzbek versions of these various hazrat or saints are Said Mir (or Amir) Kulol (1287–1370); Boboyi agalyk may be Muhammad Boboyi Samosiy (1259–1354); Hazrat-i Shoh-i Jon and Pat-abad are unattested; Khazret-i-Divan-i Bagaveddin is Muhammad Bahauddin Naqshbandi (1318–1389).

27. Authors' note: Poetry is the exception. Still, even here the ancient authors are preferred to the new ones.

28. A zolotnik is a Russian measure of weight equal to 4.26 grams.

29. This way of thinking about foods remains widespread in Uzbekistan and seems related to both South and East Asian understandings of hot and cold foods.

30. Mumiyo is also known as *shilajit* in Ayurvedic medicine, referring to a tarry, mineral-laden substance sourced from certain natural seepages in mountainous areas. Mumiyo remains a popular remedy in Central Asia.

31. Roller birds are in the family Coraciidae; the Uzbek name given here is "blue crow." All of the remedies use something *ko'k*, or blue.

3. Houses and Utensils

1. Loess are deposits formed from windblown sand and silt.

2. A vershok is a Russian measure of length equal to 1.75 inches or 4.5 centimeters.

3. This is equal to 60 × 90 or 90 × 120 feet.

4. The word we translate as shrub is Russian biriuchina (*Ligustrum vulgare*), common privet.

5. At some point in the twentieth century, these clay supas were almost entirely replaced with wooden platforms of the same dimensions.

6. Sprinkling water on the courtyard and in the entrance area to the house several times a day remains a common practice, a way of keeping the dust down.

7. In Uzbek, this roofed porch is called *aivan*.

8. Jigit or yigit is young man.

9. Authors' note: Sometimes, mostly in towns, a *bala-xona* (a high room), which is sort of a mezzanine, is built above one of the buildings of the external courtyard; it is a tiny room that is built there because there is no space for it downstairs, in the yard, or in order to have a room above other buildings that would get more breeze in summer. In the second case, the windows and doors of the bala-xona are oriented to receive a draft.

10. Authors' note: "So when you enter houses, greet each other, wishing peace, asking God's prosperity. . . ." Koran, chapter 24, verse 61.

11. The piyola is a tea-drinking bowl, lacking handles, with a volume of about 0.5 cup or 150 milliliters.

12. Authors' note: "As-salam-alaykum!" "Alaykum-as-salam!" "Are you healthy?" "Thank God. I should ask you how you are doing?" "Thank God, we are doing well and are healthy." "Is your family doing well?" "Thanks to God." "Are you calm? Are you in full health?" etc.

13. "Marhamat qiling" means "You are welcome." "Nonga qarang" means "Behold the bread." "Mirvan bo'ling" is unattested but may be a variant of *mehribon* (Tajik for kind, loving), meaning "Be so kind as to."

14. Authors' note: "Eat that, over which God's name has been pronounced. . . ." Koran, chapter 6, verse 118.

15. Authors' note: Sharia prescribes that if a man has several wives, each has the right to demand from her husband a completely separate room that can be locked with a key.

16. English manufacturer Francis Gardner established a porcelain factory in Russia in the 1760s.

17. The Nalivkins referred to the Russian beliefs that going barefoot results in catching colds, as does sitting on cold surfaces, that any draft will make one ill, and so forth.

18. Authors' note: In some kishlaks of the Namangan region (among the migrants from near the city of Turkestan who came here about one hundred years ago), they build a so-called *yer-uchak* (clay oven). A small stove is constructed under the earthen floor of the hut; the chimney of that stove is installed into one of the walls and goes through it outside. The stove is used to cook food, and the chimney pipe heats much of the floor, where the whole family sleeps. A similar heating system—i.e., warming the floor—is practiced in Kul'dzha and, probably, in Kashgar.

Editor's note: This arrangement, known as the *kang*, was typical of traditional northern Chinese architecture.

19. The qibla indicates the direction of the Kaaba in Mecca, the direction toward which one prays.

20. Authors' note: The blankets are always padded [filled with cotton batting and quilted], from 2½ to 3 arshin per side, square, sewn from chintz, ticking, or the native cotton or silk fabrics.

21. A cauldron, a cast-iron cook pot, has connotations that do not quite fit the Uzbek qozon/kazan, which is cast iron but has no neck (narrowing at the top) and has sides that slope rather gradually.

22. The Nalivkins explain how the oven is built but not how it is used to bake bread. A fire is built inside the tandir, and when it dies down to coals, the rounds of non (bread dough) are moistened on one side and then pressed against the sides or top of the tandir. The opening at the front of the tandir is covered with a lid or a blanket, and the bread inside bakes within minutes.

23. An oftoba or obdasta is a long-necked water pitcher used for pouring water over the hands; it is not a bowl.

24. Authors' note: There is a superstitious belief that an osh-taxta placed not on its legs but on its side presages someone's death. Sart women say that the so-called *goguchi* [*yuvgich*], women that specialize in washing female dead bodies for a special fee, never miss an opportunity to turn the osh-taxta in a stranger's house on its side.

25. The Nalivkins use dacha, a Russian word for a vacation house or cottage.

4. Woman's Appearance and Her Clothing

1. This expression may indicate a dust-covered boot, perhaps tan or khaki.

2. Authors' note: The temperature in most of the native homes is below 0 [degrees] Celsius in winter.

3. The Nalivkins were describing variolation, inoculating by using live virus, putting the pus of a smallpox pustule into a small cut on the hand of a person who lacked prior exposure, a practice recorded in medieval Arab and Chinese sources. Gulten Dinc and Yesim Isil Ulman, "The Introduction of Variolation 'à la Turca' to the West by Lady Mary Montagu and Turkey's Contribution to This," *Vaccine* 25, no. 21 (2007): 4261–4265. The Nalivkins' wording is not precise enough to differentiate vaccination (in the manner pioneered by Edward Jenner, using cowpox) from variolation. In fact, the Russian administration provided very few hospitals.

4. The Nalivkins' descriptions of fabrics indicate that Russian-manufactured chintzes were common in Central Asian markets, where they sold alongside local handwoven cotton and silk fabrics.

5. Brilliantine was a lightweight fabric made with a mixture of cotton or silk and wool or mohair; the fabric had a glossy finish.

6. Nalivkins use *ichigi* (Russian) for *mahsi* (Uzbek)—soft leather boots with a soft sole. Uzbeks refer to the combination of soft-soled boot and overshoe as *mahsi kalish*.

7. Authors' note: An abbreviation of *chashm-band*.

Editor's note: Chashm-band (Persian) is a strip of cloth that goes around the forehead; but in Turkestan a chimbet, chashm-band, or *chachvon* was a very large veiling cloth made of woven horsehair that covered both face and chest.

8. Paranji (Uzbek) is from Arabic/Persian *feraj*, which means robe or shirt.

9. Authors' note: "They should not stamp their feet so that they show off their covered adornments." Koran, chapter 24, verse 31.

10. Kir means both dirty and laundry. Shakar may be a variation of *shikilmoq*, to make the sound "shik-shik," a way of describing a rubbing sound.

11. Tsushtan is not attested; perhaps this refers to *sutqon*, a plant that seeps a noxious milk. Potash can be made from plants and wood ashes.

12. Here the Nalivkins inexplicably use the term *baba*, a disparaging term for an older, lower-class woman or widow, someone perceived as backward. For more on the connotations of this term for someone of Maria Nalivkina's era and class, see Elizabeth Wood, *The Baba and the Comrade: Gender and Politics in Revolutionary Russia* (Bloomington: Indiana University Press, 1997), 15–28. The use stands out against their usually more neutral terminology for women.

13. Mosh-xo'rda is a stew with mung beans, which the Nalivkins identified as lentils (*yasmiq* in Uzbek).

14. Ramadan is the month of fasting. The last three days of Ramadan are celebrated as Eid al-Fitr; Uzbeks call this holiday Ro'za Hayit. Eid al-Adha, or the festival of the sacrifice, is known as Qurbon Hayit.

15. The Nalivkins again use baba.

16. Hayit is the three-day-long holiday.

17. The figure adds up to costs estimated for one woman's clothing per year. Obviously the family's annual expenditure on clothing would be multiplied by the number of people in the family.

18. Central Asian cotton, *g'oza*, ripens in a closed pod. The pods were picked and dried so that they would crack open, and then the cotton was extracted and its seeds removed by hand. The Russian administration of Turkestan began supporting the spread of American upland cotton in the 1880s, because it had longer fiber and was more productive and because the pods open on their own.

19. The Russian term is *perelozhnoe khoziaistvo*, allowing a field to rest for several growing seasons by planting grasses there. In American farming, this is known as planting a cover crop, something that will keep the soil from blowing away and restore nutrients.

20. The authors refer to a scholarly work on Sharia by the German-Russian nobleman and diplomat Baron Nicolaus von Tornauw, *Das Moslemischen Recht aus den Quellen dargestellt* (Leipzig: Dyk'sche Buchhandlung, 1855).

21. The authors may be referring to dyeing hands with henna, a practice associated with holidays and weddings. They do not explain the source of their perception that henna on hands had been used more frequently in the past.

22. This may refer to niello, a jeweler's technique of fusing a black metal onto another metal to produce contrast.

23. A zolotnik is a Russian measure of purity in metal or of weight for jewelry.

24. Bukharan Jews, speakers of a Tajik/Persian dialect, were permitted to move from Samarkand and Bukhara to the Fergana Valley after the Russian conquest.

5. Occupations and Food

1. Mastura means veiled, covered, or secluded.

2. Authors' note: "Always be in your own houses; do use your adornments to bring yourself praise from others. . . ." Koran, chapter 33, verse 33.

3. Qalin is bride price or bride wealth, a payment made by a groom's family to a bride's family as one of the financial exchanges of marriage.

4. The Nalivkins do not note this explicitly, but marriage was virilocal, meaning that husbands continued to live in the communities of their birth, while wives moved to their husband's home. This helps explain why marriage to someone from far away frightened brides and would dispute the Nalivkins' assessment of this fear as "childish." Maria Nalivkina's voice may be dominant here; after her marriage, she left her home in Russia to join Vladimir in Turkestan. We may be hearing her contrast her perception of her own situation with concerns that women in Nanay expressed when they learned how far she was from her natal family. However, the Nalivkins later acknowledge distant marriages as a more serious matter.

5. Authors' note: The latter is only a custom. According to Sharia, the wife does not have to breast-feed her children, cook the food, do the laundry, bake bread, or sweep the house.

6. Authors' note: ". . . consult with them, and do what you consider best." Koran, chapter 65, verse 6.

Editor's note: This text seems closest to sura 3:159, but this is indeed Sablukov's interpretation of 65:6, a verse that concerns making decisions with a divorced wife about the continuation of breast-feeding.

7. Dungan or Tungan was a name used by Turkic-speaking Muslims to refer to Chinese-speaking Muslims (Hui). In intercommunal fighting in Xinjiang/East Turkestan, Turkic Muslims (Uyghurs, who were at that time called Qashgaris or Taranchis) imprisoned and enslaved Chinese Muslims. See James Millward, *Eurasian Crossroads: A History of Xinjiang* (New York: Columbia University Press, 2007), for a detailed explanation of this period.

8. Uzbek choyrak or chorak was a measure of weight equal to 5 puds, or 82 kilos, but the local version of this measurement seems to have been smaller than that.

9. Uzbek chaksa is a measure of weight (obsolete); 3 chaksa equaled 1 pud or 16 kilos.

10. Authors' note: Spinning on Fridays is considered a sin. Other work can go on [on Fridays].

11. The Nalivkins refer to the fact that each town had its regularly scheduled bazaar on one day per week.

12. A paisa is a weight of about 50 grams; also, in the Bukhara Emirate, it is the name of a small copper coin.

13. An attor is a merchant who sells perfumes and fancy goods.

14. A bachcha is a dancing boy or a boy who acted as a servant at a teahouse.

15. *Khosh omad* (Tajik) means greeting, welcome.

16. Kulchatoi is a soup that includes dough in fist-size balls (*kulcha*).

17. The Nalivkins use the term pirozhki (Russian, small pie) to describe somsa, a meat or vegetable-filled pastry (palm-sized) that is baked in a tandir; somsa may be filled with greens such as hake or collard greens.

18. A sweet paste made from sprouted wheat, *samanu* or sumalak is associated with Now Ruz in Iran, Afghanistan, and Central Asia; it probably spread with Persian culture.

19. Shir-choy is milk tea, which can be served sweet, salty, or plain.

20. This is a reference to the *Baburname*, the autobiography of Babur, a sultan from Fergana who conquered and ruled much of Afghanistan and India (d. 1530), establishing the Mughal dynasty.

21. These limited-membership circles are also known by terms such as *gap*, *gashtak*, and *mashrap*.

22. Authors' note: "Eat, drink during the time when you cannot tell apart a black and a white thread. From dawn until nightfall fulfill your fast; do not interact with them (wives), giving yourself to righteous thoughts in the mosques." Koran, chapter 2, verse 183.

23. Authors' note: "It is for them a time of ailment." Koran, chapter 2, verse 222.

24. This would be about 180 to 216 pounds, or 81 to 98 kilograms of wheat.

25. It seems obvious here that the Nalivkins regarded their own cultural practices for feeding dogs leftovers, bones, and dairy products and treating them as pets as correct and as the standard by which to judge Sarts.

26. The Nalivkins use half of a Russian expression: "Golod ne tetka, pirozhka ne podnesët" (Hunger is not an aunt who brings you a pie), altering the second half. The point is that hunger forces one to figure out how to feed oneself.

6. The Woman, Her Character, Habits, Knowledge, and Behavior toward the People around Her

1. The Nalivkins use the Russian word *rugat'sia*, which can mean to curse or abuse with words or to argue and fight with words. The Nalivkins seem to associate true grief with tears and do not recognize that wailing without producing tears might also be a genuine expression of emotion.

2. Tantalus was a figure of Greek legend whose punishment was to stand in a pool of water below a tree with fruit that was perpetually just beyond his grasp.

3. The Nalivkins use a Russian expression, not taking dirt out of the *izba* (Russian wooden house), equivalent to the English expression, not airing one's dirty linen, to contrast Russian and Sart attitudes about the secrecy of family matters.

4. The Nalivkins express this by contrasting the Russian formal, plural "you" (*vy*), which is used to express some deference, respect, or difference in status or age, with *ty*, which is informal "you," used by close friends and relatives. Among adults, Uzbeks generally address each other as *siz* (formal, plural "you"); adults address only children as *san* (informal, singular "you").

5. The Domostroi is a Russian guide to household conduct, composed in the sixteenth century. In the 1880s it no longer had legal effect but continued to influence Russian behavior.

6. Karaul means guard or watchman, but "voi-dod" (Uzbek) is simply a cry for help.

7. Authors' note: "Making peace is a good deed." Koran, chapter 4, verse 127.

8. This Uzbek phrase translates as "It was a real battle!"

9. *Aurat* (Arabic) refers to private parts.

10. Dajjal, in Islam, is the anti-Christ or the dark Messiah, a figure who appears in various hadith. In Russian folk belief, the domovoi is a poltergeist living in one's home.

11. The Nalivkins write euphemistically here. Cleaning up one's backside after defecating usually was done with water, but a lump of clay or a stone might be used in the absence of water. One wonders whether in the 1880s all social classes in Russia had so much access to discarded reading material that they used paper for this purpose or whether the Nalivkins' implied contrast is again class based.

12. A *falbin* (Tajik) is one who sees the future.

13. The Spanish fly, which secretes cantharidin, was long used as an aphrodisiac.

14. Juma namaz is the Friday communal prayer.

15. "Ya, Xudo!" (Oh, Lord) is Uzbek ; "Ya, Karim" (Oh, Generous One) is Arabic.

16. "Ya, Xudo, Ya, Falak!" (Oh, Lord, Oh Fate) is Uzbek.

17. Authors' note: Dzhai-namaz [joy—place; place of prayer] is made of a special kind of cotton, the so-called *mulla-guza*, whose fiber has a yellowish color. The same cotton is used to make fabric for light yellow robes worn by many of the more pious elderly men.

18. The Nalivkins express this as *naveshivat'*, to hang; these fabric strips are always tied to branches.

19. Aravan is now in Kyrgyzstan, and the site of the horseman petroglyphs is both a place of archeological research and a shrine. Numerous shrines in Central Asia claim a relationship to ʿAli ibn abu Talib. For more recent scholarship on rites at mazars, see Gulnara Aitpaeva, Aida Egamberdieva, and Mukaram Toktogulova, eds., *Mazar Worship in Kyrgyzstan: Rituals and Practitioners in Talas* (Bishkek, Kyrgyzstan: Aigine Research Center, 2007).

20. The pilgrimage sites of Padsha-ata (or Padysha) and Bobo-ata are located in present-day Aksy district, Jalalabad province, Kyrgyz Republic.

21. Taxt-i Sulayman is in the center of present-day Osh, Kyrgyz Republic. Anthropologist David Montgomery's description of present-day worship there is found in "Namaz, Wishing Trees, and Vodka: The Diversity of Everyday Religious Life in Central Asia," in *Everyday Life in Central Asia: Past and present*, ed. Jeff Sahadeo and Russell Zanca (Bloomington: Indiana University Press, 2007), 355–370.

22. They say siz (you, formal) to their father and may say san (you, informal) to their mother.

23. To refer to a father by his son's name, a mother might call the father "Ikrom otasi," Ikrom's father, or shorten this to "otasi," "his father." The Nalivkins write "moi muzh, moi khoziain"; in Uzbek this would be "erim, xo'jayinim," which translates as "my man/husband, my owner/boss/husband," with husband having similar connotations to its old English meaning of owner.

24. Authors' note: The same name is used to elder sisters and sometimes mothers. Besides, it is customary to also give other epithets or titles to women of different social statuses. Wives of khans, beks, and wealthy men are addressed with *ayim*; wives of hokims are called *baibiche*; wives of ishans are called *atun*; wives of parish imams are *maglum* [ma'lum]; etc.

25. The Nalivkins' implicit comparison is with Russian practice, where exchanging kisses on both cheeks was the normal form of greeting one's friends or relatives, regardless of gender.

26. The Nalivkins use the term pel'meni (Russian), dumplings. Central Asian cuisine has meat or pumpkin-filled dumplings, manti, but they differ from pel'meni in that they are larger, round, and cooked over steam rather than boiled or fried.

27. The Nalivkins use *edinoplemenniki*, literally, those of the same tribe. However, they may have meant something less precise, like ethnic group or social group or fellow townspeople, given that Sarts defined themselves as nontribal, in opposition to Kyrgyz, Kuruma, Karakalpaks, and the other nomadic or seminomadic people.

7. Pregnancy and Childbirth: A Girl

1. Authors' note: "To the believers and their heirs who follow them in faith, we grant that they will be rejoined with their progeny." Koran, chapter 52, verse 21.

2. Authors' note: Local Kyrgyz have a habit of riding only the pregnant mares, in the spring, until they give birth, because of some economic reasons that we will not discuss here.

3. Authors' note: Food (like medicines and disease) is divided into hot and cold. The former includes mutton, sugar, butter, fat, black tea (*choy-pamil*), molasses, plov, soup, and rice porridge with milk, as well as bread in wintertime; in summer, the latter becomes cold. The second category includes bread in summer, beef, milk, qatiq, all meatless dishes made with qatiq (sour milk), and stewed fruit that is only consumed as medication.

4. Authors' note: Such festivities have a common name here, *to'y*, and are organized on a large scale for a son's circumcision and similarly on the fortieth day or one-year anniversary of a death and on a smaller scale for weddings and the birth of any child, on the occasion of placing a baby in its cradle for the first time, six or seven days after birth, and on the occasion of six weeks after the woman has given birth. All these to'ys, except for the circumcision and wake, are organized only by wealthy people, and since the Russians arrived in Fergana, they have been growing smaller in scale every year with the general loss of local Muslim piety.

5. The authors do not describe this, but a wooden tube, shaped specifically to conform to either a girl's urethra or a boy's penis, guides urine through the hole in the bottom of the beshik.

6. The Nalivkins contrast a normal Russian way of asking about age with this Central Asian way of asking about age. The twelve-year animal cycle is not only Chinese (as is generally known) but also is used by Mongolians and Central Asians.

7. The term that the Nalivkins use, *lishai*, can be understood as herpes but is also used for psoriasis and ringworm, both of which seem more likely.

8. A vasiqa is a document similar to a deed, stating permanent or temporary ownership of property.

9. *Buvi* can mean mother, grandmother, or other female kin or simply be a feminine honorific suffix, like bibi; both have many dialectical variants. Standard Uzbek uses *ota* as father and *ona* as mother, but there are many regional variations.

10. Here the Nalivkins use the term *baryshnia*, referring to Russian gentry girls; Maria Nalivkina was herself from this class.

11. The authors use the term *babki*, a Russian children's game that involves throwing bones or sticks at arrangements of sticks of bones to dislodge them. It goes by many names.

12. The Nalivkins' translation misses nuances: lo'q-lo'q indicates the pulse of a drumming sound, boom-boom; achchiq can mean bitter or spicy, but it can also mean bad tempered.

13. A more accurate translation would be "Kyrgyz, Kyrgyz all died out, / crowded into a corner. / When they almost died, / they took up spades to attack (protect themselves)."

14. Khidr or Khizr (Arabic), also known as "the Green One," is a figure of Arab legend mentioned in the Qur'an.

15. Under Kokand ruler Umar Xon (r. 1810–1822) a poet named Fazliy compiled an anthology of poetry titled *Majmua-i shoiron*, including Maxzuna's poems. Interestingly, the Nalivkins do not mention the more famous women poets of Kokand, Nodira and Uvaisiy. D. M. Kamalov, *Uzbekskaia khudozhestvennaia kul'tura* (Tashkent, Uzbekistan: Izd-vo Ibn Sino, 1995), 123–124.

8. The Maiden: Marriage Proposal and Marriage

1. Throughout this chapter, the Nalivkins use two different Russian terms for girl: *devochka*, which means a little girl not yet in puberty; and *devushka*, which connotes a girl who has reached or passed puberty and who is still a virgin, unmarried. The English term "maiden" connotes this more specifically than "adolescent girl" does, so my editorial choice is to use

that rather archaic term, which also approximates the division that Uzbeks make between *qiz* (unmarried girl, virgin), *kelin* (newly married young woman), and *xotin* or *ayol* (woman).

2. Authors' note: The same is mentioned in Sharia books that were written in Central Asia, such as *Khidaya-i-Sherif.*

Editor's note: *Hidoya* (Uzbek)/*Hidayah* (Arabic) is a commentary on hadith by Burhan-nudin Marghinani, a scholar from Marg'ilon, Fergana Valley, written in Arabic in the twelfth century CE.

3. In Sunni Sharia, this is known as *khul'* divorce, divorce initiated by the wife, who has to return any bridal gifts to her husband and cannot claim any mahr. This is sometimes seen as buying her way out of an unwanted marriage.

4. Authors' note: Muslim legislation sets the rules regulating only mahr—i.e., the wedding gift that is given by the groom to the bride according to the ancient Arabic custom. It can consist of several objects of varying value. But the Sarts also have their own ancient Uzbek custom of *kalyn* [qalin], paid by the groom not to the bride but to the bride's parents, which symbolically reimburses them for their expenses made during the time they were raising their daughter.

5. Authors' note: We have mentioned above that Sharia, Muslim law, recognizes only mahr and that qalin is one of the ancient Uzbek customs that is not of Muslim origin, which is not rejected by the local clergy because in its essence it does not contradict the basics of Islam. Below are some Sharia regulations about mahr found in these books: *Jam-ur-ramuz* [*Jami' al-rumuz*, by Shams ad-Din Kuhistani], *Khidaya-i-Sherif,* and *Radd-ul-mukhtar* [*Radd al-muhtar*, by Syrian jurist Ibn 'Abidin, d. 1836].

1. Mahr is divided according to the way it is paid into *mahr-i-mua'jal,* which is paid in cash when the marriage is performed [prompt mahr], and *mahr-i-muajal,* which remains as a husband's debt [delayed mahr].
2. Both amounts of mahr are based on mutual agreement.
3. If the amount of each mahr was not negotiated when the marriage agreement was concluded, then if necessary (upon divorce) it is defined by the qozi according to local custom.
4. Before the wife receives the mahr-i-mua'jal, she can refuse to live with her husband or accompany him in travel.
5. If the amount of mahr has not been defined before marriage is contracted, the wife has the right to demand *mahr-i-misl* from her husband as soon as they start living together.
6. Mahr-i-misl means mahr equal to the mahr received by women of a similar status.
7. A given woman's equals are defined as her relatives descendant in the male line, equal to her in beauty, age, wealth, mental skills, belonging to the urban or peasant population, virginity (or lack thereof), and her contemporaries. (A given woman cannot be compared to those that lived before her and had different living conditions.)
8. In case of an illegal marriage (for instance, with the fifth wife, to a relative within the restricted degree, etc.) the payment of mahr is not obligatory if there was no copulation.
9. If at the time the marriage is contracted, the size of the mahr was set and the wife was given away as a virgin but she was discovered not to be one, she can retain her right to receive the full measure of the mahr that was set when the marriage was contracted.
10. If after the marriage was contracted, there was no copulation, the wife can (at the time of divorce, for instance) demand only half of the mahr that was set in the marital arrangement.

6. Authors' note: These are the signs of being of age: (1) ejaculation of semen for a man or fertilization for a woman; (2) the appearance of *regul'* [menses]. According to most of the

Muslim legislators these signs appear about the age of fifteen. According to some, maturity is evidenced by the appearance of whiskers among men and the development of breasts in virgin girls, in which case the minimal limits of maturity are taken as twelve for men and nine years of age for girls.

7. Authors' note: Here are the stipulations of Sharia:

1. If a person was engaged to a bride, paid the qalin or part of it, and was rejected after that, he has the right to demand everything back: either the things he gave or their value.
2. If the father of the bride gave gifts to the groom, they must be returned (or money equal to their value).
3. In the same fashion, all the presents made to the bride by the groom and to the groom by the bride are returned.

8. These parties are now known as *qiz to'y*, the girls' party.
9. Authors' note: Here are the articles of Sharia:

1. The marriage is concluded with *ijab* (proposal) and *qobul* (agreement) that must be expressed with a verb in the past tense. (For example: "Have you married him?"—"I have married him.")
2. Both of the parties must hear the ijab and the qobul.
3. Two witnesses must be present when the ijab and the qobul are pronounced: free men (not slaves) or one free man and two free women.
4. Only Muslims that are of age and possess common sense can be witnesses.
5. The witnesses must hear the pronouncing of the ijab and the qobul at the same time.
6. When marriage is performed, one of the parties can be represented by an authorized delegate.
7. When a maiden's agreement to the marriage is asked, the name of the groom must be announced, but the amount of the agreed mahr may be left unmentioned.
8. When the father asks a maiden who is of age but who has never been married before whether she agrees to the marriage, the following signs can be accepted as her agreement: silence, a smile, or quiet crying but without shouting.
9. If the person asking the maiden about whether she agrees to the marriage is not her father but a male relative, the agreement must be expressed in words.
10. A woman who is marrying for the second time or more must express her agreement in words.
11. Girls who have lost their virginity though adultery [*preliubodeianie*] or in some other way are equated to unmarried girls when their agreement is requested. [Editor's note: This is the Nalivkins' wording, though it makes no sense; by definition, a girl who had not been married could not have committed adultery; they may have mistranslated *zina*, fornication.]

10. Authors' note: Such marriage contracts are rarely found in Fergana.
11. "Here she comes with her eyes / Yar . . . do'st (rhythmic syllables) / My lover's father is following (to protect her)."
12. Authors' note: This is what Sharia says about this:

1. The parents can visit their married daughter, and she can visit them once a week (Friday).
2. She can visit her other relatives once a year.

13. The authors use *babenka*, a rather scornful term for young woman.
14. Authors' note: This ailment is very widespread in Fergana, especially in the Qo'qon region.

9. Polygyny, Divorce, Widowhood, and Death of a Woman

1. Authors' note: Here are some excerpts from Sharia regarding this issue.

    1. All the wives of the same person, Muslim women or women of the Book (Christians and Jews) have the same right for food, clothes, and cohabitation with their husband; whether they are sane or insane, virgins or not, they are all equal, regardless whether their husband is of sound mind or not.
    2. The above-mentioned rights of the wife for food, clothes, and cohabitation with her husband are acknowledged by everyone, but the question of performing his spousal obligations (the actual physical relationship) is open to debate.
    3. Some interpreters of the law say that if there is one wife, she can demand from her husband that he spends a night with her every four days, but there is no obligation of sexual intercourse.
    4. Having two and more wives is allowed only for a person who is capable of fully satisfying his wives with regard to food, clothes, and physical relations with them.

2. The Nalivkins do not clarify where they heard this. It is not stated in Sharia, but it may have been a common understanding among Fergana Valley ulomo.
3. This is a French phrase with a misspelling, *qui vivra verra*, or "time will tell."
4. Authors' note: Since every Muslim state is first of all a theocratic state.
5. Authors' note: The reader knows already about the attitude of the natives toward childlessness [and] bearing children in general and boys in particular, as well as the belief that a divorcée or a widow who was taken as a wife would belong to her first husband in the afterlife. Such a husband first is worried about being left without a wife in the afterlife and, second, wishes to take a virgin for his second wife.
6. If the Nalivkins were reporting local practice, then it differed substantially from Sharia as understood in most places. It is generally understood that only a husband can utter "taloq"; a wife cannot gain a divorce by uttering "taloq" but instead has to seek a divorce by appealing to the qozi.
7. Authors' note: Among the nomadic populations, women are treated differently. There she must remarry a brother of her deceased husband.
8. Authors' note: The funeral is usually arranged on the same day or the following morning.
9. Authors' note: This ritual seems to be nonexistent in other parts of Central Asia.

10. Prostitution

1. Authors' note: See Koran, chapter 4, verse 19; and chapter 24, verses 4–9.
    Editor's note: These verses require that four witnesses attest to having caught the adulterous pair in the act of sex.
2. Croesus was a Lydian ruler who possessed infinite treasures.
3. The Nalivkins use the term *grazhdanstvennost'*, which they must be using in the most general sense of the term, as natives of Turkestan were not recognized as *grazhdanin* (citizens) of the Russian Empire. Still, the prostitute was now subject to Russian law, meaning that she could legally sell sex. The khan's Islamic law, which severely punished fornication or adultery, was gone.
4. Authors' note: These requests have always been fulfilled by our administration at the first possibility.

5. Parents of a virgin daughter probably preferred arranging a marriage for her to placing her in a brothel for many, many reasons; the tone of the Nalivkins' commentary here is remarkably cynical.

6. Authors' note: Local countryside festivals.

7. A jallob is a woman who has been divorced and remarried countless times.

8. This story appears to have been censored, unless the Nalivkins simply forgot to tell what happened when the troop of gymnasts and dancers came to town or what it had to do with tightfistedness and visiting prostitutes.

9. When Russia legalized prostitution, the terms were that prostitutes had to be associated with a registered brothel, pay taxes, and undergo health checks. The administrative crackdown mentioned here was specifically on secret, unregistered prostitution.

Bibliography

Abashin, Sergei. "The 'Fierce Fight' at Oshoba: A Microhistory of the Conquest of the Khoqand Khanate." *Central Asian Survey* 33, no. 2 (2014): 215–231.

———. *Natsionalizmy v srednei azii: V poiskakh identichnosti* [Nationalisms in Central Asia: In search of identity]. St. Petersburg, Russia: Atelia, 2007.

———. "Problema sartov v russkoi istoriografii XIX–pervoi chetverti XX v" [Problem of the Sarts in Russian historiography, nineteenth to first quarter of twentieth centuries]. In *Natsionalizmy v srednei azii: V poiskakh identichnosti* [Nationalisms in Central Asia: In search of identity], by Sergei Abashin, 95–176. St. Petersburg, Russia: Atelia, 2007.

———. "Vozvrashchenie sartov? Metodologiia i ideologiia v postsovetskikh nauchnykh diskussiiakh" [Return of the Sarts? Methodology and ideology in post-Soviet scholarly discussion]. *Antropologicheskii Forum* [Anthropological Forum], no. 10 (2009): 252–278.

———. "V. P. Nalivkin: 'Budet to, cho neizbezhno dolzhno byt'; i to chto neizbezhno dolzhno byt', uzhe ne mozhet byt'" [V. P. Nalivkin: "That which unavoidably must be, will be; and that which unavoidably must be, is already impossible"]. *Minaret* 12 (2008). http://www.idmedina.ru/books/history_culture/minaret/12/abashin.htm.

Adams, Laura. *The Spectacular State: Culture and National Identity in Uzbekistan*. Durham, NC: Duke University Press, 2010.

Aitpaeva, Gulnara, Aida Egamberdieva, and Mukaram Toktogulova, eds. *Mazar Worship in Kyrgyzstan: Rituals and Practitioners in Talas*. Bishkek, Kyrgyzstan: Aigine Research Center, 2007.

Ali, Abdullah Yusuf. *The Meaning of the Holy Qur'an*. Brentwood, MD: Amana, 1991.

Alimova, Dilarom. *Zhenskii vopros v srednei Azii: Istoriia izucheniia i sovremennye problemy* [The woman question in Central Asia: History of studies and current issues]. Tashkent, Uzbekistan: Fan, 1991.

Arapov, D. Iu., ed. *Musul'manskaia sredniaia aziia: Traditsionalizm i XX vek* [Muslim Central Asia: Traditionalism in the twentieth century]. Moscow: Rossiiskaia Akademiia Nauk, 2004.

———. "Vladimir Petrovich Nalivkin." In *Musul'manskaia sredniaia aziia: Traditsionalizm i XX vek* [Muslim Central Asia: Traditionalism in the twentieth century], edited by D. Iu. Arapov, 7–17. Moscow: Rossiiskaia Akademiia Nauk, 2004.

Benson, Linda. "A Much-Married Woman: Marriage and Divorce in Xinjiang." *Muslim World* 83, nos. 3–4 (1993): 227–247.

Bernstein, Laurie. *Sonia's Daughters: Prostitutes and Their Regulation in Imperial Russia*. Berkeley: University of California Press, 1995.

Bikzhanova, M. A. *Sem'ia v kolkhoza Uzbekistana: Na materialakh kolkhozov namanganskoi oblasti* [The family on the kolkhoz in Uzbekistan: Based on materials from kolkhozes in Namangan province]. Tashkent, Uzbekistan: Izdatel'stvo Akademii Nauk Uzbekskoi SSR, 1959.

Bregel, Yuri. "The Sarts in the Khanate of Khiva." *Journal of Asian History* 12 (1978): 121–151.

Brower, Daniel. *Turkestan and the Fate of the Russian Empire.* London: Routledge/ Curzon, 2003.

Budagov, L. Z. *Sravnitel'nyi slovar' turetsko-tatarskikh narechii* [Comparative dictionary of Turkish-Tatar dialects]. 2 vols. St. Petersburg, Russia: Tipografiia Imperatorskoi Akademii Nauk, 1869–1871.

Burton, Audrey. "Bukharan Jews, Ancient and Modern." *Jewish Historical Studies* 34 (1994–1996): 43–68.

Clements, Barbara Evans. *A History of Women in Russia.* Bloomington: Indiana University Press, 2012.

Dinc, Gulten, and Yesim Isil Ulman. "The Introduction of Variolation 'à la Turca' to the West by Lady Mary Montagu and Turkey's Contribution to This." *Vaccine* 25, no. 21 (2007): 4261–4265.

Engel, Barbara Alpern. *Mothers and Daughters: Women of the Intelligentsia in Nineteenth-Century Russia.* Cambridge: Cambridge University Press, 1983.

Ewing, Thomas. "From an Exclusive Privilege to a Right and an Obligation: Modern Russia." In *Girls' Secondary Education in the Western World: From the 18th to the 20th Century*, edited by James C. Albisetti, Joyce Goodman, and Rebecca Rogers, 165–179. New York: Palgrave Macmillan, 2010.

Fedchenko, A. P. *Puteshestvie v Turkestan* [Travels in Turkestan]. 2 vols. St. Petersburg, Russia: Knizhnyi sklad M. Stasiulevicha, 1874–1880.

———. *Puteshestvie v Turkestan* [Travels in Turkestan]. Vol. 1, bk. 2, *V Kokandskom Khanstve* [In the Kokand Khanate]. St. Petersburg, Russia: Knizhnyi sklad M. Stasiulevicha, 1875.

Finke, Peter. *Variations on Uzbek Identity: Strategic Choices, Cognitive Schemas and Political Constraints in Identification Processes.* Oxford, UK: Berghahn, 2014.

Frank, Allen. *Bukhara and the Muslims of Russia: Sufism, Education, and the Paradox of Islamic Prestige.* Leiden, Netherlands: Brill, 2012.

Geraci, Robert. *Window on the East: National and Imperial Identities in Late Tsarist Russia.* Ithaca, NY: Cornell University Press, 2001.

Il'khamov, Alisher. "Arkheologiia Uzbekskoi identichnosti" [Archaeology of Uzbek identity]. In *Etnicheskiii atlas Uzbekistana* [Ethnic atlas of Uzbekistan], edited by Alisher Ilkhamov, 268–302. Tashkent, Uzbekistan: Institute Otkyrtogo Obshchestva, 2002.

Jersild, Austin. "From Savagery to Citizenship: Caucasian Mountaineers and Muslims in the Russian Empire." In *Russia's Orient: Imperial Borderlands and Peoples, 1700–1917*, edited by Daniel Brower and Edward Lazzerini, 101–114. Bloomington: Indiana University Press, 1997.

Johanson, Christine. *Women's Struggle for Higher Education in Russia, 1855–1900.* Montreal: McGill University Press, 1987.

Kalter, Johannes. *The Arts and Crafts of Turkestan.* London: Thames and Hudson, 1984.

Kamalov, D. M. *Uzbekskaia khudozhestvennaia kul'tura* [Uzbek artistic culture]. Tashkent, Uzbekistan: Izdadtel'svo Ibn Sino, 1995.

Kamp, Marianne. *The New Woman in Uzbekistan: Islam, Modernity, and Unveiling under Communism.* Seattle: University of Washington Press, 2006.

Kazem-bek, M. M., *Obshchaia grammatika turetsko-tatarskago iazyka* [General grammar of Turkish-Tatar language]. Kazan, Russia: Universitetskaia Tipografiia, 1846.

Khalid, Adeeb. *The Politics of Muslim Cultural Reform: Jadidism in Central Asia*. Berkeley: University of California Press, 1998.

Khoroshkhin, A. P. *Sbornik statei kasaiiushchikhsia do turkestanskago kraia* [Collection of articles regarding Turkestan Territory]. St. Petersburg, Russia: Tipografiia i Khromolitografiia A. Transhelia, 1876.

Kisliakov, N. A. *Ocherki po istorii sem'i i braka u narodov srednei azii i kazakhstana* [Sketches about the history of family and marriage among the peoples of Central Asia and Kazakhstan]. Leningrad, Russia: Izdatel'stvo Nauka, 1969.

Knight, Nathaniel. "Nikolai Kharuzin and the Quest for a Universal Human Science." *Kritika: Explorations in Russian and Eurasian History* 9, no. 1 (2008): 83–112.

Kostenko, L. F. *Turkestanskii Krai: Materialy voennostatisticheskogo obozreniia Turkestanskogo voennogo okruga* [Turkestan Territory: Materials of the military-statistical survey of Turkestan military district]. St. Petersburg: Tipografiia Transhelia, 1880.

Kuxhausen, Anna. *From the Womb to the Body Politic: Raising the Nation in Enlightenment Russia*. Madison: University of Wisconsin Press, 2013.

Laruelle, Marlene, Sergei Abashin, Marianne Kamp, Adeeb Khalid, and Alisher Il'khamov. "Constructing a National History in the Language of Soviet Science after the Collapse of the USSR: The Case of Uzbekistan." *Ab Imperio*, no. 4 (2005): 279–359.

Levi, Scott. *The Indian Diaspora in Central Asia and Its Trade, 1550–1900*. Leiden, Netherlands: Brill, 2002.

Liushkevich, F. D. "Traditsii mezhsemeinnykh sviazei Uzbeksko-Tadzhikskogo naseleniia srednei Azii (k probleme bytovaniia *kalyma* i drugikh patriarkhal'nykh obychaev)" [Traditions of interfamily ties of the Uzbek-Tajik population of Central Asia (toward the issue of the existence of bridewealth and other patriarchal customs)]. *Sovetskaia Etnografiia* [Soviet Ethnography] 4 (1989): 58–68.

Lukashova, Natalia. "V. P. Nalivkin: Eshche odna zamechatel'naia zhizn'" [V. P. Nalivkin: Another remarkable life]. *Vestnik Evrazii* [Messenger of Eurasia], nos. 1–2 (1999): 38–59.

Lunin, Boris V. *Istoriografiia obshchestvennykh nauk v Uzbekistane: Bio-bibliograficheskie ocherki* [Historiography of social science scholarship in Uzbekistan: Bio-bibliographic sketches]. Tashkent, Uzbekistan: Fan, 1974.

———. *Sredniaia aziia v dorevoliutsionnom i sovetskom vostokovedenii* [Central Asia in prerevolutionary and Soviet Oriental studies]. Tashkent, Uzbekistan: Nauka, 1965.

———. "Svet i ten' odnoi zamechatel'noi zhizhni (Vladimir Nalivkin)" [Light and darkness of one remarkable life (Vladimir Nalivkin)], 1999. O'zbekistan Davlat Arxivi [Uzbekistan State Archive], F. 2409, op. 1, d. 13, ll. 1–29.

Maev, N. A. *Russkii Turkestan: Sbornik izdannyi po povodu politicheskoi vystavki* [Russian Turkestan: A collection of articles on the occasion of the political exhibition]. Moscow: Universitetskaia Tipografiia, 1872.

Manchester, Laurie. *Holy Fathers, Secular Sons: Clergy, Intelligentsia, and the Modern Self in Revolutionary Russia*. DeKalb: Northern Illinois University Press, 2008.

Marshall, Alex. *The Russian General Staff and Asia, 1800–1917*. London: Routledge, 2006.

"Materialy k biografii Vladimira Petrovicha Nalivkina" [Materials for the biography of Vladimir Petrovich Nalivkin], 1957. O'zbekistan Davlat Arxivi [Uzbekistan State Archive], F. 2409, op. 1, d. 7, ll. 1–6.

Middendorff, Aleksandr F. von. *Ocherki Ferganskoi doliny* [Sketches of the Fergana Valley]. St. Petersburg, Russia: Tipografiia Imperatorskago Akademii Nauk, 1881.

Millward, James. *Eurasian Crossroads: A History of Xinjiang.* New York: Columbia University Press, 2007.

Montgomery, David. "Namaz, Wishing Trees, and Vodka: The Diversity of Everyday Religious Life in Central Asia." In *Everyday Life in Central Asia: Past and Present*, edited by Jeff Sahadeo and Russell Zanca, 355–370. Bloomington: Indiana University Press, 2007.

Morrison, Alexander. "Metropole, Colony, and Imperial Citizenship in the Russian Empire." *Kritika: Explorations in Russian and Eurasian History* 13, no. 2 (2002): 355–356.

———. *Russian Rule in Samarkand, 1868–1910: A Comparison with British India.* Oxford: Oxford University Press, 2008.

Mukhamedov, Sh. B. "Vzgliadi V. P. Nalivkina na problem islama v turkestane" [V. P. Nalivkin's views on the problem of Islam in Turkestan]. In *Tarixshunoslik o'qishlari 2010: Konferentsiia materiallar to'plami* [Historical studies 2010: Collected conference materials], 186–192. Tashkent, Uzbekistan: Yangi Nashr, 2011.

Nalivkin, Ivan Borisovich. "Vospominaniia o V. P. Nalivkin" [Remembrances about V. P. Nalivkin], 1957. O'zbekistan Davlat Arxivi [Uzbekistan State Archive], F. 2409, op. 1, d. 9, ll. 1–21.

Nalivkin, N. P. "Posluzhnoi spisok" [List of positions]. In *Musul'manskaia srednaia aziia: Traditsionalizm i XX vek* [Muslim Central Asia: Traditionalism in the twentieth century], edited by D. Iu. Arapov, 276–280. 1906. Reprint, Moscow: Rosiiskaia Akademia Nauk, 2004.

Nalivkin, Vladimir P. *Kratkaia istoriia kokandskago khanstva* [A short history of the Kokand Khanate]. Kazan, Russia: Tipografiia Imperatorskago Universiteta, 1886.

Nalivkin, V., and M. Nalivkina. *Russko-sartovskii i sartovsko-russkii slovar' obshcheupotrebitel'nykh slov, s prilozheniem kratkoi grammatiki po narechiia Namanganskogo uezda* [Russian-Sart and Sart-Russian dictionary of commonly used words, with appendix of a short grammar regarding Namangan district dialect]. Kazan, Russia: Tipografiia Imperatorskago Universiteta, 1884.

Nalivkina, Z. Untitled notes about her grandfather, Vladimir Nalivkin. O'zbekistan Davlat Arxivi [Uzbekistan State Archive], F. 2409, op. 1, d. 12.

O'zbek tilining izohli lug'ati [Uzbek language explanatory dictionary]. 2 vols. Edited by Z. M. Ma'rufov. Moscow: Izdatel'stvo Russkii Iazyk, 1980.

Penati, Beatrice. "Beyond Technicalities: Land Assessment and Land-Tax in Russian Turkestan (ca. 1880–1917)." *Jahrbücher für Geschichte Osteuropas* [Yearbooks for the history of Eastern Europe] 59, no. 1 (2011): 1–27.

Pervaia vseobshchaia perepis' naseleniia rossiiskoi imperii, 1897 g. [First general population census of the Russian Empire, 1897]. Vol. 89, *Ferganskaia oblast'* [Fergana oblast]. St. Petersburg, Russia: Izdatel'lstvo Tsentral'nago Statisticheskago Komiteta Ministerstva Vnutrennikh Del, 1897.

Peshkova, Svetlana. *Women, Islam, and Identity: Public Life in Private Spaces in Uzbekistan.* Syracuse, NY: Syracuse University Press, 2014.

Poujol, Catherine. "Approaches to the History of Bukharan Jews' Settlement in the Fergana Valley, 1867–1917." *Central Asian Survey* 12, no. 4 (1993): 549–556.

Privratsky, Bruce. *Muslim Turkistan: Kazak Religion and Collective Memory.* London: Routledge, 2001.

Pugovkina, Ol'ga. "M. V. Nalivkina: Pervaia zhenshchina-etnograf sredei azii (na osnove vpechatlenii zhizni v ferganskoi doline)" [M. V. Nalivkina: The first woman ethnographer of Central Asia (on the basis of impressions of life in the Fergana Valley)]. *O'zbekiston Tarixi* [Uzbekistan history], no. 1 (2011): 62–69.

Ransel, David. "Abandonment and Fosterage of Unwanted Children: The Women of the Foundling System." In *The Family in Imperial Russia*, edited by David Ransel, 189–205. Urbana: University of Illinois Press, 1978.

Robinson, Geroid. *Rural Russia under the Old Regime.* Berkeley: University of California Press, 1932.

Russkoe Geograficheskoe Obshchestvo [Russian Geographical Society]. "Perechen' nagrazhdennykh znakami otlichiia russkogo geograficheskogo obshchestva (1845–2012)" [List of those awarded with the Russian Geographical Society's recognition of excellence (1845–2012)]. 2012. http://www.rgo.ru/sites/default/files/upload/spisok-nagrazhdennyh_8.pdf.

Sablukov, Gordii Semenovich. *Koran: Zakonodatel'naia kniga mokhammedanskago veroucheniia; Perevod s arabskago.* [Koran: The law-giving book of Muhammadan faith; A translation from Arabic]. Kazan, Russia: Tipografiia Imperatorskago Universiteta, 1877.

Sahadeo, Jeff. *Russian Colonial Society in Tashkent, 1865–1923.* Bloomington: Indiana University Press, 2007.

Said, Edward. *Orientalism.* London: Penguin, 1977.

Schimmelpenninck van der Oye, David. *Russian Orientalism: Asia in the Russian Mind from Peter the Great to the Emigration.* New Haven, CT: Yale University Press, 2010.

Semenova Tian'-Shanskaia, Ol'ga. *Village Life in Late Tsarist Russia: Ol'ga Semyonova Tian-Shanskaia.* Translated and edited by David Ransel. Bloomington: Indiana University Press, 1997. Originally published as *Zhizn' Ivana* [The life of Ivan], 1906.

Severtsov, N. *Obshchye otchety o puteshestviiakh 1857–1868 godov* [General report on travels in 1857–1868]. St. Petersburg: Trubnikov, 1873.

Shaniiazov, K. Sh. *Etnograficheskie ocherki material'noi kul'tury Uzbekov konets XIX-nachalo XX v.* [Ethnographic sketches of material culture of Uzbeks in the late 19th and early 20th centuries]. Tashkent, Uzbekistan: Fan, 1981.

Steinwedel, Charles. "How Bashkiria Became Part of European Russia, 1762–1881." In *Russian Empire: Space, People, Power, 1700–1930*, edited by Jane Burbank, Mark von Hagen, and Anatolyi Remnev, 94–124. Bloomington: Indiana University Press, 2007.

Stites, Richard. *The Women's Liberation Movement in Russia: Feminism, Nihilism, and Bolshevism, 1860–1930.* 1978. Reprint, Princeton, NJ: Princeton University Press, 1990.

Tornauw, Baron Nicolaus von. *Das Moslemischen Recht aus den Quellen dargestellt* [Muslim law based on its sources]. Leipzig: Dyk'sche Buchhandlung, 1855.

Uzbeksko-russkii slovar' [Uzbek-Russian dictionary]. Edited by S. F. Akobirov and G. N. Mikhailov. Tashkent, Uzbekistan: O'zbek Sovet Entsiklopediiasi Bosh Redaktsiiasi, 1988.

Wagner, William G. *Marriage, Property and Law in Late Imperial Russia*. Oxford: Oxford University Press, 1994.

Wood, Elizabeth. *The Baba and the Comrade: Gender and Politics in Revolutionary Russia*. Bloomington: Indiana University Press, 1997.

Zanca, Russell. "Fat and All That: Good Eating the Uzbek Way." In *Everyday Life in Central Asia*, edited by Jeff Sahadeo and Russell Zanca, 178–197. Bloomington: Indiana University Press, 2007.

Zununova, G. Sh. "Osobennosti instituta braka v sisteme vostochnoi tsivilizatsii (na materialakh makhallia g. Tashkenta)" [Peculiarities about the institution of marriage in the system of Eastern civilization (based on materials from the Tashkent neighborhoods)]. *International Journal of Central Asian Studies* 9 (2004): 278–289.

Index

abortion, 129, 142–143

administration: in creditor-debtor disputes, 126; divisions of, 31, 68; *mudarrise*s and, 73; prostitution and, 185–186, 187–189; religion and, 42, 66; Sarts and Russian, 7, 8–9, 16, 19, 23, 92–93, 105, 115, 123–124, 203n23, 209n11; Vladimir Nalivkin in Russian, 5, 7–8; women involved in, 136

adultery, 62–64, 66, 185

agency, 15, 161–162, 177

agriculture, 9, 13, 14, 15, 16, 32–35, 37–48, 52, 99, 103, 109–110, 118, 140

a'lam, 68, 73

alcohol, 8, 11, 12, 54, 115, 129–130

amulets, 101–102, 128

*araba*s, 32, 50, 80, 160, 169, 205n4

Arabic language/script, 5, 16, 24, 41, 70, 71, 74

ariq, 32, 34, 37, 39, 49, 80, 84, 149

artisans, 47–49

atlas, 33, 206n9

auls, 36, 40

bachcha, 22, 33, 112, 116, 140–141, 158, 179, 189

bathing, 127, 146, 149

bazaars, 18, 33–34, 45, 47, 49–55, 72, 78, 97–98, 104, 108, 110, 112–113, 125–126, 139

beauty, 12, 18, 89, 91, 94, 100–101, 157, 159

bedding, 37, 82, 84–86, 89–90, 92, 126, 145, 164, 184

beggars, 33, 97, 125, 127

bek, 34, 39, 71

beliefs, 128–130, 132–133, 142–143, 145–148, 156, 161, 182, 211n17, 211n24

beshik, 89, 98, 128, 145, 147, 163

body, 13, 18, 20, 89–92, 127, 159–160

boys, 11, 22, 32, 49, 51, 68–69, 111, 139, 143, 146, 157, 169, 186

bread, 22, 40, 48, 55, 68, 74, 83, 86, 103, 110–111, 113, 115–118, 126, 206n20

breast-feeding, 93, 117, 127, 145–146, 148

bride, 142, 157–160, 162–170, 180

brothels, 15, 21, 171–172, 186–188

brothers, 62, 134, 157

Bukhara, 2, 12

butchers, 48–52, 115, 160

censor, 9–10, 21, 29

character, 12, 19–20, 90, 120, 124–125, 140, 159, 173

charity, 16, 137, 146

childbirth, 8, 10, 20, 65, 89, 91, 128, 134, 142–145, 159, 160, 171

children, 7, 16, 19–20, 32, 156–159; clothing of, 91, 93, 99, 146–147; fathers and, 116; marriage arrangements for, 163; parents' treatment of, 133–135, 137–138, 145–151, 176–177, 179, 181–182; playing, 140–141, 151–156; Qur'anic verses on, 60–63; schooling of, 68–69, 156–157; stealing, 99; working, 106

chimbet/chachvon, 94–95, 99, 111, 122, 139–140, 157, 158, 162, 168, 212n7

chorikor, 24, 43–45

citizenship, 9, 186, 219n3

civilization, 9, 11, 16, 18, 22, 41, 206n21

class, 4, 6, 17, 18, 19, 20, 23, 84, 94, 104, 138, 146, 150, 183

clergy, 57, 66–67, 74, 76, 178, 187, 209nn9–10

climate, 34, 35, 37–41, 47, 81, 93, 96, 107

clothing: changing attitudes about, 100; of children, 93, 94, 146–147, 150, 157, 158; of men, 32, 33–34, 37, 39, 40, 49, 51, 98, 109, 127, 132, 136; and religion, 17; storage of, 84; of women, 12, 18, 22, 32, 34, 49, 51, 89–102, 109, 111, 132, 137–138, 157, 158, 168, 183

colonialism, 2, 8, 9, 41–42

conquest, Russian, 2, 8, 10, 11, 54, 115, 185, 201n2, 213n24

consumption, 17, 19, 99, 107, 109, 111, 113–119

cotton: bags made from, 50; candle wicks made from, 87; cleaning and weaving of, 46–47, 99, 105–107, 156, 158, 164, 212n18; clothing made from, 32, 33, 39, 51, 93–96, 99, 100, 183; fabrics made from, 50, 52–53, 82–83; farming of, 9, 31, 35, 39, 43–45, 109; mats made from, 89, 132; string made from, 91; used to cause miscarriage, 142–143; use of, in cosmetics, 101

MARIANNE KAMP is Associate Professor of History at the University of Wyoming. She is author of *The New Woman in Uzbekistan: Islam, Modernity, and Unveiling under Communism*.

MARIANA MARKOVA is an editor, translator, instructor, and researcher. She holds a PhD in anthropology from the University of Washington.

Lightning Source UK Ltd.
Milton Keynes UK
UKHW020754020821
387960UK00002BA/82